PRACTICAL PLANNING BUSINESS 2020/21

HOW UK ENTREPRENEURS & INVESTORS CAN SAVE TAX LEGALLY & ETHICALLY

ALAN PINK FCA CTA

Pink
Proactive
Publishing

Practical Tax Planning for Business

For information contact:

Pink Proactive Publishing

44 The Pantiles, Tunbridge Wells TN2 5TN

PPPublishing.co.uk

Book and cover design by Here Be Dragons Ltd

ISBN: 978-1-9163566-1-0

First Edition: November 2020

10 9 8 7 6 5 4 3 2 1

To Louise

CONTENTS

About this book

Far from being a stuffy text book, this is intended to be a highly practical guide to the tax system of the United Kingdom, which guides the reader in non technical language through the mazes of one of the most complex and intimidating tax codes in the world. Arranged by topics rather than by taxes, the book sets out simple and non aggressive strategies for businesspeople and investors, who bear the main brunt of taxation in this country, to reduce this burden in a sensible and ethically acceptable way. The work has been revised, updated and expanded from last year's edition, and contains an entirely new chapter on saving tax offshore.

Alan Pink FCA CTA

Alan Pink is a well known writer on tax planning, having published articles both in the professional press and in publications aimed at the lay person. He has been the technical editor of The Schmidt Tax Report for over twenty years, and combines writing with a consultancy role with niche accountancy practice APT at Tunbridge Wells, Kent.

Whilst every effort is taken to ensure that the contents of this book are technically correct and up to date, inevitably inaccuracies may creep in due to the highly technical and fast changing nature of the subject. Tax planning is based on interpretation, and advice should be taken on specific issues before action is taken based on any of the recommendations in this book.

www.pppublishing.co.uk

CHAPTER 1

INTRODUCTION

This book aims to do exactly "what it says on the tin". That is, it aims to give clear and practical advice, in non technical language, on things which business people and investors can actually do in order to reduce their tax burden. It aims to cover the whole range of taxes which afflict the average family business or investment portfolio, and do so in a non specialist way which I hope will be easily understood by the lay person.

Unfortunately, a lot of books which purport to be about tax planning are little more than a regurgitation of the rules. It's very often left to the reader to take the logical step from understanding the rules to thinking out what can be done to work round them. This is obviously something which it is extremely difficult for the non expert to do in reality, because whatever you do in your financial or tax planning life is likely to have repercussions in other areas which it's not easy for the non expert to anticipate.

What this book isn't

What this book isn't, then, is some kind of textbook or encyclopaedia running through our tax system in the UK in a systematic way. And you won't find in it any "aggressive" tax planning schemes. These are outside the scope of this book, for a number of reasons which I'd better explain.

First of all, what is so called aggressive tax planning? And what other sort of tax planning is there?

Aggressive tax planning tends to be the sort that exploits loopholes in the law: areas where the law has been constructed badly, or perhaps badly expressed, such that a result can be obtained for the taxpayer which looks much more favourable than the legislators probably intended. You can usually tell this sort of planning, too, from its following features:

- It's "off the peg": that is, it tends to use the same structure, and the same paperwork, for everyone. Often all the planners do is change the names at the top of the documentation;
- It tends to make use of a complex series of transactions;
- It tends to achieve a perverse result, for example loss relief when you haven't really suffered a real loss, or a profit that's real but is artificially taken out of tax;
- The promoters tend to be secretive about the details; and
- The fees charged by promoters tend to be very high, often a percentage of the amount of tax sought to be saved.

Why aren't I giving the details of any aggressive tax planning schemes in this book? It's not so much because of ethical qualms about aggressive tax planning, but more about prudence. I'll have more to say on the ethics of taxation in the Afterword at the end of the book, but one fact of which you have to be aware is that aggressive tax planning tends to be high on HMRC's hit list, for obvious reasons. Even where your scheme is technically unassailable, the taxman can make life very uncomfortable for you if you make use of arrangements that he doesn't approve of. And it's worthwhile bearing in mind that you will have the whole world against you: including not just tax officials but also appeal judges, and the vast bulk of the general public.

Most cogently, though, the reason why we aren't giving any aggressive tax planning schemes in this book is because they are constantly being devised by promoters and stopped by HMRC. Almost anything we could put forward of this type would be likely to be obsolete before you read about it.

Who should read this book?

First of all, it's aimed at the owner managed business. Finance directors of large quoted companies will need to look elsewhere for guidance (and no doubt will). Their needs tend to be completely different from those of the person who is not just running the business, but owns it. So you'll find nothing in this book about the new Digital Services Tax, for example, which only applies to groups with a worldwide turnover of more than £500 millionAnd secondly, I'm using the term "business" in its very widest sense here. What follows isn't just aimed at the proverbial widget manufacturer, but at everybody who has tax affairs which are in the slightest bit out of the ordinary. So, personal investors, and those who own buy-to-let properties, are very much part of my target audience: and I hope will find a lot to interest them, and to use, in the various chapters.

Anyone who pays tax in the UK under self-assessment, as opposed to the army of workers on PAYE, should be aware of the possibilities for them to reduce their tax in a sensible and practical way. What has sometimes been called "sensible" tax planning tends to be the sort which, as it were, "goes along the grain" of the legislation rather than, as aggressive planning does, seeking to defeat what the law seems to be trying to do. Non aggressive tax planning is possible because of the huge, and ever increasing, complexity of the tax law, which lands taxpayers with a number of choices, all of them giving potentially different tax results. For example, income received by limited companies is currently taxed at the all time low rate of 19%, contrasted with income received by individuals which can be taxed at as high a rate as 45% (or more, if you count national insurance as a tax). The law gives you the choice between whether to receive your income through a company or to receive it as an individual: and the art of tax planning involves considering all of the repercussions of that choice, not just on other tax issues but also on financial, legal and practical matters.

Again, there are a number of claims and reliefs built into our tax system which have to be actively sought, and aren't just given automatically. Sometimes two equally valid ways of doing something can give very different tax results because one of them involves the availability of an important tax relief. I'll be coming on to give a number of examples of this situation in what follows.

My background

This work is born of an interest in, and enthusiasm for, tax planning for owner managed businesses and investors which I've had throughout my career as a Chartered Accountant and Chartered Tax Adviser. Whilst, like many OMB advisers, I've spent some time working in a large firm (then called Touche Ross, since renamed Deloitte) the bulk of my career has been spent in the specialist tax function of more down to earth, medium sized, firms of accountants. I've never regretted my move out of the big firm environment, where £20 million is "immaterial", and into the local accountancy scene where saving a few thousand pounds for a client can make a difference to their lives. On the one hand, you've got numbers written on a piece of paper, which may be very large but don't have any major impact on anyone. On the other, you can make the difference between somebody deciding to carry on in business, if they can get their tax liabilities under control, and giving up.

This book also comes about as a result of my own passion for writing about tax, and tax planning. For many years now I've been the Technical Editor of The Schmidt Tax Report, which is a practical tax planning publication aimed at the non specialist. I've also written more technical articles for Taxation Magazine, and for Business & Property Tax Insider magazines. I published The Entrepreneurs' Tax Guide in 2013, and, whilst this is still available, an awful lot has happened in tax since that work was published. Hence, the need I have identified for an entirely new and fresh look at the subject.

How to use this book

It'll be clear, I hope, from what I've said already that the book isn't laid out as a set of rules, on a tax by tax basis. Instead, a glance at the contents list will show you how the different topics are considered in the round in the various chapters. Inevitably, because life doesn't come in watertight compartments, there's a degree of overlap between them. Similar tax planning ideas arise in different contexts.

If it isn't too grandiose to say so, this work aims to act as a kind of partner in your trading or investment business activity. It doesn't look to take the place of your professional adviser, such as your accountant or tax consultant. A book can't look at all your circumstances, consider them in the round, and advise you in the light of that, as an adviser can. So, as is an almost universal caveat in publications of this kind, I would like to stress that anything you consider doing on the strength of this book should be checked up on with the benefit of professional advice where the numbers are big enough.

Unlike The Entrepreneurs' Tax Guide, I've chosen the annual format for this guide. The reason I have done this is, I hope, sufficiently obvious: tax changes at an alarming rate, and nothing written "once and for all" can help getting out of date. As well as a new edition each year, our website www.pppublishing.co.uk will be updated from time to time for important changes in the law and HMRC practice.

Finally, do please let me have your feedback on anything that you read here, or perhaps have failed to read here, which you think should be taken into account in a future edition.

CHAPTER 2

KNOW THE ENEMY: A SUMMARY OF UK TAXES

When Sir Geoffrey Howe was Chancellor of the Exchequer in the 1980's, he once boasted that he abolished a tax at every Budget. Unfortunately, his successors didn't continue with this good work, and indeed have reversed it!

Not all of these taxes, new and old, are going to be of relevance to the average owner managed business or personal investor. For example, this year's new Digital Services Tax is clearly aimed at the Googles of this world, and I don't suppose there will be many finance directors of oil companies combing these pages to find out more details about Petroleum Revenue Tax. And the same applies to insurance premium tax and the whole host of excise duties, where either OMBs aren't affected by them, or they have no real scope to make savings by doing things differently.

Instead of turning this into a boring textbook I'm going to single out the taxes which are a real threat, and which you're likely to be able to do something about.

What I'll be doing here is giving an overview of each tax by way of introduction, and just looking at a few straightforward ways of planning to reduce your exposure to the tax. There will be a lot more detail about specific tax planning ideas in the chapters that follow, but you can't run before you can walk, and this part of the book is intended as a foundation on which to build the rest of my structure.

So, what are the main taxes which pose a threat to your financial health as a businessman or investor? In rough order of importance, these are:

- Income Tax
- National Insurance
- Corporation Tax
- "Loans to Participators" Tax
- Capital Gains Tax
- Inheritance Tax
- VAT
- Business Rates
- Stamp Duty Land Tax
- The Annual Tax on Enveloped Dwellings

Income Tax

You'll find the facts and figures re this granddaddy of all taxes in the Appendix at the end of this book, but let's look first at the overview. It may sound silly to make the point that income tax is a tax on income; but would you be surprised if I said that this is a point which sometimes has to be made, fairly forcibly, to HM Revenue & Customs (HMRC) themselves?

It's obvious, when you think about it, that not all receipts of money are income. For example, if you loan someone money and they pay you back, that repayment isn't income and is therefore outside the scope of Income Tax. If you sell your house and realise a gain it isn't income, and isn't chargeable to Income Tax. The first distinction you have to make, when looking at this question, is between income receipts and capital receipts, because by long convention capital receipts aren't treated in the same way as income either for accounting or tax purposes.

A fairly topical example is the compensation which banks have recently been paying to customers for various misdemeanours. Are they income or capital? Well, the jury's out on at least one type of compensation, which is a compensation paid to customers who were persuaded to buy interest rate hedging products, which it apparently turned out weren't in their best interests. I am not going to go into the ins and outs of this dispute with HMRC here, but suffice it to say that not all amounts received of the sort are income, and you shouldn't ever assume such without questioning it.

The feature of Income Tax which makes it eminently plannable is its "progressive" nature – that is, the way the rate of tax increases as your total level of income goes up. The rate (at least in England, Wales and Northern Ireland) goes up from 20% to 40% for all income over £50,000, and there is even a band, over £100,000 of income, where you're paying an effective marginal rate of 60%. As has often been remarked, the effect is that, in a household of two people, an income of say £100,000 in a year is taxed much more highly if it's just one of the couples who is earning it. In fact, you are looking at something like £10,000, or 10% more tax in this situation than if the income were spread equally between two partners. So, straightforward income tax planning takes the form of "spreading" the income to use up as many individuals' personal allowances and lower income tax bands as possible. This is likely to be pretty difficult for your "ordinary" taxpayer, who simply receives a salary taxed through PAYE. But for most readers of this book, the situation is likely to be different. Unlike the poor downtrodden PAYE employee, people in business have usually got a choice as to how to structure that business, and I'll give just one example based on an actual case where some fairly straightforward structural planning was proved to succeed in saving a very considerable amount of tax each year.

Mr Jones was a one man consultancy business, effectively; the sort of person who, in years gone by, would probably simply have taken a job with the recipient of his consultancy services. This being the late twentieth century and early twenty first century, there is now much more of a freelance culture, and this was how he operated. Rather than simply sending an invoice each month, though, he formed a limited company, Arctic Systems Limited, and billed through that. What this enabled him to do (apart from saving National Insurance, of which more below) was to share out the income between himself and his wife. She had a substantial shareholding in the company alongside him, and the company paid them dividends in roughly equal proportions. In this way, her allowances and lower rate bands, which would presumably otherwise not have been used, were utilised in reducing the overall tax burden of the household. Simple but effective.

The reason I am singling out this particular instance of tax planning for mention is because this became a cause célèbre of early twenty first century taxation. HMRC argued that Mrs Jones' dividends should be taxed on her husband, on the basis of specific rules concerning "settlements", which, they said, made it difficult or impossible for her husband to divert income to his wife in this way.

It has to be said that a lot of judges, on the way up the appeal process, thought the same. Fortunately for us, though, the final arbiters of the question were the House of Lords, which was the top court in the UK (since renamed The Supreme Court by trendy Mr Blair). They decided, using published material about the original process of legislating for separate husband and wife taxation, that the diversion of income to Mrs Jones was effective for Income Tax purposes. HMRC, being ever bad losers, almost immediately announced that they would change the law. But their proposals gave rise to so many difficulties that they were dropped. All this was going back over ten years now, to 2008, and as a result it's got to be regarded as being "open season" for tax planning of this sort. Hopefully, it's easy to see how the basic principle which Mr Jones used can be extended to other, different circumstances. If, for example, you have a family where one of the couple is a high earner, perhaps on PAYE, but the couple also own an investment property which gives rise to rent, transferring the rental property, or an interest in it, from the high earning partner to the low earning partner can result in a healthy reduction in the tax burden.

I'll be saying more about Income Tax planning of this sort in Chapter 14 below, on "Tax and the Family", and it only remains, perhaps, to ask the question as to whether this kind of tax planning, which we have seen is legal, is also ethical.

One argument in its favour is that it could just be seen as correcting an anomaly in the way Income Tax works. In some other foreign systems of taxation, it isn't the individual so much that gets taxed as the household. If a household were given allowances as a whole, you wouldn't have this problem of an unequal distribution of income resulting in higher tax.

Apart from spreading income, there are various straightforward ways of saving Income Tax which involve paying amounts out. These include:

- Making pension contributions (broadly of up to £40,000 a year)
- Donating to charity under "Gift Aid"
- Investing in Enterprise Investment Schemes (EIS) companies, which give you effective relief of 30% (or 50% if it is a small new "Seed EIS company")
- Laying out capital expenditure which creates Income Tax losses (of which more below)

National Insurance

It may raise eyebrows in some circles referring to National Insurance (NI) as a "tax". But in my view that is very clearly the reality of the situation. Any idea that your contributions go into some kind of ringfenced "National Insurance fund", which is then used to provide you with pensions and other benefits, is a romantic delusion. The government spends National Insurance contributions as soon as it receives them; or, indeed, a long time before it receives them because of the current level of UK government borrowing. And not all payments of National Insurance even give rise to any entitlement to benefits.

For example, the misnamed "Employer's National Insurance" doesn't seem to count towards any benefits for the employee (and certainly none for the employer, who now has to add further statutory pension contributions on top under the "Stakeholder Pension" regime). Also, "Class 4" NI, which is payable based on profits made by self-employed people, doesn't give any entitlement to benefits – it's the humbler fixed Class 2 contribution that does that.

NI is another example of the chaotic nature of tax policy. You would have thought that unearned income, if anything, should be taxed at a higher rate than earned income, based on traditional thinking anyway. However, the result of the imposition of NI is that the reverse is the case. NI doesn't apply to investment income, but does apply to earned income, whether employed or self-employed.

Another seeming anomaly is the fact (set out detail in the Appendix) that employment relationships are subjected to a very much higher level of NI contributions than self-employed.

Here are a couple of simple and straightforward ideas for reducing your NI contributions.

If you are an employee, consider whether there is scope for you to go self-employed. You might think that this isn't as easy as it sounds: but, in fact, it's often actually easier than it sounds. Many people will be wrongly undergoing employment taxation whose real relationship with their "employer" is one of self-employment.

This is a big subject, and there's a lot of case law precedent, guidance etc to confuse the issue. But fundamentally, where a person acts under his own initiative rather than under the control of the "employer" it is likely to be the case that the true relationship is one of self-employment.

Purely from the tax point of view, this is good news both for the individual and the business he works for. The main "casualty" of switching from employment to self-employment is the Employer's National Insurance contribution for which there is no equivalent in the self-employed arena. At 13.8% of gross earnings, this effectively means the individual can have a fairly stonking pay rise without it costing the "employer" a penny.

Alternatively, consider forming a company in the same way that Mr Jones did in Arctic Systems (see Income Tax, above). If you are running your business (which may just be a one man consultancy) through a limited company, the business income will, of course, be free from NI liability of any kind. You can then extract the income from the company by way of dividends, which are also normally NI free. There's more on this in Chapter 9.

Corporation Tax

This is a very simple tax in terms of the rate charged. The current rate is a flat 19% regardless of the level of profits. So, there is no discrimination against larger earners in the corporate sphere, as there is with individuals in Income Tax.

There are several types of tax deduction available to companies that aren't available to individuals, that is they only apply for Corporation Tax purposes and not for Income Tax purposes. These are:

- Tax relief for research & development. For your average small company, expenditure on research & development which is truly innovative in global terms receives an eyewatering 230% deduction.
- Amounts written off intangible assets acquired (like computer software rights, trademarks, but not, generally, goodwill) are allowed as expenses under the "Intangible Assets" regime.
- Write offs of loans to other unconnected persons. In the individual sphere, these are normally allowed only as capital losses at best, depending on capital gains to give any relief; but in the corporate sphere such write offs are available against the company's total profits.

An obvious piece of planning, in connection with the third of these deductions which are unique to limited companies, is to make any loans you decide on to other, unconnected persons via your limited company, if you have one, rather than making them personal loans. If you have made personal loans, consider transferring these to the company so that relief would be available for any future loss in value of this loan as an asset.

Loans to Participators Tax

This isn't exactly Corporation Tax, but it is always paid by companies. Where a close company (one controlled by 5 or fewer "participators" and their associates) makes a loan to a participator or associate (the latter term includes relatives and others), and where this loan is still outstanding nine months after the company's accounting period end, a payment of "tax" equal to 32.5% of the loan is due. This tax is repayable by HMRC to the company after repayment of the loan by the participator/associate to the company, so in a way it is more like a loan to HMRC than a permanent tax.

Despite the comparatively high rate of the tax at 32.5% (and it's not allowable against the company's other tax) making a loan can be quite a tax efficient way of extracting funds from a company, and I'll come back to this in Chapter 8, on tax efficient profit extraction.

Capital Gains Tax

I've already talked about the difference between income receipts and capital receipts. Income receipts are generally chargeable to Income Tax: but is it true to say that capital receipts are generally liable to Capital Gains Tax (CGT)?

Not at all. What triggers a charge to CGT is the disposal of an asset. Generally speaking, the assets within the scope of CGT are real property, shares and other investments, and assets used for the purposes of a trade. Assets like trading stock and debtors are outside the scope of CGT, as are most "chattels" (tangible moveable property).

The rates of CGT, and the available annual exemption, are set out in the Appendix.

The most straightforward method of CGT planning of all, of course, is to refrain from making a disposal of assets! A lot of property owners go in for this sort of "planning", because they know that, if they sell that buy-to-let property investment, they won't be able to buy a comparable one with the proceeds after having paid 28% tax.

Again, as with Income Tax, there can be an advantage in spreading gains round the family. To take a simple example, if an investment property is owned not just by mother and father, but also by their three children, five annual exemptions could be available on a disposal of that property in the future.

Capital Gains Tax, anomalously, is payable on gifts as well as sales, and if the gift concerned is not of a business asset, consider making it to a trust rather than to an individual directly. Transfers into trust are eligible for deferral of CGT in the form of "holdover relief".

Consider whether you have ever invested in anything in the past which didn't work out, and on which losses arose. Very often these tend to have been forgotten about, but losses can be claimed back from a number of years ago, depending on whether they arose pre or post 1996 (when self-assessment was introduced).

Finally, consider the availability of the various CGT reliefs which I've made the subject of a separate chapter (no. 13) below.

Inheritance Tax

Unlike Capital Transfer Tax, which it replaced in 1986, Inheritance Tax (IHT) is generally only payable on death. The one exception is this is gifts into trust which exceed the nil rate band (currently £325,000: see Appendix). The rate of tax is 40%.

The most obvious way of saving Inheritance Tax is to give your assets away before you die, and, broadly, so long as you do this with at least seven years to spare you will have effectively sidestepped the tax.

Do have a look at my chapter on Practical Inheritance Tax Planning (Chapter 21 below).

VAT

This is the "simple tax", as it was described on its introduction in the early 1970's, which arguably gives business more trouble than any other tax. Matters of interpretation are rife, and it can make a huge difference whether your particular type of business fits within a narrow wording in the VAT legislation or not.

A simple, and very widespread, form of VAT planning consists in avoiding going over the VAT registration threshold, which is currently at £85,000 turnover. There are a number of ways of doing this, and you should have a look at Chapter 18, headed "VAT – Should I Join the Club?". On a more down to earth level still, it's true to say that most VAT problems encountered by businesses and investors arise simply due to a careless approach to administering the tax. As entrepreneurs, we are forcibly recruited into the ranks of the unpaid tax collectors, both in VAT and PAYE, and are made to administer a highly complex set of rules ourselves, with only intermittent guidance from the authorities and with massive penalties if we get things wrong.

Unfortunately, the tendency in most businesses is to relegate its VAT affairs to a fairly lowly member of staff, such as a book-keeper, who finds himself or herself making all kinds of decisions based on an incomplete knowledge of the law. So, if you do nothing else as a result of reading this book, do get your VAT position checked out carefully: perhaps by way of a "mock VAT audit".

Business Rates

Make no mistake about it, Business Rates is a big tax. Raising somewhere between 3% and 4% of the total tax revenue in this country, it's yet another levy on business (who already pay, effectively, most of the Income Tax, all of the National Insurance, and all of the Corporation Tax and PAYE out there).

Because Business Rates are levied on rateable value, the most likely form of planning you could undertake to reduce this levy would be to appeal, where possible, against your rateable valuation.

Stamp Duty Land Tax

This replaced the old Stamp Duty for properties in 2003. The rates are set out in the Appendix, and you will see that residential property again gets a battering in this area (as well as by the infamous "Osborne tax" which I'm discussing in a subsequent chapter).

But there are some reliefs from SDLT that you should be aware of, including the relief for purchase of multiple dwellings, where, in essence, you don't have to pay the rate which applies to the value of the whole block you are buying, but can pay it based on the average price per dwelling unit.

SDLT can apply in some situations where you wouldn't have expected it to. For example, take the case of the mortgaged property owned by one spouse, where an interest is transferred to the other spouse. Whilst the basic rule is that there's no SDLT on gifts, the law treats the transferee spouse, in this situation, as giving valuable "consideration" for the transfer in the form of assuming liability on the mortgage. So, SDLT can apply even where the essence of what you are doing is making a gift.

A perhaps not quite so simple and straightforward way of avoiding this would be to transfer the property into a Limited Liability Partnership (LLP), which has its own separate rules, superseding the basic rule just stated.

The Annual Tax on Enveloped Dwellings

This was introduced a few years ago as a way of "getting at" wealthy investors, often non UK resident, who had the temerity to buy UK residential property. It applies wherever you have a dwelling owned by a limited company, or by a partnership/LLP which includes a company member.

Any dwelling owned in such a structure which is not held for the purpose of a property letting (to unconnected tenants) business, or a property development business, will give rise to the tax, and the moral in terms of how to structure such property holdings is obvious.

The rates of ATED are given in the appendix.

So, hopefully all of the above gives a little enlightenment on the basic framework of our tax system as it applies to UK businesses and investors, and is useful in pointing out various straightforward ways of planning to reduce liability to these taxes.

CHAPTER 3

DEALING WITH HM REVENUE & CUSTOMS

It's essential to have a basic understanding of how our highly idiosyncratic national tax levying authority – HM Revenue & Customs (HMRC) – works, in order to get on well in today's tax environment. In this chapter I'll be looking at ways to work with HMRC (rather than against them), and the important things you need to do to stay out of trouble. If you're unlucky enough to have attracted their attention in the form of an enquiry into your affairs, that's a different matter. I've devoted another chapter to this, later on in this book.

How are HMRC organised? Resisting the temptation to give a sarcastic answer to this question, I would say that, apart from specialist departments which deal with non mainstream taxes such as Inheritance Tax and Stamp Duties, the important dividing line to grasp is that between self-assessment and PAYE.

A substantial majority of taxpayers in this country have their tax deducted under the Pay As you Earn (sometimes referred to as "pay all you earn" or "pay before you earn") system, and generally speaking the tax affairs of such people are straightforward. So, there's no need for someone on PAYE, generally speaking, to complete an annual self-assessment tax return unless they have other sources of income which aren't taxed at source, or they are higher rate income taxpayers.

HMRC's concentration, with regard to PAYE, is all on the employer. By contrast, for those of us who have to prepare self-assessment tax returns, their concentration is all on the individual or corporate taxpayer. Almost by definition, the target readership of this book are going to fall into the self-assessment category, because trading businesses and substantial investment activities fall outside the neat and easy PAYE tax collection method.

New Kid on the SA Block

Inevitably anyone with a new business or investment activity is going to have to tackle the red tape. If it's any comfort, my strong impression is that red tape in the UK for new businesses is still nothing like such hard work to deal with as it is in other countries, particularly in continental Europe. On the tax side, HMRC go out of their way to appear friendly, at least. But, there's still the iron hand hidden away in the velvet glove, for those who don't go through all the appropriate entrance formalities for this club.

The basic rule is that anyone with a new source of untaxed income, such as a trading business or an investment like a buy-to-let property, has to notify HMRC within 6 months of the end of the tax year in which the income first arises. So, Susan, who has always up to now just been a PAYE taxpayer, but has acquired a property which she first lets out on 1 September 2019, has until early October 2020 to notify HMRC and register for self-assessment. If she doesn't, the taxman is likely (although not certain) to charge her penalties.

The second piece of red tape the new business person/investor needs to consider is Value Added Tax (VAT). Susan in my example doesn't need to worry about this, because letting residential property is exempt from VAT, but everyone in her position needs at least to ask the initial question or questions, which are:

- Is my business exempt or taxable?
- Has my turnover exceeded the VAT registration threshold of £85,000?
- If my turnover is below this level, and likely to remain so, might it nevertheless be worth my while to register for VAT?

You'll find in the Appendix a summary of the various types of "supply" that a business person or investor might make, with how these are treated for VAT. The general rule is that everything you do in the course of business is vatable unless it is specifically exempted. You don't have to register compulsorily for VAT if your turnover is below the threshold, or until it goes over that threshold. However, if all of your customers/clients are VAT registered, the advantage of registering voluntarily, below the threshold, is that you can reclaim VAT on your expenses.

For small traders whose taxable supplies are below the threshold there is always the choice to make between registering voluntarily or not. The upside is the ability to get some money back from HMRC: but the downside is the administrative hassle of having to comply with the VAT accounting rules.

If your customers/clients are not VAT registered (for example if they are members of the public who are not in business) it simply makes you more expensive to be VAT registered, because they can't in turn reclaim the VAT charged to them.

Whilst VAT is described as a tax on the "final consumer", because the tax can be reclaimed at each stage along the line of business to business charges, this is only partly true: because VAT exempt businesses can't reclaim the tax themselves.

Taking on Staff

A managing director, a foreman, and an apprentice are standing beside a high wall. This may sound as though it's the beginning of a joke, but unfortunately, it's based on a real life event, with only the names missed out. High up on the wall is a lamp which is flickering and clearly faulty. Next to the wall, lying full length on the ground, is a ladder long enough to reach the lamp. The apprentice suggests the obvious expedient of leaning the ladder up against the wall, and going up to fix the lamp – a five minute job at most.

The managing director, who has obviously been in the business for many years, enters a veto. "No" he says, "you stay here and don't move. The foreman and I will go around the corner and organise a tower scaffold". When they return quarter of an hour later with the men bringing the scaffold pieces, they find the apprentice lying on the ground groaning.

Readers of Greek tragedy and other students of inevitability will know exactly what has happened, and what is going to happen. The apprentice has disobeyed orders, leaned the ladder against the wall, climbed up it, and fallen. He has injured himself in direct contravention of instructions issued.

Anyone who has ever been on the employer's side in a tribunal case will be unsurprised by what comes next. The apprentice sues the employer, and of course he wins his case and gets compensation. But the amusing part of the story (if you are not an employer) was the argument raised by the apprentice.

"The fact of the matter is", he said, "I'm stupid! - when you went away and left me, you failed to take into account the fact that I'm stupid!"

At this, the tribunal president presumably nodded his head sympathetically and rubber stamped the award of compensation.

This isn't, of course, an isolated instance of the way our legal system bends over backwards to favour the employee against the employer. And taking on employees brings with it not just this ridiculous bias but also a raft of obligations to employees, both tax and other.

So, I do most seriously suggest to new businesses that, if there is a way of securing the input to your business that you need without entering into an employment contract with anyone, you should do so. For example, in some industries it is customary for employment bureaus to provide staff, and take on all the obligations of the employment relationship. This won't always necessarily get the end user out of trouble derived from incidents like that of the stupid apprentice, but it will provide something of a cushion.

If you have to employ staff, though, and getting back to our relationship with our friends at HMRC, you will need to register with them as a PAYE employer. With registration as a PAYE employer comes the requirement to keep appropriate records, and make the appropriate end of year returns.

Here I would very much recommend, if economically viable, that a new business considers using the services of a payroll bureau. These specialist organisations, if they are worth their salt, will take off your shoulders the burden both of making appropriate tax deductions and paying the appropriate amounts to the staff member and HMRC respectively; but will also keep you clean with regard to the various other financial obligations which anyone stupid or unfortunate enough to employ staff is loaded with in this country. Just as one example, in the face of the total inadequacy of the state pension, employers have recently had imposed on them a requirement to provide a "workplace pension" for staff, unless they opt out – on top of the National Insurance contributions which were originally designed to provide the same thing. The ins and outs of these rules are likely to be something of a nightmare for your average small start up business to get its head around: so, hand over responsibility to a professional bureau. Many of these are surprisingly economical in terms of what they charge for an essential service.

Making Tax Digital

"Making tax digital is a key part of the government's plans to make it easier for individuals and businesses to get their tax right and keep on top of their affairs... [it] is making fundamental changes to the way the tax system works – transforming tax administration so that it is:

- More effective
- More efficient
- Easier for taxpayers to get their tax right."

I am quoting from the government's policy paper "Overview of Making Tax Digital", which is a beautiful example of a velvet glove containing an iron hand below. You'd have to be pretty naïve to take this sort of "spin" at its face value. The reality of the situation is that HMRC want to collect more tax, and this becomes clear later on in the policy paper where they talk about the benefits of MTD in reducing the so called "tax gap". But what does MTD, or Making Tax Digital, actually consist in?

The good news for those who dislike red tape is that the planned commencement date of MTD of 6 April 2019 has mostly been deferred. The rules apply from that month as far as VAT accounting is concerned, but the extension of this to income tax has been deferred, with a current anticipated start date of April 2023.

Put very briefly, MTD involves two radical changes from how tax has always been dealt with in this country up to now:

- There is an absolute obligation to keep your records on computer (if you're in MTD); and to use specified software which has been explicitly approved for MTD; and
- The keeping of records on computer is linked up with a much more frequent (quarterly) disclosure of your numbers to HMRC – or rather HMRC's computer. VAT accounting has always been quarterly or more frequent, however for Income Tax this will be a significant departure, and the aim is to do away with the annual tax return completely.

To sum up, for VAT MTD consists of no more than a slight tightening up of procedures, and forceable admission of the last few manual record keepers into the digital "club". And this is all that is currently in force.

Self-Assessment Tax Returns

Until the utopian objective of abolishing tax returns is a reality, when HMRC's benevolent intentions towards businesses (which they have to apply legal compulsion to introduce) are fully with us, there is still the need for all self-assessment taxpayers who receive a notice to that effect, to complete the annual tax return. The UK tax year ends on 5 April, for historical reasons, and if you are one of the dwindling minority of individuals who wish to submit a manual return, this has to be done within about 6 months of the end of the tax year, in October. If on the other hand you do your tax return on computer, either using HMRC's own software or one of the brands you can buy, your deadline is 31 January, approximately 10 months after the tax year end.

Confusingly, you don't just work out your tax for a year and then pay it on the 31 January date following. You have to make payments on account of that tax liability in the course of the preceding 12 months, with the first payment on account for the year ended 5 April 2020, for example, being due on 31 January 2020. A second payment on account is then due on 31 July 2020 for that year, with any balance paid or refunded on 31 January 2021. The amount of the payments on account is based on your last year's total liability, unless you put in a formal application to reduce it (which should be based on some proper assessment of your position).

It should be too obvious to need saying that, if you want to stay out of trouble with HMRC as is the declared intention of the advice in this chapter, you should get your tax return in on time. Late tax returns are a very good way of attracting HMRC's unfavourable attention in the form of investigations: and there are also financial penalties which follow on from a late tax return submission as surely as day follows night. But what's perhaps not so obvious, to judge from the every day experience of accountants and tax advisers, is that no one need ever submit their tax return late, except in cases of serious illness.

This isn't some sort of sermon about not leaving things to the last minute. Sometimes it does take a long time for the information you need to complete your tax return to become available, particularly if you are in business – and even more particularly, if you are in business with others. Sometimes the information doesn't come through at all, or not by the 31 January tax return deadline.

But what do you do in this situation where everything has got behind? Do you sit on your return and watch the 31 January deadline going by?

Absolutely not! There is a perfectly well established system under which you or your adviser can enter a provisional figure in the absence of the definite information. Where provisional figures are entered, you then have to make an undertaking as to when you intend or hope to provide the final numbers. So, you've no excuse at all for just leaving it, and if you end up with a penalty, perhaps an HMRC investigation, and invalid professional fee insurance, you've only yourself to blame!

Should I be Afraid of HMRC?

My answer to this question would be an, admittedly not very helpful, "yes and no".

It's undoubtedly the case that they are a government department with apparently bottomless pockets, who have extensive powers given to them by the law. These powers include not just the ability to require you to supply information (within limits), but also to raise "assessments" on you which it is your legal obligation then to disprove. So, if a tax inspector forms the suspicion, even on quite tenuous grounds, that your income was actually £100,000 more than you declared on your tax return, the onus on you is to prove that he's wrong, rather than being on him to justify his £100,000 additional assessment.

This is powerful artillery. However, the powers of the Revenue are not, as I've said, absolutely unlimited and there are circumstances where they can and should be reminded of those limitations.

Despite what some people think, and HMRC would like you to believe, they are not the law, but are subject to the law like any other person or government department.

Another weakness of HMRC is their low staff numbers, which are not much than half the total they were 15 years ago. Often the problem with low staff numbers in HMRC becomes a problem for the taxpayer, because it's much more difficult to get hold of anybody sensible at HMRC now than it used to be. But lack of resource is undoubtedly also hampering HMRC's efforts to bring in the maximum possible tax. Despite sporadic advertising campaigns suggesting that HMRC are some kind of all seeing "big brother", the reality is more akin to the medieval castle which is "garrisoned" by spears with empty helmets hitched on top, peering between each of the crenellations.

Also, which some may find surprising, we have seen a dramatic deterioration in the quality of technical training within HMRC. Many years ago when I was first practising in tax, the inspector was a formidable opponent technically, who had received at least as good, if not much better, a training than your average accountant. The situation now seems to be very different, with school leavers being put on to technical work at an early stage, and some quite breath taking gaps in technical knowledge revealed in correspondence with HMRC. So, you certainly shouldn't assume that any technical information given by an HMRC officer is correct, without checking it with your accountant or tax adviser.

The Role of the Accountant/Tax Adviser

And that brings me on to an important issue with regard to how you relate, as a business person, to HMRC. The majority, but not all, businesses make use of an accountant. The main reason why clients use accountants is not for their services in adding up columns of figures, but for their understanding of the tax system and the way HMRC works. I would certainly recommend anyone whose affairs are not of the very simplest to use a professional in their interface with HMRC from year to year. The problem is: how do you find a good one?

It's obviously no help looking at their own advertisements or websites. Every firm is the same according to these, and they are all brilliant. The best way to find a good accountant, still, is probably word of mouth, as with other professionals.

This has probably always been the case, but a situation which is new is the emergence of the tax adviser as a separate profession. In the 1980's, when I trained, it was completely routine to go to your accountant for all tax queries. Since then, however, the volume of tax legislation and practice rules etc, etc has become something like 7 or 8 times as much. No accountant, who has to keep up to date with non tax issues such as accounting standards, auditing standards, company law, insolvency law etc can possibly keep up to date with this enormous Niagara of tax legislation as well. Hence, accountants and lawyers whose main interest is in tax have effectively formed a new profession (although its governing body, The Chartered Institute of Taxation, dates back to the 1920's).

When should you turn to a tax adviser, rather than to an accountant, for advice? Obviously, an accountant who is worth his salt will know his limitations, and will know when to invite a tax adviser in, so to speak. However, the problem with this is that, whilst an accountant can easily react to specific questions and issues in this way, he can't necessarily see the tax planning possibilities in your situation which a tax adviser could.

If you have a general and uneasy feeling that you could be paying less tax, then, it's probably up to you to find a specialist tax adviser and put your situation to him or her for an initial view. Often, they will give this to you free of charge.

CHAPTER 4
CLAIMING YOUR DUE

One of the most obvious ways of saving tax legally and ethically, you'd have thought, must be claiming all the deductions against profits that you are legally due. But I'd lay money that not one business in a hundred actually claims all of their entitlement.

In this chapter I'm going to look at some of the less obvious deductions you can and should make in arriving at your taxable income. None of us needs to be told that the basic costs of making sales, staff salaries, and overheads of running the business premises, are allowable. But there are a lot of types of expense which aren't at all obvious, and I'm going to start with the somewhat recherché world of Capital Allowances.

Relief for "Capital" Expenditure

Let's start with the basic principles. If you have a business which turns over £20,000, incurs overhead costs of £5,000, and acquires a new car for £12,000, is your profit, for that year, £3,000? No, because the cost of the car doesn't get written off 100% in the first year. Instead, you'd put the depreciation of the car down as an expense, perhaps £3,000 in the first year, and you show a profit, therefore, of £14,000.

The reason you don't claim the cost of the car as an expense all in one hit is because the car lasts for a lot longer than one year – it is to be hoped. In their wisdom, those who framed our tax rules decided that depreciation wasn't an allowable expense, although it's not at all clear why they came to that conclusion. So, instead of this, they introduced a system called Capital Allowances, which set out specific rules about exactly how much of the cost of capital assets like cars you could claim in each period.

In general terms Capital Allowances can only be claimed on buildings at the fairly unexciting rate of 3%, but they can be claimed on "plant and machinery". I put that phrase in quotation marks because it doesn't just refer to things like JCB's and sausage machines. It's not even restricted to movable items. But you have to ask the question, of any fixed asset you acquire, as to whether it is an asset you use for the purpose of carrying on your trade or business, or a building or part of a building which is the setting in which you carry on the business. So, the basic fabric of a building, and the doors, windows etc aren't claimable as plant and machinery. But furniture and fittings, computers, electrical systems, heating and hot water systems and the like do come within the claimable category. You'll find a list of what constitutes plant in the table which forms part of the Appendix at the back of this book.

Start Up Businesses

One of the most interesting and unexpected examples of Claimable Allowances comes up in the case of a new business. Take the example of John, who leaves his employment with a big tech company to set up in business as a supplier and consultant in the home computer market. He fills his garage up with boxes of equipment, and converts one of the rooms in the house into an office. (In ten years time, although he doesn't know it, he'll be occupying a plush office building in the city, and will own ten big warehouses: but we've all got to start off small.) The point of this illustration is that John can claim, not just the cost of new equipment, office furniture, and so on that he buys, but also he can claim for what he's already got: desks and chairs in his home that he puts to business use, computers that were previously just used for home purposes like looking at funny cat videos on YouTube, the broadband system already installed at home, his mobile phone, and even the car he already owns.

What John can do, with the full blessing of HMRC, is take the market value of all these items on the day he started his new business, and claim what are known as "writing down allowances" (mostly at 18%) on this value.

For "integral features" in his home (and the same applies to any building from which a business is carried on) he can claim an 6% per annum allowance, and these features include:

- Space and water heating systems;
- Air conditioning and air cooling systems;
- Hot and cold water systems (but not toilet and kitchen facilities);
- Electrical systems, including lighting systems

This is where I make good my claim that not one in a hundred of business-es claim all that they're due. How many, I wonder, strike a market value for their home boiler, and claim allowances on it when they start a business from home? This is obviously a rhetorical question!

If the items concerned had VAT added to them when they were originally purchased, you can even go back and claim that VAT, subject to certain conditions – of which more in my chapter on VAT below.

The Annual Investment Allowance

The way writing down allowance, of 18% and 8% respectively, works is that you write that amount off the expenditure each year, so the allowance gradually dwindles in the absence of new assets acquired. And it can take a very long time indeed, as any mathematician will tell you, to get relief for the whole expenditure – indeed theoretically an infinite amount of time. The rules these days are extremely stingy in comparison with a blanket 25% writing down allowance which used to apply: but, at the other extreme, we now have a very generous allowance which applies, not to the assets you had on hand when you started the business, but to items of "plant and machinery" that you acquire after you've set up in business. This can be made the subject of a 100% claim to the Annual Investment Allowance: that is, the whole expenditure is written off in the first year. This very generous allowance is available for most sorts of plant and machinery except cars. For the calendar years 2019 and 2020 the maximum amount of expenditure you can claim the AIA on is £1 million, scheduled as I write to reduce to £200,000 on 1 January 2021: but this amount should do very nicely for most small businesses!

Capital Allowances for Landlords

If you are a landlord of commercial property, the same rules as above will apply in principle. It's less likely, in most circumstances, of course, that a landlord will be owning or acquiring a lot of plant: he usually leaves that to the tenant. But the ability to claim relief on fixtures and integral features, which may have been in the building before the tenant moves in, and indeed will probably still be there when the tenant moves out, is potentially very useful.

Landlords of residential property are in a completely different situation – unless the residential property counts as "Furnished Holiday Lettings" (FHL). FHL is closely defined, and means accommodation which is let for holidays for at least 105 days a year, and which is available to be let for at least 210 days – with no individual letting in these periods lasting for more than 30 days. These are treated as a trade for tax purposes, and, whilst their tax planning "wings" have been clipped quite a bit recently, they are still an interesting enough sort of asset and business activity to deserve a whole chapter to themselves: which I've given them later on in this book. For the average run of the mill residential landlord, though, who's probably let out the flats and houses on assured shorthold tenancies, there's no Capital Allowance relief for the plant etc within the let dwellings. What residential landlords used to get instead was what was called the "wear and tear allowance". This basically was in place to provide a very rough approximation to the cost of furnishing a residential property, and the allowance wasn't available to property that was let unfurnished. This was done away with four or so years ago now, and in its place there is a kind of replacement allowance. This is how it works. You get no allowance for the initial cost of the furniture, when you are furnishing the property from nothing, but you do get the cost of replacing items of furniture. If you replace an old item by a much better new item, then in principle you can only claim a proportion of the costs of the new piece of furniture, equivalent to what the old piece would have cost (allowing for modern improvements).

Rupert furnishes his new flat from Ikea, including a flatpack table. Inexplicably, this gives up the ghost after only a few years heavy use by the "don't care" type of tenant, and Rupert replaces it with an antique mahogany dining table which he bids £10,000 for at Christie's. The chances are, he'll only be able to claim a very small proportion of this £10,000 as a replacement!

The Byways of Expense Claiming

In this country we've got a very strange rule that expenses can only be claimed for tax if they are incurred "wholly and exclusively" for the purposes of the business concerned. This is a strange rule because the purpose, and use, of a particular type of expenditure might be overwhelmingly motivated by business purposes: but if there's any non business purpose, however tiny, this means that the whole expense – not just a proportion of it – is disallowed. It is in fact such a stringent and, let's face it, inequitable rule, that HMRC sometimes turn a blind eye to a less than strict application of the rule by taxpayers.

Of course, some kinds of expense are partly used for business "wholly and exclusively", and partly not. By this, I'm referring to such things as the phone bill, where some of your calls will be 100% business and some will be private. There's no conflict with the wholly and exclusively rule in claiming a proportion of your phone calls as relating to business, therefore. Strictly, the line rental is a mixed purpose expense and has to be disallowed, but I wouldn't be surprised if a lot of people quietly ignore this sort of subtlety.

By contrast, take the example of the taxi driver who needs to buy a new pair of spectacles. It may be that he doesn't wear them much other than when driving, but this is a classic case of an expense which HMRC will dig their heels in and deny relief for. Inevitably, being able to see clearly is something you do not just for business purposes. The same is true of most eating and drinking, and expenditure on clothing. There's an irreducible minimum of non business purpose behind any such expenditure.

Another sort of expenditure that HMRC will throw out as a direct profit and loss account deduction is "Capital" expenditure. This means not just the purchase of assets which will last for a long time – which would generally qualify for Capital Allowances depending on whether they are "plant and machinery" – but also things like legal advice relating to the structure of the business (for example issuing shares in a company) and relating to the acquisition of assets. There's a very important distinction between expenditure on a property which is "capital" on the one hand and ordinary repairs on the other. Capital expenditure normally involves an element of improvement to the property, and if this is predominant, HMRC will disallow the expenditure as capital. (Incidentally, there's a lot of talk about how wicked and unfair taxpayers are who go in for avoiding tax: but nobody ever mentions the wicked and unfair rules imposed by HMRC which disfavour the taxpayer. A classic example of this, in my view, is "capital" expenditure which gets disallowed for tax purposes even though the expenditure is wholly and exclusively for the business – and often doesn't get allowed for any other purpose (for example Capital Gains Tax) either.

Thirdly, expenditure on entertaining is usually verboten. The only exceptions to this are entertaining your own staff and entertaining if you are a pub or restaurant or similar business.

So, as I've already mentioned, we're taking the obvious sorts of expenditure, such as cost of sales, staff costs, and premises overheads, as read: what follows is a short list of some of the less obvious allowable items.

Travel & Subsistence

Expenditure on travelling in pursuance of your business (for example a landlord travelling to his properties to mend a door handle) does come into this category, of course. But what exactly does "subsistence" mean? Well, basically, it's eating and drinking. Surely, you might say, eating is a classic example of expenditure which can't ever be "wholly and exclusively" for business purposes? You eat to live. But despite this, in practice HMRC will allow costs of meals bought whilst away from home on business. You have to be away not just from home, but also from your main place of work, if these are different. Lunch taken at the restaurant down the street from your office doesn't qualify.

"Wife's Wages"

If other members of your family (not just a "wife") help in any way in your business, it can make a lot of tax sense to pay them for doing so. If, say, they have little or no income of their own, this results in an overall reduction in the tax paid by the business and by the household as a whole. This is easiest where the amounts involved are below the threshold at which the dreaded PAYE needs to be applied, of course. But do watch out for one trap: HMRC can and do disallow amounts put in business profit and loss accounts for family wages where the amounts concerned are not actually paid, but just put down as a claim. (This is surprisingly frequent practice, nevertheless, in the real world.)

Home Expenses

I've already talked about the possibility, easily overlooked, of being able to claim Capital Allowances on home equipment and plant generally, and of course the same principle applies to the day to day costs of running the home, including heating, lighting, insurance, home repairs, broadband subscriptions etc, etc. These are the sort of expenses which you can claim on the basis of a fair apportionment between the business and private benefit. The art lies in a method of apportionment which, whilst being fair and justifiable, is as favourable to you as possible.

HMRC will sometimes suggest that you do it on a square footage basis. So, let's take the example of John and his garage full of boxes of computer equipment; and the room at home converted into an office. They might suggest taking a square footage of those two rooms and dividing it by the total square footage of the house, and then using that as your fraction for claiming allowances. But there can be different methods of doing it which are a lot more favourable, especially taking into account the fact that you may be spending the majority of your time, and things like electricity and gas, on your occupation of the home whilst working. All it needs is a little common sense and imagination.

One concern that people sometimes raise with me is about losing some of their Capital Gains Tax exemption for the home. Surely, they say, if I am claiming say 25% of my home expenses as relating to business, this means that 25% of my home is now business premises which would be taxed on the gain, when I sell?

Well, I tend to answer, you can conceivably bring about that fairly disastrous result (with more Capital Gains Tax payable than you've ever saved in Income Tax by claiming home expenses), but it's actually very easy to avoid this happening. The sale of your home is completely exempt from Capital Gains Tax if the property has been your main residence throughout your period of ownership, and no part of the home has been used exclusively for business purposes. So, it's quite easy to avoid any restriction in your CGT exemption, by making sure that you use all of the house, at some time, for private purposes. What the CGT rule is really designed to catch is the "flat over the shop" scenario, where the shop is taxable on any sale but the flat exempt.

This issue is one reason, though, why I would not recommend claiming a proportion of the mortgage interest on your home against tax. The logical implication of such a claim is that part of your home is exclusively business.

Protective Clothing

I've made the point above that clothing is almost inevitably disallowable under the "wholly and exclusively" rules. There was even a case about this which a lot of us felt the taxpayer was unlucky to lose. This was the famous leading case of Mallalieu v Drummond. Ms Mallalieu was a barrister who only wore the regulation dark clothes in court, and wouldn't have been seen dead in them in ordinary life. Surely, you would have said, this is an example of these particular clothes being bought wholly and exclusively for her business? In one of the finest pieces of logical hair splitting in the whole of tax case law, the House of Lords decided that her purpose "must have" included that of preserving warmth and decency, and therefore her claim was chucked out.

Despite this, and with doubtful logical consistency, HMRC do specifically allow the cost of protective clothing, like overalls, steel toe-capped boots, and presumably milkshake proof suits for politicians.

"Company Only" Expenses

As I've already commented elsewhere, there are some types of expense which can only be claimed by limited companies, and these are:

- Losses on financing loans to non connected parties;
- The 230% (for small companies) allowance for research and development; and
- Amounts written off intangible assets (like trademarks, computer software and many other types) by way of depreciation or "amortisation".

Claiming Taxes Against Tax

You can't claim the Income Tax or Corporation Tax on your profits as an expense, unfortunately, but there are some sorts of tax which can be claimed as an expense of the business. If you're not VAT registered, or can't claim all of your VAT back because some of your turnover is VAT exempt, the irrecoverable VAT becomes part of your overheads and can be claimed as a reduction in your profits as worked out for direct tax purposes. Stamp Duty Land Tax can also be claimed where the cost of the property itself is an expense (as, for example, it is for a property developer).

Provisions

The last in my little list of the byways of expense claiming may also be the most interesting and potentially lucrative one. One of the interesting things about provisions is that they aren't expenses, laid out in money, at all. Rather, they're accounting adjustments to the profit. There are three different types of provision which can reduce your reported, and therefore taxable profits:

Stock Provisions

Where your business is the sort which buys and sells goods of any kind, you should always do a review of your stock list at the end of each accounting period, and write down the value of any items which are no longer saleable, or saleable at a figure less than cost. The good thing about this process, from the point of view of tax planning, is that you don't need to do a corresponding write up of stock items which are worth more than their cost (carrying value in a stock list is normally cost). So, it's a one sided exercise in your favour.

Bad Debt Provisions

If a debtor is definitely not going to pay you, or even if you reasonably anticipate that he will not pay you in the event, you are quite a liberty to delete the value of that debtor from your balance sheet, resulting in a reportable loss in the profit and loss account.

Warranty Provisions

If you are doing any kind of work, or supplying any kind of goods, which might give rise to uninsured claims by aggrieved clients or customers, you can, and indeed should, make a properly calculated provision for such future claims – even if they cannot be worked out accurately at the time the accounts are prepared. The only sort of provision for losses of this kind which does get disallowed is a provision which hasn't been calculated sufficiently scientifically (the case on this is Owen v Southern Railway of Peru).

As a general principle, look through all your balance sheet items, particularly in the current assets category, to see whether the carrying value should be written down to a more realistic recoverable value. The difference will reduce your taxable profits.

CHAPTER 5
TAX PLANNING FOR LANDLORDS

In a way it's odd that the term "landlord" is still universally accepted as the term for a person who lets property out for rent. Why haven't the language police been out hunting down this old fashioned, patriarchal, elitist etc, etc word? Perhaps it's because of the problem of finding a suitable substitute – although that doesn't normally bother our boys and girls in blue at the language division. But you could hardly talk about a "land person", even nowadays, if you wanted to be taken seriously.

I found out an interesting fact recently, which is that, apparently, anyone who owns land in Scotland can be called a laird or lord if they are male, or a lady if they are female. So, there is quite an industry going selling small plots of land in Scotland to people so that they can put "lord" or "lady" on their cheque books and credit cards. They say it gets you priority in booking restaurant tables.

Anyway, I'm going to follow the very convenient tradition and refer to the people whose tax affairs are the subject of this chapter as "landlords". In many ways, the tax system treats landlords just the same as any other recipient of untaxed income (by which term I mean income which doesn't have tax deducted from it at source). For example, in working out how much rental profit you've made, you are allowed to deduct much the same sort of expenses as you can in calculating the profits of a trade. But there are also a number of points of considerable tax planning interest, to say the least, that affect landlords uniquely: hence the need for this chapter, which summarises these points, refers to other parts of this book where you can find them discussed in more detail, and elaborates one or two of them that aren't examined elsewhere.

Taxation of Investment Activities

The first thing to get clear is that being a landlord is an investment activity, and not a "trade" within the meaning of that word accepted for tax purposes. And one of the first things you realise, when you go into the rules of our tax system in any depth, is that our tax legislators seem to like trades; and don't seem to like the investments and investors. The only type of property letting which is treated as a trade is furnished holiday letting: and this is such an important exception that I'm devoting a separate chapter to it later on. But here are some of the more important ways in which our tax system discriminates against "ordinary" property letting, as it does against other investment type activities like owning shares:

- The sale of let property is generally chargeable to Capital Gains Tax at the full rate, with gains on commercial property being charged currently at 20% for higher rate taxpayers, and gains on residential property at the higher rate of 28%. By contrast, the sale of assets (including properties) which form part of the disposal of a trading business are only subject to 10% tax (because of "Business Asset Disposal Relief" - formerly "Entrepreneurs' Relief");

- If you make a gain on selling a property used for a trade, rather than used for letting to a tenant, you can "roll over" that gain against the acquisition of a new trading property. That means no tax is payable until you subsequently go on to sell that replacement property at a gain – unless you then replace it with property number three, and so on. It's a common misapprehension on the part of property investors that, if they sell one of their properties and buy another one with the money, they don't have to pay tax. Unfortunately, doing this means that you have less available to invest in a replacement property, because of the tax which you definitely can't "roll over";

- If you give away an investment property, you are treated as making a capital gain even though you haven't received a penny for it, perhaps. With property or other assets used for a trade, on the other hand, this imaginary "gain" can be "held over", so that no tax need become payable on the gift. The same principle applies to gifts of shares. If the company is an unquoted trading company, you can hold over the gain, whereas if it is a property investment company, you can't;

- Trades are generally completely relieved from inheritance tax, whereas investment properties are fully taxable: meaning HMRC, all other things being equal, will take 40% of its value from you on your death; and

- It's a lot easier to get relief for losses incurred in a trade than in a property investment activity.

Loss relief for trading losses is such an important subject (like furnished holiday letting) that it deserves a chapter to itself, which I've given it below in Chapter 16. But losses from renting property have their own peculiar and fairly restrictive regime, which I'll have a look at now because it isn't dealt with elsewhere.

It may seem counterintuitive that property rental losses are more likely to happen in boom periods for investment property ownership. But actually, the reason for this is quite clear. When people are buying to make a capital gain, they are quite happy to pay large capital sums for a comparatively smaller income return. Very often the rental return won't actually cover the expenses, but the landlord who is really investing for capital growth rather than income doesn't mind this: because your returns from capital growth can be many times as great as anything you can get in the way of rent. So, it's by no means unusual to see losses accruing year after year.

What can you do with these losses for tax purposes? Well, the answer is "precious little"; because all that's allowed is to carry these forward against future rental profits from the same rental "business".

The Revenue tend to interpret this last phrase very restrictively, too: if, say, you own and let out property in two different "capacities", you can only offset the losses made in one capacity against future profits from the same. The example HMRC give in their manuals is of somebody who lets out a property personally, but also has a share of property income from a partnership. Losses from one can't be offset against profits from the other. Whether HMRC are right in taking such a strict line as they do (and I have my doubts, personally) it's obviously better, if you can, to organise your landlord activities in one "entity" if you can, rather than it being fragmented between a number of different businesses.

HMRC will also disallow losses if a property business ceases, perhaps because you've sold your only investment property. What happens to the losses here is, unfortunately, that they evaporate into thin air. But it's a question of fact as to whether your property business has "ceased": so if you are only going through a short period between owning properties, and you were always intending to buy another one after you sold the first, then you may well be justified in claiming to carry forward any losses from property one against property two.

Now Read On

The unique challenges and opportunities facing landlords, as I've said, are considered in detail in various parts of the book, including in particular:

- Chapter 4 considers the claiming of expenses and the way you claim relief for capital expenditure. All landlords should have a working knowledge of these;
- A tax efficient business structure is just as important for landlords as it is for people carrying on a trade, so have a look at Chapters 7 and 8 on how to structure your business, and how tax efficiently to extract the profits personally from that business;
- I've already mentioned furnished holiday accommodation, and how important this is for running tax efficient property businesses;
- Chapter 17 examines the all important distinction between trading

and investing: basically whether you are fundamentally a landlord or a property developer or dealer;

- I've devoted two chapters to VAT, and one in particular considers how you can come a cropper, without proper planning, in the sphere of VAT on property;

- Inheritance tax is of major concern to property investors, for obvious reasons: see my chapter on practical inheritance tax planning (Chapter 21) for some ideas on minimising the effect of this killer amongst capital taxes;

- Towards the end of the book, where the planning is getting perhaps slightly more advanced, I'm considering the merits and perhaps otherwise of Limited Liability Partnerships (LLP's) with limited company partners, as a tax efficient structure. This has a particularly interesting angle with regard to such LLP's which own investment property; and

- Of course there's the infamous "Osborne tax" to consider: easily the biggest tax headache which landlords are facing at the moment. See Chapter 25 for a solution – or rather more than one possible solution.

Property Holding Limited Companies

For the rest of this chapter, though, I'm going to be looking at providing an answer to the question: should I hold my property investments through a limited company? This is a question which is raised very often in practice, and no wonder: the differences in your tax treatment using a property investment company on the one hand, against holding property direct or in partnership on the other, can be huge. I say that this is a question which is raised frequently in practice: but sometimes it isn't raised at all, and the tacit assumption is made that a property investment company is a Good Thing – with sometimes disastrous consequences.

Why Form a Property Company?

I should make it clear once again that the target audience of this chapter is those who invest in property rather than hold property as a trader i.e. to sell it for short term profit. The distinction is considered carefully in the chapter on trading versus investing which I've already referred to.

Sometimes, no doubt, a property company is set up for non tax reasons: such as providing a formal structure through which to hold a family's wealth. But my suspicion is that tax is overwhelmingly often the driver.

Put briefly and simply, a limited company currently (2019/20) pays no more than a flat 19% tax on its rental (as other) profits: individuals who own property directly can pay rates as high as 40% or even 45%. So, is it a "no brainer" to hold your property portfolio through a company?

Far from it! Because what I've just said glosses over the fact that companies pay dividends to their shareholders, and those dividends are then personal income for the individuals. In the straightforward case where a company receives rental profits, pays Corporation Tax on them, and then distributes what's left as dividends to its shareholders, the company isn't actually saving any tax at all on the income.

In fact the reverse is the case, because passing the income through a limited company in this way will usually actually increase the tax. Let's have a look at a simple example to illustrate.

Walter and Dennis are both 40% income tax payers. Walter has a property company, Walter Investments Limited, which owns a single property, yielding rent of £20,000 per annum after expenses. Dennis also has a property yielding net rental profits of £20,000 per annum, but he owns this direct rather than through a limited company. Both men require the post tax rental income to live on.

Dennis's tax liability on his rent is simply worked out: it's 40% of £20,000, that is £8,000. Walter, on the other hand, has two layers of tax to pay, firstly at company level and secondly at personal level when the company pays him out as a dividend. So, Walter Investments Limited pays tax at 19% on the £20,000 rental profit, and sends its cheque for £3,800 to HMRC. The balance of money is then paid out to Walter as a dividend of £16,200. Walter being a higher rate taxpayer, the dividend rate (which is lower than the rate on other income, because the dividend is paid out of post company tax profits) is 32.5%. His personal tax, then, is £5,265, meaning that he has £10,935 left after these two levels of tax. This is actually an effective overall tax rate of just over 45%, as against the straight 40% paid by Dennis.

Of course one example can't establish an unbreakable rule which applies in all circumstances. If there is substantial borrowing on the property, the interest on which is now completely disallowable under the "Osborne tax" rules, the position might be different – depending on the final tax effect of the disallowance in the case of the individual property owner. Also, not every property investor needs to distribute all of the income, and instead chooses to reinvest it in the purchase of new property. I wish I could say it was just a case of "doing the sums", but in the case of the company which ploughs its profit back into new property investments, there are so many variables that it isn't really realistic to do a single sum and act on the basis of the answer; because ultimately, arguably, profits retained in a company are going to have to be distributed at some point.

In fact there's no right or wrong answer, if one looks purely at the tax rates or effective tax rates on income: but it is fair to say that in a lot of cases the income tax "benefits" of holding a property portfolio through a limited company are a complete illusion.

Short Term Versus Long Term

In many cases, nevertheless, the reduction in the immediate or "headline" rate of tax on the rents will be a short term advantage. But I would like to suggest that there can be some very serious long term disadvantages of a property company too, which are so serious, and so likely to apply, as to create in my personal opinion a presumption against the use of property companies.

Read the following "Cautionary Tale" and see what you think.

Minnie and Susan each buy a property in year 0 for £100,000. Minnie simply buys the property in her own name, but Susan acquires it in the name of Susan Investments Limited, in which she holds the shares. Ten years later, both properties have doubled in value, and are sold in year ten for £200,000. Both ladies use the gain/proceeds to build an extension to their homes.

Because this is a residential property, Minnie's tax charge on the £100,000 gain is at 28%, that is £28,000. Susan, by contrast, has a corporation tax charge (which we'll take at 19%, the current rate, for illustration); so that the tax payable by the company is £19,000. This leaves £81,000 to be extracted from the company by Susan, and we will assume (which is most often the case in practice) that there are reasons why she is unwilling to do this by way of winding up Susan Investments Limited. So, she takes the £81,000 profit out as a dividend, on which she is taxable, as a higher rate taxpayer, at 32.5%. So, she has a fairly substantial £26,325 income tax bill to pay.

The end result is that, of her £100,000 capital gain on selling the property, Susan has £54,675 left – whereas Minnie has £72,000 after her personal CGT charge of 28%.

But the situation can actually be many times worse than this, because of the principle which states that a person dying, and leaving assets to their beneficiaries, leaves those assets at probate value for Capital Gains Tax purposes – that is, the market value of the asset on the date of death. Let's show how this could impact on the straightforward situation I've just illustrated.

The facts are the same as in the example above except that, most unfortunately, both Minnie and Susan die in a fight about 6 months before the properties are sold, the sales being organised by their respective executors. A valuer decides that the properties were each worth £190,000 on the date of the ladies' demise.

In Susan's case, assuming that the company pays the profit out as a dividend, the overall tax burden is exactly the same, that is there is tax to pay in total of £45,325. (There's also inheritance tax to pay, but as this is basically the same for both Minnie and Susan I'll pass over this aspect)
The position with regard to the property formerly owned by the late Minnie could not be more different. The sale is actually not by the company in her case, but by her executors, and the base cost for CGT purposes is the value on the date of death: £190,000. So, not only is there only one layer of tax in Minnie's case, but the gain on which the tax is levied is tiny in comparison with what it would have been if Minnie had been alive. Ignoring the annual exemption, and assuming her beneficiary is a higher rate taxpayer, the tax will be £2,800.

Dumb question time: would you rather pay £45,325 or £2,800 tax on what is essentially the same gain?

A critic might make the counterargument that, if Susan is dead, it is likely to be much more tax efficient to wind up the company, because although, as the example illustrates, you get no uplift to market value on death with properties held by a company (because the company itself doesn't die) you do get an uplift to market value on the shares in the company itself. So, the gain can actually be extracted from the company, in all probability, with very little tax; because the capital gain on winding up starts with a probate value of £190,000. Unfortunately, though, what this argument ignores is the fact that it is likely, in practice, that a property investment company that is held over a long period will actually have several properties, not all of which will be sold. And when you wind up a company which owns properties standing at a gain, all of the gains on those unsold portfolio properties are treated as crystallising for Capital Gains Taxation purposes. Winding up the company is likely not to be a desirable option in most cases.

In summary, then, think at least twice, and probably three or more times, before deciding to structure your property investment activity as a limited company. The short term advantages might be non existent, but even if they are there, you could be storing up huge tax trouble to come for yourself or subsequent generations of your family.

CHAPTER 6
BUSINESS TRAVEL & ENTERTAINING

We live in an age of Spin. It's probably never been scientifically measured, but my guess would be that the vast majority of this comes from government, who seem to most of us to be more concerned about how they are viewed than what they're really like, or what they achieve. An interesting example of what might be called negative Spin is the campaign against "tax avoidance" mounted by HMRC and some of the more sanctimonious of our MP's. We get a lot of humbug – frankly – from those who think there is a "right amount of tax" and that everyone should pay it.

Underlying all of this heavy morality is the idea that our tax system, if left to itself, would produce a "fair" result. This is an idea which I suspect very few accountants and tax advisers – i.e. those who know anything about the subject – would subscribe to. Exhibit A in my testimony would be the tax treatment of business entertaining.

Disallowance of Entertaining Expenses

Within living memory of currently practising tax advisers, business entertaining has always been treated a non allowable expense for tax purposes. The reason for this almost universal disallowance (see the limited exceptions below) is hidden in the mist of time, but probably derives from a mixture of puritanism and envy on the part of those who have devised our tax system. Why should people enjoy themselves? Particularly when nobody takes the taxman out to lunch! (Of course, if they did, this would no doubt be fuel for the next big scandal – like the senior taxman a few years ago who was found out accepting favours, including free holidays, from taxpayers.) Do you think that this is unduly cynical? I wonder, given that the main exception to the rule is one of the few instances in which the taxman does get a "benefit" – the staff party exception, of which more below.

You might argue, against what I've said, that entertaining isn't, or shouldn't be, what running a business is about. Business is serious, and is about making profits – not enjoying yourself on a series of "jollies". But the point is that there's already a rule, which I've mentioned in Chapter 4, to the effect that any expenditure which isn't "wholly and exclusively" for business purposes is disallowed. So, you don't need a blanket ban on claiming entertaining expenses, where these might be purely incurred for business reasons. Take the example of Hodder, who is struggling to build up a publishing business. How does a publisher build up his turnover? The answer is, by persuading bookshops to stock his books. The slow way of doing this is to build up a reputation for producing good, saleable books, of course. But this is a very slow way. If you want to build up the business effectively, you need to grasp the nettle and take influential people amongst your potential customers (the bookshops in Hodder's case) out to lunch and/or dinner. Or you need to take a box at the local cricket or rugby match, and invite potential customers along, etc, etc.

This is what our hero does, and after the end of year one, his profit and loss account looks like this:

	£'000
Sale of books	200
Direct costs of book production	100
	100
Staff costs and premises overheads	(80)
Business entertaining	(30)
Loss for the year	(10)

If pressed, the taxman would no doubt accept, in Hodder's circumstances, that the entertaining is purely for business purposes, and not so that Hodder can enjoy himself personally. But the rule is the rule: the £30,000 entertaining has to be added back, resulting in a taxable profit of £20,000, on which the tax is, say, about £4,000. So, Hodder has a tax charge when he's made a real economic loss. The Right Amount of Tax?

Exceptions to the Rule

There are two main exceptions to this rule:

- Where the business consists of the provision of entertaining type services, for example a pub, hotel or restaurant; and
- Entertaining staff.

In both these cases, not only can you deduct the entertaining cost in your taxable profit computation, but you can even claim the VAT back if you are a VAT registered business.

There is a catch, though, where you're talking about staff entertaining. The entertaining is an allowable expense against profits, true: but it's also treated as a taxable benefit in kind, on which the staff members have to pay income tax and you, as their employer, have to pay a type of employer's national insurance (at 13.8% over a threshold). This is where the "staff party" exemption comes in.

Where staff functions over a year cost no more than £150 per head, this general rule about staff entertaining giving rise to a taxable benefit in kind doesn't apply. Could this be roughly the amount which is spent on HMRC staff parties?

If you're going to take advantage of this exemption, don't adopt a slap happy approach, though. Keep a careful record of the cost of staff functions over the year, and exactly how many staff attended each one, so that you can prove to a suspicious tax inspector, if you need to, that the £150 limit hasn't been breached.

In addition to the £150 staff party exemption, you can also provide "trivial benefits", which are benefits in kind which cost no more than £50 for each benefit. If the recipient concerned is a director, there's an annual cap of £300 on what can be spent tax free in this way.

Live it up on your Company – Tax Free

What this possibly rather provocative heading is referring to is the way business entertaining is in practice dealt with from the point of view of the relevant employees of the business which is doing the entertaining. Let's say you have an existing customer who is very important to the business, and who is known, also, as being a person who enjoys the fleshpots. As directors of your company, you and your spouse take him out to lunch at the Ritz as part of a programme of cementing relationships with crucial customers. Having lunch at the Ritz is a very pleasant experience for most people, and you would have thought that the taxman would want to charge you tax, somehow, for the pleasure that you and your spouse have received and paid for by the company. But the practical reality is that, whilst the actual bill is not an allowable expense, it's not treated as being a benefit in kind for you either – providing the entertaining is genuinely business related (this is my gloss on the practice) and is not an excuse for a personal "jolly".

Travelling Expenses

The treatment of travelling could be one of the more headbanging aspects of our complex and vague tax system. Hopefully, though, what follows will help the reader disentangle some of the complexity, and establish how to use the rules in the most advantageous way. First of all, I'll explain the principle which I label that of "the Rolls Royce and the window cleaner".

It's not surprising that the more luxurious method of travelling by air, for example, is described as "Business Class". This is based firmly on the principle I'm talking about, which is that you don't have to be a cheapskate in order to get tax relief for your travelling expenses. If you choose to travel in style, and therefore expensively, the cost is just as much allowable as if you travelled cattle class. In the case from which the term comes, HMRC tried to argue otherwise. They tried to persuade the appeal commissioners that a window cleaner should not be allowed to claim the cost of driving around between jobs in a Rolls Royce. The judge disagreed. He said that it was not up to the Inland Revenue (as they then were) to tell a person how to run their business, but merely to tax the results.

This principle extends, of course, not just to travelling at a higher class on public transport, but also to staying in the best hotels, and driving a top of the range car.

Choose Your Tax Regime

This is where I'm going to have to ask you to pay some fairly careful attention, and stop looking out of the window (if you are doing). The difference between the employed and self-employed tax regimes is particularly important where claiming travelling expenses is concerned.

If you are self-employed (a sole trader or a partner) we have the usual woolly situation beloved of the UK tax system. The tax treatment of travelling in a self-employed business depends, amongst other things, on where you are starting from. If you start from home, and home is not the main base of your operations, then the expense will be disallowed, following a string of cases which have decided this principle. For self-employed people, travelling between places of work is allowable, but not generally if the place you start from is your home.

Employees, in a rare instance of HMRC generosity to this downtrodden class, have both a clearer and, in some circumstances, a more favourable tax system. Bear in mind that you can effectively "choose" this employment regime, if you are running your own business, by running it through a limited company and becoming an employee/director of that company.

So, how do the rules work for employees?

The essential distinction is between a "temporary workplace" and a "permanent workplace". The first of these terms is defined negatively as meaning any workplace which is not a permanent one. So, it all hangs on the definition of a permanent workplace. Travelling to a permanent workplace is disallowable, as is "subsistence" when you get there. However, travelling to a temporary workplace, as defined, can be claimed even if you are travelling from home.

A temporary workplace is somewhere that you work for less than two years, and which isn't your workplace throughout the whole period of your employment contract. Let's take a practical example to highlight the difference.

Bill and Ben are both employees of Exciting Construction plc, which moves them from site to site as developments are undertaken. They both live in Clapham. Bill is taken on, on an 18 month contract to oversee the beginning of the company's development on a site in Maidenhead. Meanwhile Ben, who is a permanent employee of Exciting Construction, is finishing off their previous development in Chelmsford. Bill's contract duly comes to an end after 18 months, and he is back on the job market.

None of Bill's travelling expenses are allowable, because, whilst he was at Maidenhead for less than a two year period, this was the whole length of his employment contract with Exciting.

Ben, by contrast, who moves his place of work to Maidenhead to finish off that development, is allowed all of his travelling expenses from Clapham to Chelmsford, and then (providing there is not more than two years work there), his travelling to Maidenhead. This is because each of Chelmsford and Maidenhead are a "temporary workplace" for Ben.

I should stress, again, that the above rules apply only to employees. If Bill and Ben had been self-employed, none of their travelling would have been allowed from home to site.

Eating & Drinking

In the area of eating and drinking, or "subsistence", as it's termed, there is another example of employees being more favourably treated than the self-employed. Referring back again to the "wholly and exclusively" rule which I've discussed in Chapter 4, you would have thought that this would have the effect of making all eating and drinking expenses disallowable, because you eat to live, and not just to work. But in practice HMRC allow eating and drinking where you are travelling away from home, and therefore, no doubt, paying out more money than you would if you were at home.

The contrast between the self-employment and the employment regimes is mostly to be seen in relation to lunch. A self-employed person can rarely get tax relief for having lunch near his place of work, particularly if this is the usual one. Employees, on the other hand, can claim for eating and drinking whenever they are at a "temporary workplace". If your temporary workplace is in Piccadilly, then, can you claim for lunch at the Ritz?

This is where the vagueness and woolliness so beloved of our law makers comes back into its own, even in the context of the comparatively clear and understandable employee travel and subsistence rules. How far can you push the rule that eating and drinking at or near a temporary workplace are allowable?

Probably the key to answering this question is in the word "subsistence". This normally has connotations of minimal expenditure, as in the phrase "he was merely subsisting, not living". But adopting that extreme interpretation would probably be going too far in the other direction. A meal, with accompanying drinks, is probably not going to be questioned, by a PAYE auditor visiting the office of your business, if it is reasonable and appropriate to the job you're doing and the area where you are located. But this is obviously a potential breeding ground of arguments between HMRC and the taxpayer.

Probably the only thing I can say which is definite and categorical in this area is that I'm sure most people aren't claiming their full due with regard to the cost of restoring their tissues whilst away at work.

CHAPTER 7

HOW TO STRUCTURE THE BUSINESS

Choosing the right business structure could be the most important tax planning decision you ever make. That's because there are a number of, on the surface, equally valid options and they all tend to give a different tax result. If reading this chapter does nothing else than make the point that the "knee jerk" response of forming a limited company is not always right, but that you should consider other options first, it will have done a good job.

Some of the more obscure and recherché business vehicles we can rule out of account straight away, because these are unlikely to be relevant to the average owner managed business. It's rare, for example, for trading businesses to operate as trusts or "foundations" – a distinctly exotic growth associated normally with large offshore pots of money. Limited partnerships, too, although theoretically available and used, indeed, for certain specialist purposes, have effectively been completely superseded by their much younger cousin, the Limited Liability Partnership (LLP).

So, fundamentally it's likely to be a choice between the following four business structures:

- Sole trader;
- Partnership;
- LLP; and
- Limited company

Sole Traderships

This is the simplest form of business vehicle, comprising simply an individual carrying on business directly in their own name. In the rest of this chapter, incidentally, I will be concentrating on trading and professional businesses, rather than investment businesses, as, for example, the term "sole trader" suggests. Investment businesses have their own structural considerations, and I'll be looking at these elsewhere in the book.

Sole traderships have a comparative lack of accounting "red tape" surrounding them. It's not necessary to prepare accounts in a rigid pre-set format, or make additional disclosures as accounts which have to show a "true and fair view" have to. Whilst obviously a sole trader has to put the business figures down on the annual tax return, the accounts prepared for the sole trader's own use (if indeed they even are prepared) don't have to obey any particular rules other than adding up and balancing.

From the point of view of tax planning, the important point to make is that the profits of a sole trader business are chargeable to income tax immediately on the individual involved: that is, it makes no difference whether the individual draws money out of the business bank account or leaves it there.

So, sole traderships are quite different from limited companies, where there are two tax stages:

1. At the comparatively low (currently) rate of 19% when the company makes the profits; and
2. An income tax charge, when the company pays the profits out to its shareholders as dividend.

Partnerships

By the word "partnerships" I mean what are sometimes called "general" or unincorporated partnerships: that is partnerships which have not been incorporated as LLP's. As general partnerships the members are liable without limitation, personally, for all of the business debts, so partners can end up carrying the can for financial difficulties which are none of their own making.

On the other hand, partnerships share with sole traderships the refreshing lack of accounting red tape. Partnership accounts can be drawn up in any format that the firm chooses.

Like sole traderships, partners are chargeable to tax on the profits attributed to them as they are made, regardless of whether the partners actually draw those profits out of the business or not. From the tax planning point of view, an interesting feature of partnerships is that there is nothing like the same pressure to justify the amount a partner earns by reference to the work that partner does. If, say, husband is running a plumbing business, and pays his wife a wage for such things as administration and answering the telephone, the wage, to be allowable, must be a reasonable sum in relation to the work the wife does. If (as one suspects often happens in practice) husbands in this situation significantly overpay their wives, in order to use up their lower rates of tax and allowances, HMRC can disallow the excessive portion of the wages. Of course, whilst I am talking about husbands and wives as an example here, exactly the same principles apply wherever one member of a household pays wages to another member of the household for services to the business.

By contrast, if in that situation a husband had brought his wife into partnership, there need be no such direct relationship between her physical input of effort to the business and the amount of the profit share she receives.

LLP's

These are an interesting hybrid, introduced comparatively very recently into UK law in the year 2001. An LLP is a body corporate legally, like a limited company; and like a limited company it has its own separate legal personality, and has the capacity to enter into financial transactions, own assets, and incur debts in its own name.

Like a company it has to prepare accounts in accordance with a set format laid down by company law, and these accounts have to show a "true and fair view" of the LLP's profits, losses, assets and liabilities. (This phrase "true and fair view" has a very specific meaning, and involves compliance with financial reporting and other accounting standards.)

In all of these respects, and others, LLP's are actually more like limited companies than partnerships, despite the presence of the word "partnership" in the title. But the principal difference between an LLP and a limited company is that an LLP is taxed as if it were a partnership.

As it is treated as a partnership for tax purposes, the LLP itself has no tax liability on its profits, and virtually might as well not exist from the straightforward taxation of profits point of view. Instead, the LLP profits have to be divided between the various members (as partners are termed) and those members then have a direct tax liability on the profit share they are awarded. As with sole traders and unincorporated partnerships, the partner is taxable on his share regardless of whether or not he draws it out in cash or other asset form from the business, or alternatively leaves it within the business. And that tax charge, as with the other two business structures I've already talked about, is at the partner's individual rate of tax.

As the name suggests, the real impetus behind the introduction of LLP's into UK law was the limitation of liability that LLP's bring. Unlike the position of the unincorporated partnership, where one partner's disastrous mistake can bring down all the other partners, a member's liability is limited to the amount he has invested in the LLP. In other words, he can lose that, but will not have to contribute any more towards the losses resulting from a financial disaster – unless, in some circumstances, he is the one who is at fault in the matter.

For this reason, LLP's were immediately very popular with firms of accountants and solicitors, who had traditionally until then operated as partnerships, and taken the severe risk of financial armageddon making all the partners bankrupt. It's because of this that a common view has built up that LLP's are really "for" accountants and lawyers, rather than for other sorts of business.

This is not in fact the case at all, and any kind of business can operate through an LLP, including investment businesses (which, as I say, I'll discuss in more detail later).

Self-Employment Without Tears

But one of the reasons why LLP's are so popular with professional businesses, which involve a lot of individuals doing work at a high level, is because they combine the tax benefits of self-employment with limitation of liability – which no other business structure does.

The benefits of self-employment include the much lower National Insurance rates, which I've already discussed in Chapter 2 above, and the general ability to claim expenses in a lot more free and easy a fashion than employees are able to.

After LLP's were first introduced, people soon cottoned onto the fact that, in principle, you could extend the self-employment umbrella over a large number, or even all, of the staff of your business. In theory even the cleaner and the clerk who sorts out the rubber bands and paper clips could become a "partner": the disinclination to do this traditionally springing at least partly from the fact that partners are all liable for each other's actions in an incorporated partnership. So, everybody won: the business because it lost the obligation to pay employer's National Insurance contributions of 13.8%, and the individual because he or she was able to benefit from the lower rates of personal National Insurance contributions, and the ability to claim more expenses. (Membership of an LLP also brings with it, arguably, a loss of rights under employment legislation: but some individuals have been known to have their cake and eat it even in this way.)

You'll notice that most of the above is in the past tense, and the reason for this is that some fairly strict new rules were introduced in 2014, to stop businesses "unreasonably" extending the range of partnership to individuals whom HMRC regarded as being not "really" partners.

So, from 6 April 2014, an LLP member has to tick any one of the following three boxes (note not all of them) in order to be treated as self-employed for tax and NI purposes:

- The individual has to have capital invested in the LLP, equating to at least 25% of that individual's expected annual income; or
- There has to be a variable element of income (variable by reference to the total profits of the LLP, not the performance of the individual) which is expected to be at least 20% of his total income; or
- The LLP agreement has to give that individual the ability to exert a "significant influence" over the way the LLP was run.

What happened following the introduction of these rules was really quite interesting for tax advisers. Most of the more brash promoters of tax avoidance arrangements, who had been majoring heavily on persuading people to form LLP's and make the butcher, the baker and candlestick maker all members, suddenly seemed to go off LLP's completely, and a lot of them seem to have told their clients simply to abandon the LLP structure in favour of the limited company.

A much cooler look at the actual changes, though, suggests that the use of LLP's as business structures to save significant amounts of employment type National Insurance is still very much alive and well as an idea. Obviously, you are going to have to be careful who you admit as a member now, but there are quite a few businesses where people who would not generally regard themselves as equity owners of the business can nevertheless be brought in as self-employed LLP partners, with the beneficial effects I've mentioned.

Limited Companies

Unlike all of the other business structures I've discussed, limited companies have their own tax status, paying Corporation Tax on their income and capital gains at (currently) a flat rate of 19%. If the company then pays its profits out to the shareholders as dividends, the shareholders pay Income Tax on those dividends: but at a somewhat lower rate, to take into account the fact that the profits they are receiving have already been taxed once (see Appendix for rates).

One effect of this is to encourage people carrying on their business through limited companies to retain profits within the business rather than extracting them for personal use. All the time the funds are within the company, rather than being taken out as dividend, they will have suffered only a 19% tax rate. So, companies can be particularly suitable for the sort of business where profits need to be rolled back into the business: for example, businesses where a high stock and/or work in progress asset is held.

On the other hand, since the recent introduction of higher rates of tax on dividends, the company can actually result in a higher overall tax charge on profits which are received by it and then paid out as dividends, than would have been the case if the income had simply been received by the individual, as a sole trader or partner, in the first place. See the example below for another instance of how this can happen.

A disadvantage of limited companies is that the owner managers, rather than being self-employed, move over on to the employment side of the line. This is a disadvantage from the National Insurance point of view, as I've already commented: although this can be avoided, at a cost, by the extraction of funds in dividend form rather than as salary or remuneration. But it can also be a disadvantage from the point of view of your being taxed on benefits in kind provided by the company.

Let's take use of cars as an example. If a car is owned by a partnership and driven by one of the partners, the way personal use is taken into account in working out the tax position is by disallowing a proportion of the motoring expenses (including capital allowances) as relating to private mileage. So, the profits of the partnership subject to tax are higher in consequence of this disallowance. But this tends to be a much less unfavourable tax outcome than the way things are done in limited companies. Where a director of his own company (as any other employee) drives a company car, there will be a benefit in kind based on a percentage of the market value of the car when new, and this benefit in kind figure is then treated as income of the director concerned for tax and National Insurance purposes. With cars, in particular, some extremely anomalous and unfavourable results can come about because of the way the benefit in kind is assessed. For example, the rules take no account at all of how much business mileage is driven, how much private, and the percentage proportions of the two. Even one mile of private motoring in a year brings into play the full tax charge.

So, it's fair to say that, in general, companies are very bad news from the point of view of the taxation of private use of the business assets.

Hybrid Structures

Finally, I'll briefly mention a business structure which is sometimes referred to as the "hybrid" arrangement: briefly, because these are so interesting from the tax planning point of view that I felt it appropriate to give a whole chapter to them (Chapter 24).

Briefly, then, these are partnerships or LLP's which include a limited company as one of the partners. The company shares are typically owned by one or more of the other partners, and so you have something of a triangular structure with the individuals having direct interests as partners and also indirect interests as shareholders in the company partner.

In a nutshell, a significant advantage of these hybrid structures is that they can combine the benefits of self-employed taxation for the individuals with company taxation for the business profits, at the favourable lower corporation tax rates.

Doing The Maths

Now let's have a look at some numbers. Let's assume that Stephen is running a business which makes £150,000 profits each year. As a sole trader, Stephen will be liable at full Income Tax rates on the whole £150,000, and, assuming he has no other income in the same tax year, the total Income Tax will be £52,500. He will also pay about £6,000 National Insurance, meaning that he has a total overall "tax" rate of about 39% on average.

Now let's suppose that Stephen brings his wife Mary into partnership, and she has no other income either. Because their lower rate bands and personal allowances are both now available, their combined total tax bill will be £35,000, and they will also each have about £4,000 National Insurance to pay, meaning that the government in total get about £43,000 on this income: an overall average rate of between 28% and 29%.

Now let's assume that, instead of trading as a sole trader or partnership, Stephen passes the income through a limited company. The company will have a corporation tax liability, at 19%, of £28,500. If the company retains this, and doesn't pay it out to Stephen or Mary as personal income, this is obviously far and away the best result: a 19% tax hit rather than a 39% (for the sole trader) or 28% or 29% (for the partnership).

If, by contrast, the company pays out the profits as dividends (because Stephen and Mary need the money to live on) the dividends paid out will be the post corporation tax profits, that is they will total £121,500. If both Stephen and Mary are shareholders and receive half of this each, the Income Tax charge on these will average out at about £5,700 each, meaning that Stephen and Mary will end up with about £55,000 each post tax: an average tax rate between 26% and 27%.

In their circumstances this would seem to be the best result, and the company is cheaper than the otherwise comparable partnership structure because, firstly, £2,000 of the dividends are tax free, and secondly the Income Tax at the dividend rate is less than the combined effect of Income Tax and National Insurance on the income as earned income, which is how the partnership is treated.

A Caveat

Any example such as this has to be treated with caution, of course. If I had changed any of the assumptions (for example about other income) in the above example, I might easily have got a different outcome in terms of which structure is preferable. There's no substitute for doing the sums.

There are other factors, too, which might influence your choice of business structure, other than the simple arithmetic arriving at post tax "bottom line". For example, if your business is likely to be loss making in the earlier years, there can be huge advantages in not "trapping" these losses in a limited company – see Chapter 16 below. Similarly, if you are looking at tax efficient profit extraction using personal ownership of assets, the non limited company structure can facilitate the building up of assets, such as goodwill, in your effective personal ownership (for some interesting techniques using personally held assets, see Chapter 23 below).

But what the example does bring out is what a huge difference the business structure can potentially make to your ultimate tax burden (especially if you include National Insurance as a tax, which I think to all intents and purposes it is).

Why are the differences so great? I think the true answer to this question is that no one knows – the origin of the large difference between company tax rates and individual tax rates, for example, is lost in the mists of time. It seems to me clear that there is actually no coherent or sensible policy behind these rules, which have simply grown like Topsy.

Where does this leave us, then, in our quest for tax saving techniques which are both legal and ethical? Personally my view is that, where there is no actual connected or coherent thinking behind the tax system, there is nothing in the slightest bit unethical in choosing whatever structure you like with the ultimate tax treatment in mind.

CHAPTER 8
PROFIT EXTRACTION

Now we are coming near to the heart of sensible tax planning for owner managed businesses. As in so many areas of tax and business generally, being an entrepreneur or private investor is something which gives you choices as to how you structure things; and the method of profit extraction you use can make a huge difference to your tax bill.

So, what do we mean by the phrase profit extraction? The phrase is used where there is a limited company which conducts some kind of business activity, and makes profits on which Corporation Tax is paid. If you then want to access those profits personally, outside the company, you have to take the money out of the company somehow. And that's where the choices, and the tax planning fun, begin. Profit extraction isn't relevant where there isn't a company: for example, where the business is run directly by individuals as owners, sole traders, or partners. As I've explained in the previous chapter, structures like this give rise to only one charge to tax, at the point at which the profits are made, and there's no further tax when you take the money out of the business and into your personal bank account. Conversely, of course, there's no tax planning opportunity either, in the form of leaving the profits in the business or taking them out in some more tax efficient way.

Corporate & Personal Tax Rates

As I've already pointed out, the rate of tax on income which is paid by companies tends to be significantly lower than that paid by individuals. At 19% the current Corporation Tax rate is the lowest, I suspect, in living memory in this country. For individuals (at least in England, Wales and Northern Ireland) the lowest rate of Income Tax, after the personal allowance has been used up, is 20%, and this rate jumps to 40% above total income of £50,000, rising to a top rate of 45% above £150,000 of income in a year. So, it's easy to imagine situations where the tax on a particular income source could be considerably more than twice as much if that income is received by an individual, as it would be if it were received by a company. If that were the end of the story, it would be a "no brainer", for every individual whose income took him or her substantially into the 40% rate, to set up as a company.

But of course it's not the end of the story. If the person concerned wants to have the private use of that money, it needs to be paid out of the company and into the individual's personal bank account. If it is paid out in income form, personal tax levels then apply again, and if all of the company's profits are so paid out, all the benefit of the lower Corporate Tax rate is effectively lost.

There is the possibility of keeping money within the company, of course, and this could be described as the first and most basic level of tax planning. Any company owner is at perfect liberty to defer tax, perhaps indefinitely, by simply making the decision not to pay the money out as income, and I've never come across anybody describing this simple choice as unethical "tax avoidance".

This is particularly useful where the sort of business you are in benefits from profits being retained within the business. For example, if you are dealing in goods, it can help your business if you increase your stockholdings, and running this sort of business through a company means that the profits which you plough back into the business in this way are profits which have only borne the 19% (currently) tax rate. This is an awful lot better, of course, than having only 60%, or 55%, of your profits to reinvest. The same principle applies in any kind of business which requires capitalising, including, for example, a business of holding properties as investments. If, instead of distributing your net rents from the property owning company to the individual shareholders, the company retains them and uses them as the nucleus of an investment in new property, this is a very good and tax efficient way of expanding.

Dividends v Remuneration

But the tax benefits of retaining profits in a business aren't really what this chapter is about. What I start off with is a presumption that the individuals behind the company want to get their money out; and want to get it out in a way which doesn't cause an unnecessarily high leakage of tax etc to the government. So, let's start by looking at the two commonest methods of profit extraction.

Sometimes advisers, and even commentators, go on as though tax planning for owner managed businesses comprised simply the choice between paying out a company's profits as dividends or as director's remuneration. Certainly, as I've said, these are the commonest methods of profit extraction in practice, although they are by no means the only ones, as I'll go on to explain.

Both remuneration and dividends are income, and so chargeable to Income Tax, in the hands of the person who receives them. But they differ from each other in two very important respects, which are:

- Remuneration attracts a liability to National Insurance contributions, whereas dividends do not; and
- Remuneration is an expense allowable against Corporation Tax, and bears the full rate of Income Tax in the hands of the recipient. Dividends, by contrast, aren't an allowable deduction, and are paid therefore out of profits post Corporation Tax. For this reason dividends are taxed at a lower rate of Income Tax, although one which doesn't quite make up for the fact that the money paid out as a dividend has already been taxed once.

So, should you pay out income as remuneration or dividends? Let's give an example to illustrate the difference.

James receives a basic salary from his company which takes him into the basic rate Income Tax band. This year, there are £10,000 profits in the company, before tax, available additionally to pay out to James. Should he pay this as remuneration or as a dividend?

If he chooses the remuneration route, it has to be borne in mind that the company will have a liability to Employer's National Insurance of 13.8%. So, the gross amount paid to James needs to take that into account. Actually, the amount of gross bonus which, with the addition of 13.8% Employer's NI, will use up the whole of the £10,000 is an amount of £8,787. So, this is the starting point for working out the tax and the employee's National Insurance. With tax at 20% and an employee's contribution at 12%, this results in further deductions from James's bonus of £2,812 giving a net amount in his pocket, after all taxes (counting NI as a tax for these purposes) of £5,975.

Now let's look at what that sum would have looked like if a dividend had been paid instead.

	£
Profit available	10,000
Less: Corporation Tax at 19%	1,900
Therefore available to pay out to James as a dividend	8,100
Income Tax on dividend @ 7.5% on £6,100	
(Because the first £2,000 of dividends are tax free)	458
Therefore available to James after all taxes	7,642

In this example the dividend method of profit extraction obviously wins hands down over the remuneration method. And the reason for this isn't hard to work out: The absence of any National Insurance charge more than makes up for the small extra tax which the dividend route involves.

For this reason, as a general rule, OMB's tend to use the dividend method of profit extraction rather than the remuneration method, although there is no substitute for doing the sums in each case.

Every general rule has exceptions, though, and there are a number of reasons why in particular cases remuneration will be paid, including:

- Where the shareholdings differ in proportions from the amount of agreed profit going to each individual, for example where one shareholder works in the business and another doesn't;
- Where an individual needs to show earned income for pension contribution or mortgage reference purposes; or
- Very often, where a small amount is paid in order to make the year count for National Insurance contribution purposes. An amount somewhat under the personal allowance can be paid as remuneration without actually triggering an NI contribution liability or (if covered by personal allowance) an Income Tax liability: nevertheless, it means that you are deemed to have notched up a year's contributions for the purpose of the old age pension.

In the case of the first of these problems, where it's wished to pay an individual a greater proportion of the available profits than his or her shareholding in itself merits, an alternative way of doing this, without going down the remuneration road, is to have different classes of shares in the company, so that a different rate of dividends can be paid to that individual as compared with the others. This is relatively straightforward to organise.

Moving Off The Beaten Track

If circumstances allow, you should definitely look to move off the dividend/ remuneration beaten track. Both interest (on a loan to the company by the individual) and rent (for the company's occupation of a property owned by the individual) are arguably significantly more beneficial as ways of profit extraction, in income form, than either dividends or remuneration.

Why is this? Because, like remuneration, interest and rent are both allowable deductions against the company's Corporation Tax profits, providing they aren't excessive in amount. But, unlike remuneration, they don't give rise to any National Insurance liability. So, you haven't got the double tax charge between the company and the individual, which tends overall to give a higher effective tax rate, and you haven't got any NI either.

In fact there's only one problem with these alternative, and more tax efficient, methods of profit extraction: you need to have the loan, or the property, in order to pay them!

It's quite uncommon in practice, in fact, for directors' loan accounts to pay interest. This is probably largely down to the fact that, if a director is lucky enough to be in credit with his company, it's even more tax efficient simply to repay that loan to him, which is capital, and therefore not taxable income at all. Also, it's a minor irritation that companies, on paying interest, have to deduct tax at the basic rate and account for this to HMRC on a quarterly basis.

The rent option tends to be available more frequently, because it's quite frequent, in practice, to find the situation where the company occupies premises which are owned directly by the individual. This can even apply where the company's business makes use of some of the individual's home.

To sum up, you should always look for opportunities of using the interest route or the rent route in preference to paying either remuneration or dividends.

Unconventional Wisdom

And then there's unconventional wisdom. A lot of companies are run like this. The individual director, who is often the 100% shareholder, draws freely from the company's bank account, and uses the company credit card, for private purposes throughout the year. On paper, therefore, a balance builds up which technically is a loan to that director: or at least a payment on account of remuneration which he is due to receive at the end of the year. The conventional wisdom is that this debit balance needs to be cleared at the end of the year by voting the director concerned a bonus and/or a dividend, since nasty things happen if there is an amount owed to the company by a shareholder or an associate (broadly, relative) of a shareholder.

But actually this conventional wisdom might be not so wise after all. Whilst a debit balance to a shareholder or associate gives rise to a 32.5% tax charge (to prevent companies making loans instead of paying dividends) this can in the event be less of an imposition than the tax liability on the dividend. If a shareholder wants £100,000 out of the company, say, he will probably need to pay himself a dividend of something like £150,000 if he wants to be left with £100,000 after the personal tax he has to pay on the dividend. If instead the company loans him the £100,000, the loans to participators tax is £32,500, and this is paid by the company, not the individual. The total cash outlay, then, in the case of a loan is £132,500 rather than the £150,000 or thereabouts cost of paying a dividend in our example – and the difference is even greater if you're taxable at the higher rate of 38.1%. So it's actually cheaper, to the tune of nearly £20,000 on these numbers, to take the money as a loan rather than as a dividend.

What's more, the loans tax is refundable by HMRC if the loan itself is repaid in the future: so if some better way of extracting funds becomes available later (for example as capital – see below) loaning the money could be a good way of keeping your options open.

Finally, we should make the point that it is technically contrary to the Companies Act for a company to loan money in these circumstances: but there seems no real problem in practice, since the only come back in the case of a private company is that the loan is legally "voidable" by the company, which isn't an issue where everyone is in agreement.

Capital Drawdown

What dividends, remuneration, interest and rent all have in common, of course, is that they are income in the hands of the recipient. They all therefore suffer from the disadvantage that the company's profits, when paid out in these ways, are effectively being taxed at the personal tax rate (or even rather higher, overall) and ultimately there is no benefit to be had from the lower tax rate that companies themselves pay. It follows, then, that any way of taking money out of the company which is "capital", and therefore not income chargeable to Income Tax, starts with a huge advantage in terms of tax efficiency.

I've already mentioned the most obvious way of doing this, which is to draw down on any credit balance that the individual might be fortunate enough to have with the company. Failing that, we've seen how the company making a loan to the individual rather than paying a dividend can make use of the fact that a loan, being a capital sum, is not chargeable to Income Tax. But these don't exhaust the possibilities of capital, and therefore tax free, profit extraction. Consider the following example.

Robert owns and publishes a scurrilous publication aimed at making libellous or near libellous statements about the "great and the good". Being something of a tin pot affair, the magazine is put together and published from a property at the bottom of Robert's garden, which he built some years ago. Being a very fat man with a tremendous appetite, Robert is also a big spender, and needs to support an expensive lifestyle from drawings out of the company which publishes the magazine.

One year he comes up with a really pretty brainy wheeze. Applying for the appropriate permission, he fences off the part of the garden on which the office is built, and creates a new land registry title. He then sells the office and surrounding land to the company for its full market value. The credit, which is thereby generated in his favour, in the company's books, is sufficient to fund some fairly lavish drawings over a period of years.

In the above example, the individual doesn't even pay any capital gains tax on transferring the property to the company, because it was covered by main residence exemption from Capital Gains Tax. This obviously won't always be the case, or perhaps even often be the case. However, if you think about it, transferring a property which gives rise to a 20% Capital Gains Tax charge (as most commercial premises do) is still going to be highly advantageous, as in the next example.

Queenie owns a number of small industrial units which she inherited from her father some years ago, when each unit was valued at £100,000. One of them is used for the purposes of a design business which she has set up and runs through her own company. It is currently valued at £250,000, and Queenie transfers it to the company for that figure. Apart from the Stamp Duty Land Tax, which is relatively low because this is a commercial property, Queenie has Capital Gains Tax to pay on the transfer. This is 20% of the £150,000 gain, after allowing for her CGT annual allowance. So, she has about £28,000 to pay.

However, as a result of the sale, she can now draw down, over a period of years, £250,000 without further tax charge. Assuming she were a higher rate taxpayer, dividends of this amount would have given rise to Income Tax of about £80,000, as against the £28,000 Capital Gains Tax "upfront", which is all she has actually had to pay.

A Caveat

A decision like transferring a property into a company isn't one which should be taken in isolation from all the other relevant considerations, of course. One effect of transferring a property into the company is that, on any future sale of the property by that company, there is potentially more Capital Gains and personal tax, overall, to pay than would have been the case if you had retained the property personally. So, look before you leap.

You could also raise the objection, to the above scenarios, that putting the properties into the company exposes them to the risks of the business. If there were a major financial disaster which struck the company for any reason, and the company went into insolvent liquidation, the individuals have effectively lost the properties: a situation which would not have applied if they had kept the properties outside the company.

This objection might be more apparent than real, though. It's usually possible to safeguard valuable capital assets, like properties, from trading disasters of this sort by moving them into non trading holding companies, which own both the capital assets concerned and 100% (normally) of the shares in the trading company.

Intangible Assets

The idea of transferring valuable capital assets to the company, in order to produce a credit balance which can then be drawn down without Income Tax, is arguably more appropriate where you are looking at intangible assets of the business, like patents, know how, computer software, and goodwill, whose value may well, unlike real property, have a finite life. And there's another, quite exciting, reason why it could be highly tax advantageous to transfer intangible assets to your company. Have a look at Chapter 23 where I explore this whole area in more detail.

LLP's With Limited Company Partners

One of the issues with transferring assets to a company, of course, is the fact that the capital gains tax payable has to be paid "upfront". This may well be worthwhile, nevertheless, because of the rate of CGT being typically much lower than the Income Tax you're saving by being able to take your subsequent draw downs tax free. But the LLP with a corporate partner structure could just be a way of having your cake and eating it in this respect. For the delicious details of this, refer to Chapter 24 below.

Selling or Winding up the Company

Ultimately, company sale or liquidation is a very tax efficient way of converting its value into personal money in your bank account. The tax on this is CGT, charged at a rate of 10% in the case of trading company disposals up to the £1 million limit for Business Asset Disposal Relief, and at 20% above that limit and for non trading companies. By definition this tends to be your last bit of profit extraction from the company!

I hope I've said enough to make it clear why profit extraction is such an important subject in the area of tax planning for owner managed businesses. The difference in your overall tax burden can be massive, and you can be looking not just at deferral of tax, but permanent reduction. It all comes down to taking a creative approach to the specific situation you find yourself in.

CHAPTER 9
HOW TO USE PERSONAL SERVICE COMPANIES

It's generally true to say that the poor downtrodden wage – or salary – slave gets the roughest deal from our tax system. Subjected to high rates of National Insurance contribution and a system known as PAYE (sometimes nicknamed "pay all you earn", or "pay before you earn") that gives little or no room for manoeuvre in terms of tax planning, they are very much an underclass, although they are in fact the vast majority in terms of numbers amongst taxpayers. No wonder there was a backlash from the more savvy amongst this class, which gathered momentum during their 1990's. And the form this backlash took was the increasing use of Personal Service Companies.

There are basically three ways a person providing his own personal services to a client/employer can structure the relationship. In tax terms there is the expensive way, the very expensive way, and the eye wateringly expensive way.

The last of these methods, and the most expensive in terms of tax, of course, is to be receiving a salary from the employer taxed under PAYE. Cheaper, for reasons that the following example will make clear, is being "self-employed" in relation to the employer, whom we should now call a client. But almost always the most economical way of doing the job is to set up a personal service company.

Felicity is a high flying management consultant, whom a number of companies, large and not so large, seek out to help cover the backs of the management – sorry, I meant provide objective third party advice to the board. She accepts a job with Giant Banking Corporation plc at a salary of £200,000 per annum (ok, so she's not that high flying a management consultant). Her average tax rate in the year is 40%, and therefore the government get £80,000 Income Tax, and about £7,500 Employee National Insurance contributions, which are deducted from her salary giving net pay of £112,500 – not far off a 50% "tax" rate. In addition, the government get about £26,000 "Employer's National Insurance" contributions. So, overall the government gets slightly more than Felicity does herself out of the fruits of her labours.

And in case you thought that the Employers National Insurance contribution acted as some kind of pension or health insurance arrangement for Felicity, think again: the Employers NI is simply a payroll tax which does not give rise to any entitlement to state benefits on the part of the individual whatsoever. The very title "Employers National Insurance" is a lie.

Now let's progress to the next stage of tax planning sophistication.

After scraping along as best she can on less than £10,000 net per month from her work, Felicity leaves the Giant Banking Corporation, and accepts an assignment with a much smaller organisation, Mr Tufty's Garages Limited. The negotiations between Felicity and the managing director of the company, Ron Tufty, get round to the awkward subject of money. "What's your input going to cost me over the year?" he asks. She answers "£226,000, that's what my previous people were effectively paying." Mr Tufty thinks for a while. "Are you happy not to get any employment rights?" "Perfectly".

So, Felicity is taken on a self-employed basis at a rate of £226,000 a year, the same amount, including Employers National Insurance contributions, that her previous employer was paying in total. Felicity duly invoices the company £18,833 per month. She also registers dutifully with HMRC for self-assessment.

At the end of the year (ignoring expenses for simplicity) she has £226,000 to put on her self-assessment tax return. Assuming her average rate of tax is still 40%, this means that she has an Income Tax charge of just over £90,000. The National Insurance levy, on the self-employed basis, is much more modest than what applies in the employment sphere, and amounts to about £7,000, with no levy equivalent to the Employers National Insurance contribution.

Result: The government get about £97,000 and the person who has sweated actually to make the money gets £129,000. The scales have tipped somewhat in the favour of the taxpayer.

I must try to avoid giving the impression that it's purely optional whether you go employed or self-employed. In theory, the tax treatment should follow the facts, rather than how those facts are described. So, if the management consultant in our example is in what is sometimes referred to as a "master and servant relationship" with the payer, she and the employer would both be making a big mistake in processing the payments as if she were a freelance worker. HMRC can (and do) come down like a ton of bricks on this situation where they discover it.

So, is Felicity, in my example, employed or self-employed? To answer that question, you need to look at basically all of the features of the relationship between her and the client/employer. Does the company control how, when, and where the duties of the assignment are performed? Is she "part and parcel" of the employer organisation? Is she genuinely in business on her own account? Does she take any financial risk? Is there "mutuality of obligations", which require the business to provide her with work, and require her to do the work which they provide?

All of these questions, and a number of others, have to be asked to decide what is actually basically a factual question: is the relationship one of employment or self-employment? But arguably Felicity in our example may have been wrongly categorised by Giant as an employee, so that HM Government received more money than was properly due. What ethical stance should we take to this (I suspect very common) situation?

Finally, let's consider what happens to basically the same situation, where a Personal Service Company is set up.

Moving on, our heroine is approached by a high street firm of accountants, who want her to help them introduce a new management structure. Again, they agree the same rate of pay, £226,000 per annum gross, but unlike the previous client, they refuse to take her on a self-employed basis. The problem is, as they point out to her, that if HMRC come along and attack the situation, it's them, the accountants, who are vulnerable to a lot of extra charges, for not operating PAYE when they should have done.

So, acting on their suggestion, she forms a limited company in which she and her husband both have shares. This invoices the client, and because they are paying a limited company, they are happy that there is no issue on any possible future PAYE audit by the taxman.

The situation benefits Felicity too. Her husband, whilst he is working, doesn't earn anything like the same amount of money as her, and so when the company, having paid Corporation Tax of £43,000 on its £226,000 profit, pays the balance of £183,000 out to the couple as dividends, the average tax rate on those dividends is 25%. So, they end up with just under £140,000 in their bank account after tax.

The Lowest Tax Option

It's not difficult to see why the individual ends up with different amounts of money post tax, as a result of a different business structure, on what is basically otherwise an identical financial situation. The self-employment situation is more "tax" efficient than the employment situation, for the simple reason that the National Insurance contribution rates are less for self-employed people than for employed people. Moving on to the Personal Service Company route, there is no National Insurance at all in this context, because companies don't pay NI. Dividends, which are the method by which our people take their money out of the company, are also a National Insurance free type of income. Moreover, the company enables the income to be spread amongst at least two (sometimes more) family members, making use of their lower tax bands.

That's the mechanical explanation for the difference – and it has to be said that, in many real life cases, the difference in favour of the Personal Service Company route is even more marked than that shown in my example. But what is the actual reason, in terms of taxation policy, for this big difference?

I have to say that the reason for the differences, in the sense of why the system is set up like this, is something of a mystery to me. If you ask the average man in the street, or indeed the average MP, what the answers to the following questions were, I suspect you'd get a completely blank response:

- Why are the National Insurance rates higher for employees than for the self-employed?
- Why does National Insurance apply only to earned income and not to unearned income?
- Why is the rate of Corporation Tax so much lower than the higher rates of Income Tax?
- Why does a household with two earners pay more tax if one of the earners is more highly paid than the other?

One of the purposes of this book is to show ways in which tax can be reduced "ethically". It simply won't do to say that everyone has the duty to pay the maximum possible tax, because where does this duty come from? It seems to me that the reality of the situation is that our system is antiquated and irrational, and simply knowing how to find your way round that system in order not to pay unnecessarily large amounts is hardly culpable morally.

HMRC Fight Back

Whatever the rights and wrongs of the situation, though, the facts were that the Inland Revenue were seeing an increasing use of the Personal Service Company device over the last years of the twentieth century, and anything in the way of a system which regularly reduces tax liabilities for potentially large numbers of people brings them out in spots. So, someone in the Revenue decided that it was time to "put a stop" to the use of Personal Service Companies. (Ironically, reputedly the largest user, and beneficiary, of the arrangements whereby individuals were not employed but taken on through Personal Service Companies was the Home Office.) And the way they decided to counteract the use of such companies tells us a lot about the whole attitude to tax legislating in this country.

Did they take a step back and ask any of the above questions, or consider whether the rules have just happened completely randomly over a long period of time? Of course not. Their reaction was to patch the leaking vessel, as is almost always is.

This is where the dreaded "IR35" comes in. This was the number of the Budget press release which announced the new changes, which finally came in in Finance Act 2000. What "IR35" basically says is that, if you ignore the existence of the Personal Service Company and the result is that the hypothetical relationship between the "employer" and the individual is then one of employment, the rules would apply. Where the rules apply, the intermediary company (not the employer) has to account for PAYE and National Insurance as if it were simply a salary that was being paid. So, this takes away all the advantages, of course, of the Personal Service Company route. You have the higher, employee, level of National Insurance, and there is no ability to spread the income amongst possibly lower taxed members of your family.

An interesting feature of the new rules is the fact that it is the intermediary, personal service, company which had all the responsibility of deciding whether the rules apply. The payer escaped scot-free regardless of what the position is.

IR35 In Practice

All this sounds very good, of course, and in principle the IR35 rules mean that you can't "dress up" an employment relationship as a freelance service provider billing through a company. But the Inland Revenue found, to their cost, that the theory and the practice were very different.

The basic problem (from their point of view) is that the employment versus self-employment test is a very difficult one to assess in reality, and is arguably based on concepts which are completely out of date. In the old days, when one could talk about a "master and servant relationship", that is a relationship of employment, working practices were very different from what they are now. It is much more common these days, particularly amongst the higher paid, for there to be a freer relationship between the parties, which doesn't really fit in with old fashioned concepts of "employer" and "employee". The result was that the taxman lost almost all the cases he took to the Tax Tribunal, trying to make an IR35 charge "stick".

The Attack Intensifies

Stage two of the HMRC fight back took 13 years to come, and came in with effect from 6 April 2013. What this change in the rules was saying was that, if the individual concerned, who was providing his services through a Personal Service Intermediary Company, was also a director of the "client" company, the "employment" test would be deemed automatically to be passed. So, this brought to an end all kinds of very lucrative arrangements by directors of quoted companies, for example, who were providing their services to those companies through Personal Service Companies of their own.

So, far so good, from HMRC's point of view. But the basically problematical nature of IR35 still remained, in all other cases. IR35 doesn't apply where the intermediary company and the client company are "associated", that is under common control, so the bulk of situations where a director was providing his services to a company through his own Personal Service Company were untouched by the 2013 changes. And so they should be, you might say. However, HMRC returned to the fray again a couple of years later, and this time their changes to the IR35 rules were more fundamental in nature.

Public Sector Clients

From 6 April 2017, where the client is a public sector organisation (for example the NHS), the onus of deciding whether IR35 applies switches from the intermediary company itself to the payer.

The impact of this has been fairly predictable, and must have been cynically predicted by those bringing the changes in. No public sector payer, being a bureaucrat, is ever going to do anything which fails to cover his own back. So, we have seen, in practice, public sector clients adopting a "knee-jerk" approach to such situations, and informing contractors using Personal Service Companies that they will apply IR35.

This has been a fairly successful example of steamrollering on the part of HMRC. For example, doctors, whilst they are very unlikely to be treated as "servants" of the NHS in reality, have been subject to a widespread imposition of IR35 on payments made to their intermediary companies.

The fourth hammer blow of HMRC against what they see as this "abuse" has not yet come into force at the time of writing. However it is the fairly predictable extension of the public sector rule to large and medium sized companies in the private sector.

But it does seem as though HMRC have learnt something from the "knee-jerk" reaction of public sector payers, for whom there is no downside, effectively, in saying that IR35 applies. Under the new rules, there is a proposal that any large or medium sized private sector payer will need to share the reasons for their decision with the contractor concerned. Interesting times.

Where Are We Now?

Overall, my view is that the Personal Service Company is an extremely powerful tax planning tool whose day has not yet come to an end by any means. Firstly, anyone providing their personal services to "small" enterprises (and the word "small" is very relative here) is still effectively in the "good old days" of Personal Service Companies. Secondly, even if you number amongst your "clients" medium or large clients, it's by no means certain, even when the new rules come in, that they will simply be able to steamroller you into accepting IR35.

If your "client" is in the public sector (for example if you are a doctor providing your services to the NHS through a Personal Service Company) things might get better, but I wouldn't hold my breath. For the time being, at least, those who provide their services to the public sector have probably got to knuckle under and accept employment taxation.

You might ask, why is this last situation considered acceptable? There is plenty of odium directed at those who twist the facts to reduce their tax liability: but this is a good example of the situation where the facts are being twisted in order to increase tax liabilities!

Chapter 10
Asset Protection – Without Tax Tears

What nobody understands who isn't an entrepreneur is the chanciness of business. Outsiders tend to see the rewards when business is successful, but what they don't realise is that running a business is to be on a constant knife edge between success and failure. Not only are trading businesses vulnerable to all kinds of problems that are too big to control: like economic factors and government action, but regulators and lawmakers are constantly active in introducing new requirements which can make the difference between a successful business and one that's no longer viable.

I probably don't need to labour the point, given my target audience for this book. But the threats and vicissitudes which businesses face every day in this country give rise to an understandable interest, on the part of entrepreneurs, in the whole subject of Asset Protection.

I need to make it clear at the outset that my specialism isn't Asset Protection: I'm a tax adviser by profession. But I naturally see a lot of the techniques which people use to insure against financial disaster in practice, and the important thing to note is that these actions, and Asset Protection techniques, tend to have fairly significant tax consequences, of which you should be aware before entering into any of them.

Limited Liability

The concept of limited liability dates back to the time when lawyers were (occasionally) a help to business rather than a hindrance. As soon as more than one person becomes involved in carrying on a business, you've got the problem of the "innocent" potentially suffering for the acts or defaults of others. In an ordinary partnership, as we've seen, every partner can be made liable for the debts of the partnership, and this can mean that somebody who had no part in incurring those debts can nevertheless be forced to pay them.

The practical effect of this situation was clearly to discourage people combining together, contributing their resources to capitalising and running a business of more than a fairly minimal size. The reality of the situation where you run a larger business is that the principals are not in a position to keep their eye on every single transaction entered into from day to day, and therefore some kind of protection was urgently needed for investors who provided the essential life blood for enterprises to get off the ground. Therefore if business was to stand a chance of growing beyond this minimal size, without unacceptable risk to those who provided the essential fuel (in the form of capital) to get the business off the ground, a solution to this problem of unlimited liability was ungently required.

Step forward the joint stock company with limited liability, one of the great Victorian inventions which we are still benefiting from.

The way the system worked, and still works, is thus. An entity is incorporated which is deemed in law to be a separate person, able to own assets, enter into transactions, and hence carry on business in its own name. The members or shareholders agree to introduce a certain amount of capital each into the entity. If anything goes wrong, and the entity is wound up insolvent, all the investors lose is the amount they have contributed (or, in rare instances, agreed to contribute in the future) in the form of capital.

Of course there are limitations to limited liability. If an individual is involved, and the liabilities concerned have arisen as a result of that individual's actions, there are all kinds of ways that creditors can get at him or her. Also, there are some situations where the individual can be got at because of having given a personal guarantee, usually to a bank, on the body corporate's debts. And there are some occasions where statutory rules "lift the veil of incorporation" – although actually there aren't many of these. All in all, however, carrying on business through a limited liability vehicle seems obviously sensible, except in the case of a few businesses (perhaps holding a property portfolio?) where the risk of financial disaster is truly negligible.

The Alternatives

Until fairly recently, the only way you could get your liability limited was by forming a limited company. And the price of limited liability therefore included bringing yourself into the limited company tax regime. I have talked about this already elsewhere, but in summary trading through a company can have certain disadvantages. Earned income received by shareholders/directors of a company is subject to the employment rates of national insurance contributions, which are much higher than the rates that would have applied if the business had been run as a partnership. There is an often punitive code for taxing individuals for private use of business assets; and the "dividend tax" can have the effect of increasing the rate of income tax paid. This is why the introduction of limited liability partnerships (LLP's) in 2001 was such a boon. These were brought into UK law at the behest of the accountancy profession, and it's easy to see why. The benefits of self employed taxation (of members) can be combined with limited liability in a way which, before 2001, was simply impossible.

I am not saying, of course, that the partnership tax regime will always be preferable to the company tax regime: it depends on the circumstances, and I've discussed this in more detail in the chapter on The Business Structure. But the important point to be clear about is that, if you want to conduct your business with the benefit of limited liability, you've now got a free choice between two radically different tax regimes.

Business Assets

If your business makes use of substantial fixed assets which are in basically the same ownership, for example the property from which the business is carried on, one of the most sensible things you can do, if the business is in any way risky, is to separate out the ownership of those assets from the trade.

There are three main options for achieving this. The first is where the individual shareholders (or LLP members) own the asset in their own individual names, outside the company. I'll refer to this as "personal ownership". A second option is freestanding company ownership, where the shareholders of the trading company also own the shares in another company which owns the valuable assets. Thirdly, there's the Holding Company route, under which the shares in the trading company are owned by a holding company, which latter company also holds the valuable assets, but does not trade itself.

In all these situations, of course, you need to make sure that the individual or the company which owns the valuable assets doesn't have a liability to pay any amounts to the trading company: because, in the event of financial disaster striking the trading company, and a liquidator being appointed, the liquidator will then obviously be able to get his hands on the valuable assets, by sending a demand for repayment to the asset holding entity. Subject to that point, though, all three of these options give a similar level of protection to the valuable assets, against any financial armageddon of the trading entity. (All this assumes that the trading entity is conducted through a limited liability vehicle, since otherwise unlimited personal liability would extend to the interests the individuals have in the asset holding entity.)

As before, it's likely to be tax, therefore, that decides which of the options is to be preferred.

Personal Ownership

From the capital gains tax planning point of view, personal ownership has got a lot going for it. If the property were sold without there being a sale of the business at the same time, the individual pays capital gains tax on any gain, but after that the money belongs absolutely to the individual. By contrast, if the asset is owned by a limited company, you've got two layers of tax, potentially: once when the company makes a gain on selling the asset, and once when the money is passed out to the individual – usually as a dividend.

If the asset has been bought on a loan, on the other hand, there can be an income tax penalty of personal ownership.

Gregory has been trading for many years from office premises in the high street, when the owner offers him the opportunity to buy it. He decides to go down the personal ownership route, and borrows £200,000 from the bank to make the purchase. The loan is a 10 year mortgage, meaning that Gregory has to take out of the company as income such amount as will give him £20,000 after income tax to pay back each year's portion of the capital. This means the company has to pay him additional rent of £33,333, because Gregory is a 40% taxpayer. The repayment of capital is "generating" a tax charge of £13,333 each year which would be substantially reduced if the recipient were a limited company.

From the inheritance tax point of view personal ownership works reasonably well. With respect to properties used for the business, such an asset held outside the trading company qualifies for 50% business property relief – so that only half of its value would be chargeable to tax in the event of the individual's death.

Back to capital gains tax, and the availability of two very important reliefs: entrepreneur's relief and rollover relief. Entrepreneur's relief applies where a trading business is sold, and the benefit of it is that the tax rate is reduced from the usual 20% or 28% to a much more manageable 10%. If the property and the trading company are sold together, entrepreneur's relief is extended to the gain made on the sale of the personally held asset, so personal ownership certainly ticks the entrepreneur's relief box. Note, though, that if rent is paid as in Gregory's example, this relief is restricted – indeed completely denied if the rent is a full market one.

Rollover relief applies where you sell a trading asset as a capital gain, and reinvest some or all of the proceeds in a new trading assets. Again, rollover relief is granted for assets held personally but used by the company for its trade. Tick.

Freestanding Company Ownership

This avoids the income tax problem highlighted in the example of Gregory, but apart from this, and the fact that the trading company could be sold, if necessary, without needing to extricate the asset from it, there isn't a lot to be said, in my view, for the freestanding company ownership option. If the company sells the asset, you have the problem with the potential double tax charge on the gain, that I have already alluded to. No inheritance tax business property relief is available for the value, because the shares are treated (perversely) as being the shares in an investment company rather than a company which has anything to do with a trade. And the two capital gains tax reliefs I've made such a lot of above are both denied. If you sell the shares in the freestanding company, say, there's no entrepreneur's relief because the company is treated as being an investment company again. And if the freestanding company sells the asset and buys another one, there's no rollover available because the freestanding company isn't using either asset for the purposes of its own trade.

The Holding Company Option

Again, this solves the income tax issue referred to in the example, because the entity with owns the asset is a limited company whose top rate is (currently) 19% on income. You also get rollover relief if the holding company sells the asset and buys another trading asset; and a sale of the holding company's shares will qualify for entrepreneur's relief.

From the inheritance tax point of view, the holding company route is actually better than the personal ownership route, because the value of the asset, held within the group as a whole, is eligible for 100% business property relief, not just 50% as with personal ownership.

The one big drawback with the holding company route arises in the situation of the sale of the business, where the purchaser wants to buy the business but doesn't want to buy this particular asset. It can be quite expensive, in tax terms, to say nothing of legal fees, disentangling the asset from the group prior to sale.

Top Hatting

In comparing the three main options for owning valuable assets away from the trading company, for asset protection purposes, I've made the implicit assumption that there is a free choice in the matter. Often, though, this won't be the case. If the trading company already owns the asset concerned (which is especially likely to be the case if you are talking about assets other than real property, such as patents, computer software, trademarks and goodwill built up by the company in the course of its trade) it's not so easy to move these out into personal ownership or the ownership of a freestanding company. Any such transfer out is likely to give rise to tax both in the transferor company and in the hands of the individual. And this is where the holding company method of asset protection comes into its own.

You haven't got a holding company? Well you can create one, and this is the process often known as "top hatting". I'll illustrate this with an example.

George is a publisher whose company, Trashcan Limited, produces a specialist magazine, Talking Rubbish, for local authority cleansing executives. He's been in the game for a great many years, and the title has become very successful, and, therefore, valuable.

One of the reasons why the magazine is so popular is because it doesn't mince its words. Chief executives, industrialists, and politicians come in for a lot of stick: meaning there is the ever-imminent danger of libel actions being taken out against the company. In the event of one of these ruining the company, George, if he wanted the business to rise like a phoenix from the ashes, would need to scrape the money together, somehow, to pay the liquidator for the ongoing use of the Talking Rubbish title.

To guard against this, George forms a new holding company, Trashcan Holdings Limited, in which he also owns 100% of the shares. This company then issues further shares to him in exchange for his shares in the trading company, which thus becomes a 100% subsidiary. The last stage of the process is the hiving up, by way of legal transfer, of the rights to the valuable title.

On the face of it, you would have thought that the disposal of the shares in the trading company to the new holding company would be capital gains tax event for George. Fortunately, though, there is a relief, which applies in situations like this, which can be checked with HMRC in advance by way of a formal application for clearance. Providing the motive behind the top hatting is commercial (as here) and is not tax avoidance, HMRC will almost always give clearance with very little question.

Asset Divestment

What I have been talking about so far is the actions people take to protect themselves against financial threats caused by the business. The aim of using limited liability entities, and holding valuable assets separately from the business, is to avoid "infection" from the business causing problems with your other assets. But there are obviously situations where personal liability is threatening, or might threaten in the future, such that anything at all that you own could be vulnerable to this personal attack. One obvious way of protecting against such claims is to make a gift of assets to one's spouse or partner. If the giver and the recipient are married to each other, or are civil partners, this tends to be quite easy to do on a tax neutral basis. There is no capital gains tax, effectively, on gifts of assets between spouses etc, even if a gain has arisen on the asset concerned. The one major exception to the tax neutral nature of inter-spouse transfers is stamp duty land tax, where a property is given which has a mortgage or other loan secured on it. To the extent that the transferee spouse is taking on a share of that mortgage liability, this is treated as "consideration" subject to SDLT. So a point to watch for: although incurring an SDLT charge might be preferable to subjecting the whole property to the possible depredations of any future creditor.

Where the donor and donee are not married or in civil partnership, CGT is definitely an issue that needs to be faced. The gift, as I have commented already in other contexts, will be treated as if it were a sale of the asset concerned for its market value, with resultant capital gains tax to pay. Unless the asset concerned is a "trading asset", there is no ability to hold over the gain, and therefore tax would fall due. Trading assets include properties, goodwill etc used for the purpose of a trade carried on as a sole trader or a partnership; and the shares in a company which exists substantially wholly for the purpose of carrying on a trade.

The Use of Trusts in Asset Protection

I believe this is a big thing on the other side of the Atlantic, where the rules are no doubt more cut and dried. In principle, however, even in the UK making a gift into trust can be a powerful tool of Asset Protection. Assets held in trust, even if you yourself are one of the trustees, are generally speaking not available for the benefit of your personal creditors.

Income received by a trust is taxable at the top rate of income tax (currently 45%), unless this is a trust in which you, as the person providing the value, are an actual or potential beneficiary. In the latter case this will be treated as a "settlor interested trust", and all of the income (and capital gains) will be treated as taxable directly on you.

In the case of trusts which pay the trust rate of 45%, because they are not settlor interested, income subsequently paid to beneficiaries is treated as if it were a payment of income from which 45% is being deducted, and beneficiaries with a lower personal tax rate can therefore reclaim tax.

The big issue with setting up trusts and transferring assets to them for protection purposes is that fact that a transfer of any kind of asset other than business property (trading businesses), or agricultural property, will trigger an inheritance tax charge at 20% to the extent that the value going into trust, over a cumulative 7 year period, exceeds the nil rate band of currently £325,000.

LLP's as Asset Protection

Another reason why trusts are sometimes popular (and would be more popular but for the inheritance tax charge I have just mentioned) is because gifts to trust can benefit other people (typically younger generations) without giving those people control over the wealth concerned. A not dissimilar result can be achieved, though, by using LLP's. I should stress that the example that follows is hypothetical, since there is no decided case law on the key issues as yet. However it seems to me plausible while we are awaiting for such case law guidance.

Mrs Miggins has a portfolio of ten rented garages worth in total £1 million. She has no need of the income from the occupiers of the garages, because she is well provided for in terms of pension payments. The garages were left to her in her late husband's will many years ago, when they had a value of £500,000. The old lady wants to make a gift of 75% of the value of this little property portfolio to her grandchildren; but doesn't want to give them control over all this value, because in her view they are not yet mature enough for this.

The obvious solution would seem to be to make a trust for her grandchildren, enabling her to get the value out of her estate, and thereby save inheritance tax: but without giving the grandchildren themselves control over the property. The problem with the trust idea is that a £750,000 transfer into trust will give rise to a lifetime inheritance tax charge of £85,000.

Acting on advice, she decides instead to set up a family investment LLP into which she introduces the garages at their value of £1 million. Because she retains the right to enjoy 100% of all capital profits under the LLP Agreement, this is not treated as being a disposal by her of the properties, so there is no CGT to pay.

The next stage is to make a transfer of £750,000 of the capital to her grandchildren, who would become members in the LLP (either directly, or through nomineeships which have their parent's name on the register). It seems to me that this transfer of capital does not give rise to capital gains tax and, being an absolute gift (in principle) is also not subject to a lifetime inheritance tax charge.

Where we are uncertain, of course, is the effect of having a substantial capital account balance in an LLP on the future financial affairs of the grandchildren. Supposing one of them gets into a bad relationship, which involves matrimonial proceedings, how much will the judge take into account the fact that that grandchild has capital in a family investment LLP with such and such value?

My own view, for it is worth, is that the judge would be unlikely to value this capital at full face value, at least, if the LLP Agreement provides for others (Mrs Miggins in our example) to exercise complete control over whether any funds are ever paid out to the LLP in the form of repayment of capital. So it may be that the LLP provides a similar sort of protection to a trust: but without the inheritance tax penalty on transfers into the LLP in excess of £325,000.

CHAPTER 11
AN INSPECTOR CALLS

In Chapter 3 I introduced the subject of HMRC, and how businesses inter-
act with the government's tax raising body in times when everything is running smoothly. Now I come on to the more difficult area of what to do when
HMRC investigate your affairs.

HMRC investigations (they prefer the less combative word "enquiries")
can be very stressful, time consuming and expensive. Very often, a businessperson has to regard them as an "act of God", which descends on their business from a blue sky and the consequences of which simply have to be worked
with. But there are ways in which you can make an enquiry into your affairs
less likely.

What Triggers an Investigation?

Very often, no doubt, HMRC enquiries are set off by things you can't do
anything about, like large or unusual items in your accounts; or perhaps by
a random decision on the part of the HMRC computer to open up your affairs. But there are things which you can do (or refrain from doing) which can
have a positive impact on the likelihood of an investigation. Taxpayers who
habitually send in their returns late, for example, are increasing their changes
of being selected: because HMRC argue, no doubt with good reason, that
someone who is cavalier about getting their figures in on time may also be
cavalier about getting them right. Accounts with obvious errors in them are
also asking for an investigation to be opened: and the point is, that once a
human being in HMRC has decided to open your file, who knows what evils
might pour out, as from Pandora's Box, as a result of that decision?

Falling out with another person in a big way is also a mistake, if you can
avoid it, from the point of view of the tranquillity of your tax affairs. Although naturally we haven't got any figures, it seems likely that quite a high

proportion of investigations begin as a result of aggrieved former spouses and partners "tipping off" the Revenue about known, suspected, or invented tax irregularities perpetrated by their former partner. Sacking an employee in acrimonious circumstances can be as damaging, for this point of view, as getting divorced.

So bear in mind this danger, and if there is any scope for reducing it sensibly, take every opportunity to do so.

Types of Investigation

If you're running a business which does VAT returns, or employs staff, the tax control visit is always a possibility. Specialist VAT or PAYE inspectors will contact you with a request to come and see your records. My own impression, anecdotally, is that purely routine and random "control visits" of this sort are less frequently done nowadays than they use to be. Very often a VAT inspection, for example, will actually be triggered by some substantial VAT reclaim – perhaps because you have acquired a substantial capital asset like a property which had VAT included in the purchase price: and which you are now therefore reclaiming. PAYE visits tend nowadays to be more concentrated, it seems, on the very large employers. The reason for this is that large employers are more likely to have made repeated, systemic errors which the visiting officer can gain kudos by uncovering.

What evasive action can you as the businessperson take? You can't refuse to allow the officers on to your premises, because they have a right to visit your place of business to inspect your records. But you can take action to make sure that they find nothing amiss.

One way of doing this is to have your accountants, or a firm of tax advisers, perform a "mock PAYE audit" or a "mock VAT audit" on your records. In principle this audit should cover all the same areas that the visiting officers would, and clearly the mock auditor may well find errors which you can correct much less painfully than by letting HMRC discover them.

Self Assessment Enquiries

Both companies and individuals can also have their self assessment tax returns checked. In the old days, there was what was known as the "ERA" system. This was when every set of accounts and every tax return going into the tax office was looked at by a real, live human person (or almost human in some cases). This person, who was actually usually a fairly senior inspector of taxes, would use his judgment on whether to "examine", "review", or "accept". The accounts therefore went to three different piles, and if yours went on to the "accept" pile you could breathe a sigh of relief: the inspector would write to you a letter saying that he agreed your computations. A set of accounts which went into the "review" pile was subject to a series of targeted questions: could the revenue have an analysis of entertaining expenses, or legal expenses, or the like? It was the "examine" pile which really came in for the third degree treatment. Typically this would involve having to send in all of the bank statements of the business, and also possibly of the individuals, and justify every single receipt of money as being either declared as income of the business, or not such income. Expenses would also be gone through, often, with a fine toothcomb.

That was the good old days. Under the new regime of self assessment, there's no equivalent of the "accept" pile. If you hear nothing from HMRC, this doesn't mean they've agreed your return, merely that they don't happen to have enquired into it. If you do receive a letter, this will now be accompanied by a fairly formal notice saying that HMRC have decided to enquire.

This isn't necessarily a cue to panic. It may be that it's just an "aspect" enquiry (similar to the old "review" system), and they want a little bit more information on a few specific figures. Alternatively, they may be opening you up for a "full" enquiry, much the same as in the old days of "examine".

Are there any tips as to how to approach an HMRC self assessment enquiry? Well, the first thing, as I say, is not to panic: even if it looks as though what you've got is a "full" enquiry. It's a good idea to establish clearly what your rights are, and what the taxman's rights are. For example, running down the list of questions, are there any which can be seen as mere "fishing", with no apparent necessity for the Revenue to receive this in order to check your tax liability? They have the right to make reasonable requests for information for this purpose, but this doesn't extend to every possible question they could ask about you and your financial life. One example I have seen in the past is of inspectors asking to see a person's Will. Any such request should be jumped on from a great height; and if there is any doubt as to whether a piece of information could be justified by the taxman as being necessary, ask him why he's seeking that information. Ask the question: "What specific tax liability will this information enable you to check?" Sometimes the responses to this question are evasive and unsatisfactory!

It should go without saying that the information which the inspector is entitled to ask for should be provided as promptly as possible, correctly and in a courteous manner. There is no sense getting the tax officer's back up: although there's absolutely no need to "crawl" to them either, which is something I see too often. An obsequious approach to HMRC can in a way be as bad, or worse than an aggressive and obstructive approach.

The reason why you should not "bend over backwards" in your dealings with the Revenue is that, the more "helpful" you are, the more the officer, being only human, will regard you as an easy target. No, you should be courteous and provide the information properly requested; but do this as briefly as possible without overwhelming the officer with superfluous information. And don't be afraid to stick up for yourself if you think he's being unreasonable.

"COP 9" Enquiries

We move up another notch in the hierarchy of HMRC investigations when we get to the so called "COP 9" or "Code of Practice 9" enquiry.

This is a game with a very clearly defined set of rules, set out in the booklet which HMRC will give you at an early stage of proceedings. Basically what the tax authority is saying to you, by offering you a COP 9 basis of enquiry, is that they are pretty sure you are guilty of irregularities in your tax affairs: but they'll agree not to prosecute you on condition that you cooperate fully and provide full disclosure. That is, what HMRC are offering you here is a "deal".

The natural (and understandable) reaction of most people to this sort of approach is one of horror, and a willingness to eat out of the inspector's hand. But do bear in mind that this reaction might actually be massively over the top in terms of what is reasonable, for the following two reasons amongst others:

- It has more than once, in my experience, transpired that the Revenue's "reasonably sure" is in fact very far short of certainty on their part that they have discovered any undeclared income etc.
- Despite the extremely disturbing implications that they are on the verge, unless you are a good girl or boy, of bringing the full weight of the criminal law system against you, the reality is that HMRC actually prosecute only a very tiny, almost negligible, proportion of taxpayers each year. Unless you are a very high profile individual, or are in a position of trust like a tax barrister or tax adviser, the threat of taking criminal proceedings is very rarely fulfilled in practice.

How do you deal with a COP 9 enquiry? In the vast majority of cases, unless you are a qualified accountant yourself, you will commission one to prepare a full "Disclosure Report" for the benefit of the taxman. There's usually no need to be inventive in making up the structure of the report – the inspector will give you a very clear indication of the areas he wants covered. Hopefully this report will then form the basis for a negotiated, contract settlement of any tax liabilities, together with interest and any penalties, which will be agreed as a final lump sum settlement (even if, in practice, it has to be paid in instalments).

Criminal Proceedings

Finally, you've got what has got to be the worst case scenario on any reckoning. For whatever reason, whether it is the heinousness of your supposed tax evasion, or your high profile or responsibility as an individual, it may become clear that HMRC are indeed planning to investigate you with a view to possible prosecution. Normally speaking there won't be any doubt that this is their intention, because you will be interviewed under caution. But if there is any doubt, you (or your agent, such as your accountant) should pin the Revenue officer down on this point before any discussion at all takes place about tax.

How should you approach a criminal investigation into your tax affairs? Well, this is where this book, and indeed the advice of all accountants and tax advisers as such, gives way to a very simple imperative: you need to get proper legal representation, and straight away. And do what the solicitor advises you.

Know the Enemy

It may seem a little confrontational to describe HMRC as the "enemy", however where you are under tax investigation there's no point mincing words. The reason they are investigating your tax affairs is because they think they may be able to get some more tax out of you, which is obviously in their interest and correspondingly contrary to yours.

When you are taking on HMRC in an enquiry, you have to remember that they hold a lot of trump cards in their hand. They have reasonably extensive information powers, which enable them to require you to provide them with information and explanations which are reasonably needed to check your tax position, and they have the ability to raise assessments, if not satisfied, where the onus is on you (subject to the below) to disprove what the inspector has put into his assessment computer. It's this onus of proof which is the real killer in terms of measuring the strength of your position as against theirs.

On the other hand, remember the following points about HMRC and their position:

- They start off by knowing nothing of the facts; whereas you have all the facts, so to speak, under your control;

- Just as the inspector knows nothing about your affairs, deep down he very rarely cares much either. Spirited resistance will often lead to the inspector (or his replacement, if he gets taken off the case, as seems to happen frequently) may well decide simply to concede or compromise from sheer weariness;

- If witness evidence is important, you are likely to be the one who knows all the witnesses, who hopefully should therefore be well disposed towards you; and

- The onus of proof actually shifts back to the Revenue themselves where you are talking about periods more than four years old. They have to show, at least on balance of probabilities, that alleged problems with your tax affairs, more than four tax years ago, are reasonably assessed by them – and that you were either "careless" (for assessments up to six years old) or "deliberate" in the alleged understatement of your tax liabilities in your returns.

Meeting the Taxman

More often than not, the Revenue will want at least one meeting between you, as the taxpayer, and themselves. Do you have to agree to such a meeting?

The answer is a resounding "no". There is no obligation to meet or answer verbal questions. But might it be to your advantage?

For what it's worth, my own view is that it is only comparatively rarely that a meeting will actually be useful from your point of view. There are all kinds of reasons why a meeting might be immense help to HMRC themselves. A person speaking impromptu, so to speak, will often give away far more information than he would if he were thinking hard about his answers, in the course of a written correspondence. But the question you have to ask yourself is: will a meeting assist me? If the answer is no, then you should suggest that the enquiry be continued by way of correspondence.

Sometimes an HMRC officer will threaten you with higher penalties, effectively, if you refuse to hold a meeting. Penalties can be mitigated, it's true, if an enquiry finds there is extra tax to pay but the taxpayer has shown good cooperation. But I think that this threat by HMRC should be rejected, because a meeting is rarely the best or most efficient way of actually communicating the kind of detailed information to HMRC that an investigation requires. If you are in a meeting and the inspector asks you when you started letting a certain property, for example, you are much less likely to be able to answer accurately than if you are able to consult your records back at the office or at home. So declining to hold a meeting is not, in my view, likely to be genuinely an example of lack of cooperation.

The Knock on the Door in the Morning

But what about the much advertised ability of HMRC to make unannounced visits? These are actually very rare in practice, in my experience, however when they appear unannounced you should think twice or three times before actually letting them in. If you refuse to allow visiting officers to elbow you aside and push into your premises, the worst that can happen is that you receive a relatively small penalty for doing so: and even that only applies where they have successfully applied to the tribunal for the right to make the unannounced visit and enter your premises.

The key to dealing with this kind of very distressing situation is to be reasonable. If you find them on the doorstep unannounced, suggest that they come back at a future date which has been agreed between you as being mutually convenient.

Again, if the police are present, get straight on to a solicitor to ask for advice – but in the meantime, politely ask all the officials concerned to wait outside while you take this advice.

Penalties

I've mentioned the threat of penalties being increased for lack of cooperation, and it's as well to bear in mind the way penalties are worked out. The amount of the penalty, which is a percentage of the extra tax that HMRC find, depends on the extent of disclosure and cooperation, and the following table sets out how the maximum and minimum penalties are calculated.

	Penalty Range
Careless errors	0% - 30%
Deliberate but unconcealed errors	20% - 70%
Deliberate and concealed errors	30% - 100%

Where on the range you come will depend on how helpful you have been in disclosing the necessary information to put things right.

What to Do if you Can't Reach Agreement

In the vast majority of cases, an enquiry either ends with HMRC accepting that there's no extra tax due, or in an agreement between the taxman and the taxpayer. Just occasionally, though, the disagreement is so fundamental, and the amount of money involved is so big, that there's nothing for it but to go to the tax tribunal.

This may seem a bit of an intimidating prospect; and it's certainly true that an appeal to this first stage of the appeal process is more formal than it used to be in the days of the old General Commissioners. But if you feel that your case is a good one, you shouldn't be afraid of being prepared to go to the tribunal.

If the amounts of money are big, but not big enough to justify the use of a professional representative (still less a barrister – tax barristers cost an arm and a leg these days) you'll find, if you represent yourself, that the tribunal chairman will be anxious to ensure that your inevitable ignorance of the procedure doesn't hamper you, to the extent that he or she possibly can.

It's probably over egging the pudding to go into any great detail about tribunal procedure here, in a book which is fundamentally about tax planning. However, the formal requirements should be followed carefully, and these will be made clear to you in the course of the tribunal appeal, in the form of specific "Directions" which the tribunal will issue at various stages of the process.

What happens following the tribunal decision? The costs of the hearing are unlikely to be awarded to the victorious side, unlike the case with hearings in higher courts. But both sides have the right to appeal against the decision. This appeal is generally to the upper tribunal, and beyond that appeals are taken normally to the Court of Appeal: and, rarely, for important cases, even beyond that to the Supreme Court (the new name for the judicial committee of the House of Lords).

Using a Professional Adviser

Finally, I come on to a topic which arguably should have come first. Should you use a professional adviser, such as an accountant, a solicitor, or a tax adviser, to represent you when fielding an HMRC investigation? And if so, how do you choose the right professional to appoint?

Where the enquiry is a fairly basic one, it's normal simply to allow your accountant, even if he isn't a tax specialist as such, to deal with the HMRC correspondence. In this connection, if you don't know already, ask your accountant whether he has Fee Protection Insurance. This is fairly widespread now, and, for a small premium, you can cover the costs of the accountant dealing with enquiries on your behalf: which can be quite a boon given how much money such enquiries can run into in terms of professional fees.

If the going gets tough, though, and in particular if it gets technical, you should seriously consider using a specialist tax adviser who deals with investigations on a regular basis.

How do you choose a good tax adviser? Mostly, the best way is to find one is by personal recommendation – even if this means letting other people know that HMRC are having a go at you. The acid test of a good tax adviser is that he is clearly on your side rather than on his own, or that of HMRC. A sure sign of a representative who will let you down is the adviser who, it's clear, is afraid of the taxman, and is more concerned to please HMRC than to defend your interests.

CHAPTER 12
REWARDING KEY STAFF

I've had my rant elsewhere about all the obstacles placed in the way of businesses trying to provide jobs to others: obstacles put in the way of entrepreneurs by the government and lawyers, mostly taking the form of a series of increasingly onerous burdens and an absurdly biased approach to dealing with disputes between employer and employee. HMRC have a booklet on PAYE entitled "Thinking of Taking Someone on?" If I wrote it, this might be a very short booklet, consisting of the single word "don't!".

Extreme and ranty views aside, however, in most types of business getting above a certain minimal size inevitably brings with it the need for staff. And in the area of employing and rewarding staff, as in so many other areas, there's a right way to do it and a wrong way to do it, in the context of the tax rules.

The Bonus Culture

The purpose of rewarding key staff, and in particular how you reward them, is a subject which naturally leads on to consideration of performance related bonuses. It's seems obvious to give key staff an incentive to work hard by paying them extra if the business, or any particular aspect of it, does well. But bonus schemes are by no means without their problems. There is sometimes the temptation to manipulate figures, where a person's pay depends on them; and, arguably more importantly, there is a law of diminishing returns with bonus payments.

Put simply, a bonus will either stay the same, go up, or go down from year to year. It's probably all very fine if they go up – although you can end up paying astronomical figures to staff, beyond what you'd originally envisaged – but inevitably the time has got to come when this year's bonus is either about the same as last year's, or is less (or even non existent). If the bonus is roughly the same, it quickly becomes seen as effectively a fixed entitlement – part of the remuneration package, and therefore its action as an incentive disappears. If the bonus is less this year than last year, it is more likely (such is human nature) to act as a disincentive.

So, experienced employers will think several times before introducing any kind of formal bonus scheme. Anything which is an entitlement comes to be looked on as such. It may be better to make one off payments, not on a regular or expected basis, to capitalise on times when the business, and therefore the key staff, are riding on the crest of a wave.

Tax Favoured Benefits In Kind

These comments about bonus schemes are strictly speaking outside my remit as a tax adviser, but derive from long experience of employing people myself and acting for clients who do so. To return to the main subject of the book, are there particular ways of rewarding staff that could be said to be favoured by the tax system?

Compared with the default position, which is payment in money, provision of various kinds of benefits can give a good tax result. I'll pick out one or two of the types of benefit which are most likely to be relevant to the owner managed business, (ignoring old favourites like staff canteen and sports facilities, which tend to be associated with the larger employer). But first a word of caution. Arrangements under which an employee swaps some cash salary for benefits in kind are now caught by the so called "salary sacrifice" rules, and the advantage of doing them is therefore greatly reduced. But you can award all or any of the following as an additional incentivising benefit:

- Free car parking, not just on the premises but also at nearby public car parks, is something the provision of which you get tax relief for, against your profits, but the employee pays nothing for in tax.
- You can provide one mobile phone tax and NI free per employee, providing the phone contract is between you, the employer, and the supplier.

- The provision of your business's own services is not tax free, but is calculated on the "marginal cost" basis. This was established in a high profile case where the children of teachers at a public school received cheap or free tuition: the extra cost of having one more pupil was way less than a proportion of the total costs of the school; and still less than the amount of fees that would have had to be paid by unconnected parents.

- Cheap or subsidised living accommodation, again, is not free of tax, but is calculated on what is generally a very favourable basis. If the cost to the business of providing the accommodation is less than £75,000, the benefit in kind is worked out on the basis of its rateable value (in England and Wales). This is usually a very small figure indeed in relation to the true rental value of the property. Over £75,000, the same rules apply as for beneficial loans: that is, the value is treated effectively as if it were a loan to the employee, and to the extent that no payment is being made, a tax and NI charge arises on the basis of a notional income equal to the "official rate" of interest (currently 2.5%).

- "Cars for kids" is one of my favourite tax favoured benefits. You'll notice that the good old "company car" benefit hasn't in itself featured in this list, and the reason for this is because it is often the absolute reverse of a tax favoured benefit. Punitive rules introduced by Gordon Brown when he was Chancellor have the effect of taxing employees as if they had received a given percentage of the list price of the car when new, as income each year; and no allowance is given at all for business use, even if this is predominant. The percentage depends on how "green" the car is in terms of CO_2 omissions. The "cars for kids" idea turns this on its head and concentrates on cars whose provision is a pure "perk": where there's little or, more often, no business use of the car at all. If you compare the amount of taxable benefit of providing a youngster (usually adult child of the key employee concerned) with a small (and therefore green) car, and then consider the cost to the business of providing that car, including probably astronomic insurance premiums, you will find that very often, in practice, the amount on which the employee is being taxed is considerably less than the actual amounts that the business is shelling out – and claiming tax relief for.

The Share Dilemma

It often seems to strike majority owners of private trading companies that it would be a good idea to give the really crucial and central staff members shares in the company. What could be more natural than the feeling that a person with an equity holding in the business is more likely to be "heart and soul" behind its success? All I can say is that, after many years' experience, I'd advise company owners to think twice about the wisdom of indulging in this act of generous inclusiveness. There is nothing much more aggravating than the presence of a minority owner in a business who isn't pulling his or her weight or, worse still, is positively antagonistic to the other owners. It can be a very expensive and long drawn out process getting rid of such individuals. And this is also where what I have referred to as the "share dilemma" comes in.

The basic tax problem is this. If you give shares in the company to an employee – it doesn't matter whether you transfer them from an existing shareholder or issue them new – the employee is chargeable to tax, and the company to National Insurance, on the value of those shares; except in the rare instance that the employee pays full value for them. If, then, you wait until a late stage in the development of the business, when it is successful and the shares are therefore valuable, to transfer a shareholding to the key staff members concerned, you've got what can be a very substantial tax charge. To make matters worse, it's not always at all easy to determine how big that tax charge will be in advance, because HMRC's views on the value of shares can diverge widely from those of taxpayers.

By contrast, the tax on share awards is likely to be much less, or even nil, where the shareholdings are allocated at the outset, or at an early stage of the business's development.

So, do you give the shares early on, when the tax situation is manageable, or wait to see whether you really want this person as a minority shareholder in your business? There's no easy answer. For what it's worth, though, my own inclination would always be to err on the safe side, and look at other ways of incentivising key staff members, other than giving them shares in the company. Quite why our tax system includes such a powerful disincentive to business expansion by widening the equity base of businesses, is a puzzling question. It's another instance, in my view, of the essentially random nature of our tax system. Looking for ways round this is not in any way morally culpable on any reasonable view of the situation: and a considerable industry did indeed build up whose aim was precisely that.

Did HMRC or its political masters consider the strong brake which these rules imposed on the growth of our economy? Or did they load the statute book with many pages of detailed rules to frustrate the efforts of those looking for a tax efficient solution? No prizes at all for guessing that they chose the latter course of action!

Share Options, & Other "Schemes"

The "Employment Related Securities" rules are indeed a fearsome battery of anti-avoidance law. For example, any attempt to manipulate the value of the shares at the time they are awarded is heavily frowned on. If the value is artificially depressed on issue, or indeed if it is subsequently artificially enhanced, that enhancement is caught for Income Tax under these rules.

Are share options the answer?

These work by saying to employees: "you can't have any shares now. But we'll give you the opportunity to acquire them at favourable prices in the future – subject to conditions". The conditions often relate to the performance of the company; and, of course, for the share options to be a valuable thing to have, the value of the shares needs to be greater than the price at which the scheme allows the employee to acquire them when he exercises his option.

These may be effective in incentivising employees – I don't know – but there's very little in them in the way of tax break.

The most popular form of share option scheme around at the moment is probably the Enterprise Management Incentive, or EMI. It's easiest to explain how this works by giving an example.

James Regent owns all of the shares in Palace Limited. He decides to award EMI share options to his right hand man, John. At the time the EMI scheme is devised, the value of 10% of the company (which is what James wants John to have options over) is £100,000. So, the terms of the scheme are that John can acquire 10% for £100,000 at any time within the three years to ten years after the award of the options, providing the company meets certain turnover targets.

Three years later, the turnover targets have already been met, and so James exercises his option, and pays £100,000 for shares which, by this time, have actually gone up in value to £250,000.

Two years later, the company is sold for £10 million, and James therefore receives his share of this figure, which is £1 million. His gain is worked out on a difference between what he pays and what he gets, that is, he pays capital gains tax on a £900,000 gain, which, with the benefit of entrepreneurs' relief, means that his tax is only £90,000.

When we talk about EMI being a tax favoured scheme, we mean that, in the example of John, he has effectively received a reward for working which is ultimately charged to Capital Gains Tax (at the favoured rate of 10% in that example) rather than Income Tax. But consider the limitations of EMI. Principally, John still has to come up with £100,000 from somewhere, and if the rules were that he could acquire them for a lower value than the value when the EMI scheme was devised, then he would pay Income Tax – not Capital

Gains Tax – on any shortfall of what he pays for the shares over what they were worth when the EMI scheme terms were set.

In short what even "tax favoured" share schemes can't do is get round the basic problem of the value which has arisen in the shares before the scheme is entered into. The employee has either to pay that or pay tax on it, even under EMI.

Paying Staff in Dividends Rather Than Salary

Sometimes shares are awarded to staff for reasons which are much more basic than the fairly high flown one of incentivising them with an equity stake in the business. Sometimes the aim is simply to provide a mechanism to pay them in dividends rather than as salary, and hence eliminate the punitive National Insurance liabilities which arise from payment of salary. Dividends, in normal circumstances, don't trigger any NI.

To some extent, you can get round the problem of the value of shares on issue, here, by doing what you might describe as emasculating the shares. That is, they will often have no rights to vote or to participate in capital on a winding up or sale of the company. They are simply a mechanism to pay dividends as and when the voting shareholders see fit.

In principle, these severe restrictions on the shares do have the effect of depressing the value more than somewhat. But there's always the niggling doubt as to whether an issue of new shares, which then immediately proceed to pay substantial dividends each year, won't be attributed a value by the HMRC share valuation boys – who notoriously live in a world of their own.

As with the issue of "full fat" shares, it's going to be very much better if you can set up shares of this type at the outset of the business, before there is any value there, rather than when the business is mature.

Occasionally, it may be possible to avoid this issue even with mature businesses. Consider the following example:

Beefeater Limited has built up a highly successful business selling souvenirs at the Tower of London. Building on the successful model, the director and 100% shareholder decides to set up an outlet in Edinburgh selling kilts and tam o' shanters in the Royal Mile. Angus, who has been instrumental in helping to build up the London business, is to be moved to Scotland to work the same magic (it's hoped) on the Edinburgh outlet. The owner of the company has been meaning for some years to bring Angus in on an equity share in the company, but his accountant's dire warnings about the tax consequences of transferring 25% of a valuable company to Angus have held him back.

The new plans give a fresh impetus to this idea. A new company is formed to run the Edinburgh outlet, and, of course, at this stage it has no value because the business that it is going to run hasn't even started yet. The owner decides to reward Angus with 50% of the shares in this company, however, since the anticipated value of the Edinburgh business is likely to be about the same as that of a London business when everything has fully matured. So, Angus gets what is in effect a 25% stake in the business without any upfront tax charge.

Generous Impulses on Sale

I wish I had 10% for every time a client has come to me with some such suggestion as the following. Johann Schmidt is selling his company for millions of pounds, and he wants to recognise the input of his "right hand man" in bringing to the company to the stage where it will sell for such a large amount. Johann asks me whether he can make over to this right hand man 10% of the sale proceeds of the company.

My, admittedly very negative, response is to point to the tax effects of putting this suggestion into place. Firstly, Johann will still pay Capital Gains Tax on 100% of the proceeds, because nothing in the suggestions acts to divert any of the ownership of the company, and therefore the proceeds from selling it, to anyone else. Secondly, there is a more than insignificant danger that the payment to the right hand man will be treated as employment income (even if it's paid by Johann and not by the company) with resultant significant liabilities to Income Tax and employers NI. So, effectively the 10% of the proceeds going to the right hand man are going to be bearing tax well in excess of 50%. There's no tax relief for Johann in making the payment, but the receipt is fully chargeable as earned income on the individual receiving it.

One way that Johann could have avoided this nightmare tax/NI scenario was by entering into an EMI scheme. In fact quite a high proportion of these, in my experience, as implemented by owner managed businesses, consist of an agreement that shares may be acquired by key staff only in the event of a sale of the whole company. On such a sale, the fact that they have to come up with money sufficient to pay the market value of the shares on original establishment of the EMI scheme is not a problem: because this can be paid out of the sale proceeds. But the effect of the scheme is that the shares are actually being sold by the right hand man (to use the terminology in my example) rather than by "Johann". So, there is no Income Tax charge and no Capital Gains tax charge for Johann on the shares that he has "given away".

Personal Service Companies

One alternative to the highly expensive employment relationship is to allow your key employees to bill you through a Personal Service Company. I don't intend to go into all the detail of these, as there is a chapter given over to them, but suffice it to say that there are huge potential advantages, particularly in the National Insurance arena, to rearranging things in this way, providing the individual concerned passes the so called "IR35" test. As well as National Insurance benefits, the individual has the potential benefit of sharing the income amongst members of his household to reduce the overall average tax rate on the earnings.

LLP Membership

Another potentially very useful piece of lateral thinking is to explore the possibility of the key individual being not an employee of your limited company, but a member of your LLP. As with self-employment generally, LLP membership can result in a significant saving in National Insurance on the individual's earnings. As a self-employed individual, he would also have the more benign regime which applies to many benefits in kind, particularly the provision of cars.

If you object that your business is run by a company and not by an LLP, the response is to consider whether a restructuring of the arrangements could change this. Your company could, after all, hive down its business into an LLP, in which it would become a member. Or it could hive down a portion of its business in this way. The cost and administrative hassle of making this structural change could be less than you think – and could result in a seriously more motivated staff member or members

CHAPTER 13
MAXIMISING CAPITAL GAINS TAX RELIEFS

The basic idea of Capital Gains Tax (CGT) is simple. If you sell a capital asset for more than you bought it for, the gain is chargeable to tax. And yet, anecdotally, Capital Gains Tax questions are responsible for most of the mistakes which accountants and tax advisers get sued for; and the reason for this is the abundance of available reliefs against this simple scenario.

I am going to be having a look at the more important of such reliefs for business people and investors, concentrating on the following:

- Business Asset Disposal Relief (formerly Entrepreneurs' Relief)
- Investors' Relief
- Roll over Relief
- Exchange of Joint Interests
- Main Residence Relief
- Loss Relief
- Substantial Shareholdings Exemption
- Incorporation Relief

As this isn't an encyclopaedia or a text book I'm not going to bore you (I hope) by a systematic exposition of all of the rules, but instead point out the practical ways in which you can maximise the availability of these potentially very valuable reliefs.

Business Asset Disposal Relief

This is the relief which was known as Entrepreneur's Relief until the 2020 Finance Act, and you could write a book about this relief – in fact I think someone has. It's of considerable importance to people in business – trading businesses, anyway – because it secures a uniquely low rate of tax at 10% for business disposals which qualify. Before the 2020/21 tax year, there was a lifetime limit of £10 million per individual of gains that would be given the relief, but this was drastically reduced to £1 million on Budget Day 2020. It's available for sale of unincorporated businesses, and for the sale of trading companies. If the business is unincorporated (for example a partnership, sole trader, or, effectively, LLP) the relief is given against the gains made on the individual assets which you sell as part of the whole business. Unfortunately, unlike the old "Business Asset Taper Relief" which it replaced in 2008, the relief isn't given for the sale of individual assets which have been used for the purpose of a trade, but only for gains made when the whole business (or a definable part of it) is being sold. Hence farmers, for example, who sell a few fields for development don't get the relief, because the fields don't comprise "part of a business" in themselves, but merely assets of the business. I'll come on to this point again shortly.

With a company sale, there are three specific requirements for the sale of the shares in that company to qualify for the 10% tax rate which BAD relief gives. (I wonder did the legislators think about the inevitable use of this acronym?) Firstly, the selling shareholder must have at least 5% of the shares. Secondly, he must be an officer (director or secretary) or employee of the company. And thirdly the company must be a "trading company" as defined.

What Is A Trading Company?

I'm glad you asked me that! In fact, given the immense importance of this question for BAD Relief and other CGT reliefs too, the definition of what is meant by a trading company is supremely, even criminally vague. It is defined, believe it or not, as a company whose activities don't comprise to a substantial extent activities other than trading activities. No definition is attempted of the word "substantial", and it's almost as if the lawyer writing these rules was rubbing his hands with glee at the idea of all the lucrative (for the legal profession) litigation this extremely imprecise word was likely to cause.

HMRC came in with their size elevens, shortly after the original introduction of the rules, and said that in their view "substantially" meant "20%". Unfortunately, they ceased to be forthcoming beyond this point, and the question of whether this is 20% of the assets of the company, its income, or the time given to the various activities, has no kind of answer, satisfactory or not. When asked about this, HMRC gave the un-useful answer that it depends on the facts and circumstances of each case.

So, making sure that your company doesn't undertake non trading activities is an important planning point, as an example I'll give demonstrates.

You should bear in mind that all of the above three requirements need to have been fulfilled for at least two years (formerly one year) prior to the date of sale. Again this raises some interesting planning points which I'll illustrate with an example.

How To Lose BAD Relief

It's clear from the above list of very prescriptive rules that this is an easy relief to foul up if you're not careful. Take the very common case of husband and wife shareholders, for example. Mr has 51% of the shares and Mrs has the other 49%. Mr is a director of the company, but Mrs has no office, and doesn't work for the company either.

Have you spotted the problem? On any sale of the business, BAD Relief won't be available for Mrs's 49% of the company, because she hasn't fulfilled the "officer or employee" criterion. Or take the case of Mr Philoprogenitor, who has transferred 20% of his company to his five children, who have 4% of the shares each. It doesn't matter that the whole company is held by the same family: the five individuals in question have failed to come up to the

5% shareholding necessary to get the relief, so 20% of the sale proceeds of the company won't qualify.

Or, again, consider the "success" story of Moneybags Limited in the example below.

Moneybags Limited makes a lot of profit each year: upwards of £1 million after tax. The 100% shareholder, Mr Midas, has very frugal lifestyle needs, and takes only minimal dividends out of the company each year. So, the natural result, of course, is that cash builds up and up in the company bank account.

Cash sitting around in a company deposit account is effectively dead money, because the banks will only give a pathetic rate of interest. Mr Midas decides that the money can be put to better use (it could hardly be put to worse use). So, he starts investing the surplus cash, that the business doesn't need, in a buy-to-let property portfolio. Soon this portfolio is worth several million, and is contributing a substantial – note the word – part of the company's bottom line profit.

Predator plc approaches Mr Midas to buy Moneybags Limited from him. The price tag is the modest sum of £20 million, and Mr Midas reckons that he will get BAD Relief of £1 million (which is the individual lifetime limit), resulting in a reduction in the overall tax bill on sale of £100,000 – with the rest of the shares paying the CGT rate of 20%.

Mr McNasty, the tax inspector, thinks otherwise. The company has "substantial" investment activities, and the effect of this is "all or nothing". The company fails to qualify as a trading company, even though most of its value derives from its trade, and BAD Relief is denied completely.

What should Mr Midas have done? One possible solution might have been to lend the money across to another company which Mr Midas also owned, which other company then made the investment in the buy-to-let properties.

It's very arguable that a simple balance with an associated company – especially if it doesn't pay interest – is not a non trading "activity" as such, because it's not an activity at all. So, BAD Relief might quite likely have been saved by these means.

All this talk about how to lose Entrepreneurs' Relief is obviously a bit negative. So, let's turn to a story with a happier ending, to illustrate one very interesting aspect of the Entrepreneurs' Relief rules:

Provident Construction started as a pure building contracting company, but, after some years successful trade at this, it started doing property developments. As with many property developers, they tended to build out a series of units, sell some of them, and keep some of them as rental properties long term. So, you have here a company with a mixture of trading (property development and general building) and investment (holding rental properties) activities. In our example Provident Limited has roughly 50% of its value in investment properties and 50% in the trading "stock" and work in progress of their development trade. So, this company doesn't stand an earthly chance of getting BAD Relief if it is sold. Moreover, this has been the position for many years. In due course of time, the shareholder, Edward, dies and leaves the shares to his son John. He decides that the business needs shaking up, because it can be made much more profitable (the young always know better) and built up to a substantial company with a view to selling to some large property development/construction group. Softly, softly is the name of the game, though, and John undertakes a very gradual programme of selling off the investment property stock and ploughing the money back into new developments, which are mostly, very fortunately, successful. Finally he gets to the stage where the investment properties are worth less than 20% of the total company assets, and at this point he starts putting out feelers with a view to sale of the company.

Just over two years later, the company is sold and John achieves BAD Relief on his capital gain. The fact that, for the majority of his period of ownership, the company didn't qualify as a "trading company"; but has only so qualified for the last two years, matters not a jot.

Planning to maximise BAD Relief

The reduction of the lifetime limit of the relief from £10 million to £1 million on Budget Day 2020 made the following tax planning strategy much more relevant for a large number of entrepreneurs. If you have a family you should bear in mind that every family member has their own £1 million allowance, which you can tap into by bringing them into part ownership of the business with you. So Mother, Father and three children collectively could secure the 10% tax rate on £5 million of gains – but only if they are brought into ownership etc at least two years before the sale. The saving of tax, in this example and assuming that the business sells for at least £5 million, is £400,000 as compared with the frequently found scenario of one family member, such as Father, owning 100% of the business.

Finally on BAD Relief, I mentioned, at little while ago, the case of the farmer who won't qualify for Entrepreneurs' Relief for selling a few fields. You have to sell a "business or part of a business". So, consider the device used (based on a real life case) in the following case study:

Mr Gallagher is a very successful farmer. On his 300 acres, he seems able to turn in very reasonable profits by intelligent use of the land and as a result of his good business head. Even successful farming is nothing like so profitable, though, as being in the fortunate position of owning land which gets planning permission for residential development.

This is exactly what happens, with an acre of the farmland lying within the local development plan of an adjoining village. The value of the land suddenly jumps up, almost overnight, from the agricultural value of £10,000 an acre to £1 million per acre.

Mr Gallagher takes advice, and is displeased to be told, by his accountant, that he will be paying 20% tax on the £6 million. This is because he's not selling part of a business, only a few assets of an existing business; and therefore BAD Relief is denied.

Mr Gallagher decides, therefore, that he will sell the whole farm, and thereby realise a gain, including the development gain, with the availability of BAD Relief. Fortunately, the rest of the land has not gone up in value very much since he acquired it, and so the overall tax bill is less for selling the whole farm that it would have been for just selling the 6 acres.

You might say that the above example is a bit contrived and unlikely. It's not so easy, after all, to sell a complete farm, or indeed any other type of business, just like that. But what I forgot to say in that example was that the sale was an engineered one, to a connected company which Mr Gallagher had set up for the purpose. The relief applies just as much to a sale to a connected person as it does to a third party. Alternatively, Mr Gallagher could have considered bringing in a partner and giving that partner an interest in the partnership capital gains – which is also treated as a disposal for capital gains tax.

Investors' Relief

In most ways this is like BAD Relief as it applies to selling shares in trading companies, but differs in that, whereas with BADR the individual must be an officer or employee of the company, with Investors' Relief they must not normally be such. Also, there is no 5% minimum shareholding, but the shares must have been subscribed for, not bought from someone else; and must be held for at least three years. Like BADR Investors' Relief reduces the tax rate to 10% (from 20%) on up to £1 million of gains.

Roll Over Relief

A CGT relief which is often overlooked is Roll Over Relief, and it's often misunderstood too. When you sell an asset that you've used for trading purposes, and buy another, you can "roll over" the capital gain on the old asset against the acquisition cost of the new asset, as per the simple example below.

> Speedy Motors Limited has outgrown its premises, and sells them for £300,000, realising a gain of £200,000 (because the original base cost was £100,000). They buy a replacement garage for £500,000, and claim roll over relief for the gain on the old one. So, there's no tax to pay on the gain on the old premises, and the base cost of the new premises is reduced, for the purpose of calculating future capital gains, from the actual £500,000 laid out to £300,000 (by deducting the £200,000 "rolled over gain").

The new asset has generally to be bought at some point in the period of one year before and three years after the disposal of the old asset. It's clear from this timing, though, that it doesn't need to be actually the same money that you get from selling the old asset that you reinvest in the new. In fact, it doesn't matter how you finance the acquisition of the new asset. Nor does the trade need to be the same trade, but another trade carried on by the same person works just as well.

If you like, that's the good news. The bad news is that Roll Over Relief only applies to trading assets, as in the example of the trading premises of the motor business. It doesn't apply to investment assets, like properties which are let to third party tenants; and it also doesn't apply to trading stock – because trading stock isn't an asset within the scope of CGT.

But to counter that bad news, there's some potential good news with regard to the time limits: which is that HMRC can extend these at their discretion if there is good reason to do so. Consider the following two examples.

Tick and Bash are an old fashioned firm of accountants. They sold their old offices in 2015 with a view to moving to spanking new premises in a more bustling part of the town. Unfortunately, whilst the sale of the old offices went through, the negotiations foundered for the acquisition of the new, so they were forced to move out into rented property. A year later, a suitable property was identified, and negotiations began. Unfortunately again, there turned out to be all kinds of structural problems with the new building, which had to be sorted out before Tick and Bash could buy it. As these things do, the negotiations dragged on and on, and it wasn't, in fact, until 2019 that the purchase was finally completed.

Tick and Bash go cap in hand to HMRC and explain the situation. They've been trying to acquire this replacement asset for three years, and it was only due to exceptionally bad luck that they took more than the statutory three years to reinvest the proceeds from the old property sale. HMRC are feeling in a good mood that day, and grant the extended relief.

A company has as its trade providing serviced offices to other businesses. One particular property has been earmarked for this purpose for some years, and the work has been going on gradually, as money is available and as planning hurdles are overcome, to convert the property for that purpose. When it is ready, the company decides to move out of its current HQ and move into this property, because it's much too nice to let out to other people!

On a "cap in hand" claim to the Revenue, the company manages to get them to agree that the improvement expenditure on the offices can be claimed for Roll Over Relief against the gain on the sale of their previous offices – even though a lot of this expenditure was taking place a lot more than one year before this sale.

Exchange of Joint Interests

This is going to be a relief, I suspect, which is of considerable interest to property investors. In a way, it's a form of Roll Over Relief, but, unlike Roll Over Relief proper, it works when the properties concerned are purely investment in nature and not the base of any kind of trade carried on by the owner. The following example takes a married couple, but there's no requirement for there to be any particular legal or other relationship between the owners.

Janet and John own a fairly large buy-to-let property portfolio, with a total value of £10 million. Unfortunately things aren't going well for Janet and John's marriage, and they separate in early 2017, finally getting divorced two years later. As part of the divorce deal, it is agreed that £5 million worth of the jointly owned properties should be transferred into Janet's sole name, and the rest of the portfolio should be transferred into John's sole name. This is what is known as an "exchange of joint interests". Because of the availability of Roll Over Relief, the capital gain that would otherwise have arisen, by reference to the value of what each was getting and giving up, is treated as held over indefinitely until any of the properties are actually sold to third parties for cash.

There's also a similar relief from Stamp Duty Land Tax that's available in the above kind of situation.

Main Residence Relief

It might be questioned what a section on Main Residence Relief is doing in a book aimed at traders and investors; but actually, there is a lot of cross over between business properties and personal properties in the real world.

The basic relief is well known. If you sell a house which has been your only or main residence throughout your period of ownership, the gain on that sale is exempt from CGT. If the property has only been occupied by you as a main residence for some of your period of ownership, a corresponding fraction of the gain is exempt, and the rest taxable. Where any of the gain is exempt under the Main Residence rules, the last nine months of the period of ownership is treated as if it were a period of occupation as a main residence: even if in fact this wasn't the case.

You can nominate a given property as your main residence where you have more than one home. Nominating does not mean you have to pretend that it is your main residence in fact: if anything, you are saying precisely the opposite to the taxman when you enter your nomination. You are saying that "I have residences A and B. I actually live in A for most of the time, but I want B to be treated as if it were my main residence for tax purposes".

An interesting planning point arises with the timing of this nomination. It can only be made within two years of the question "which is my main residence?" needing to be answered. So, consider the following example of how this time limit can be organised to your advantage.

Bartholomew has a flat in London and a house in the country. He's owned the house in the country for ten years, and the flat in London for the last four years, and has no other residences. The reality of the situation is that the house in the country is the main base of his existence, with the London flat being little more than a pied-à-terre.

As it happens, it's the London flat which is really shooting up in value, and Bartholomew decides to "cash in his chips" by selling the flat.

When his accountant tells him how much Capital Gains Tax he's going to have to pay on the sale, as and when it goes through, he nearly falls off his chair. Is there anything I can do about it he says?

Acting on the accountant's advice, Bartholomew takes on a tenancy of a second London flat, and moves some of his things into it. He now, therefore, has three residences, and it's necessary to determine which of them is his main residence. So, he elects for the London flat which he owns to be the main residence, and this therefore starts accruing an exempt period. When the London flat eventually sells two years and nine months later, that much out of his total period of ownership of six years and nine months is treated as exempt from CGT.

Loss Relief

It may not seem to need saying that capital losses can be offset against capital gains, but there are occasions when the existence and availability of losses has been overlooked (I've seen this happen in real life myself).

The important point to note, with regard to Loss Relief, is that, for any loss accruing since 1996, when self-assessment came in, it's necessary to put in a formal claim, within four years, or the availability of the loss disappears. But correspondingly, for the period before 1996, it wasn't necessary to make a claim at the time. Let's show how significant this can be in another case study.

> Ebenezer wants to sell one of his buy-to-let property portfolio, because he's seen another property he desperately wants to buy. Unfortunately, if he does sell the CGT bill is massive, because he bought it years ago for a low price. He goes to see his accountant, who asks him if he can cast his mind back over his whole financial history since 1982. Ebenezer realises that he invested £300,000 in a company which went wrong in the early 1990's. It was one of those situations where the company kept just needing another £10,000 to turn the corner: and then eventually turned the corner into the insolvency practitioner's office. Gathering together all the evidence of this, Ebenezer's accountant is able to put in a claim for the £300,000 loss incurred in 1992, and this then is available to offset against the forthcoming sale of the buy-to-let property.

The Substantial Shareholdings Exemption

This is an exemption from CGT (or rather, strictly, from Corporation Tax on Chargeable Gains) which doesn't seem to loom very large in advising small and medium sized businesses in practice.

On the face of it, this is puzzling, because the Substantial Shareholdings Exemption completely eliminates any Capital Gains Tax charge when you sell a trading company, and the only requirement is that you, the owner, are a limited company and that you have held at least 10% of that company for at least one year. It really is as simple as that. No tax.

So, why aren't we jumping up and down and promoting this relief for all we're worth?

Well, it's fundamentally a question of structural choices in the way you hold companies. If you are an average OMB with one or more trading companies under your control, you fundamentally have the choice as to whether to own these companies directly yourself, as an individual, or hold them through some kind of holding limited company. If you hold them through another limited company, the sale of the shares, when it comes along, is completely tax exempt. So what's the problem?

The answer is, of course, that it's your company which has the sale proceeds, from selling the trading company shares, and not you. In order to get the money out of that company, you're either going to have to wind it up (which is possible if it doesn't also hold other assets) or, much worse in tax terms, pay the money out as a dividend. By contrast, if you had owned the shares directly yourself, you'd have the proceeds in your own bank account, with only a 10% (assuming Entrepreneurs' Relief is available) tax charge.

So, the Substantial Shareholdings Exemption presents us with a dilemma as to how to hold trading company shares. In some cases, where a person is a "serial entrepreneur" and wants to continue to plough back proceeds from selling businesses into their general business holding portfolio, a limited company holding structure makes very good use of the Substantial Shareholdings Exemption. But for most people, I suspect, the outcome of personal receipt of the sale proceeds subject to only 10% tax is going to be more attractive as a prospect.

Incorporation Relief

Finally, a relief which has come to the fore recently with the widespread incorporation of people's buy-to-let property portfolios. When you transfer a "business" to a limited company in exchange for shares, you get relief from the Capital Gains Tax that would otherwise have been paid, with the gain being "rolled over" into the deemed cost to you of the new shares.

> Jean-Paul transfers his thriving buy-to-let property portfolio business to Potiphar Limited in exchange for shares of the same value issued to him by that company. The value of the portfolio, and therefore the shares issued by Potiphar Limited, is £10 million. The portfolio originally cost Jean-Paul only £2.5 million, and therefore the gain rolled over under Incorporation Relief is £7.5 million.
>
> For the purpose of any future sale or winding up of Potiphar Limited by Jean-Paul, the shares, although they "actually" cost him £10 million, will be treated as only having cost him £2.5 million for CGT purposes.

So far, so dull. But the really interesting feature of this situation, to continue with my illustrative example of Jean-Paul, is that the company itself is treated for tax as having acquired the portfolio for what it was actually worth, that is £10 million. The rolled over gain has no effect on the company's tax position as such. So, in principle, the company could sell the whole portfolio shortly afterwards, for £10 million, and there would be no tax to pay at all.

For those who aim to sell business assets at a gain in the foreseeable future, Incorporation Relief effectively gives them a tax free step up to market value in the cost of those assets. You may say that there is a catch in all this, which is that the money then ends up in the company, and tax has to be paid after all if you are going to get it out. But it's not always necessarily part of a person's game plan to take the money out of the company. He may be quite happy to leave it in there and reinvest it, in whatever it was going to be reinvested in, in any case, within the company's ownership.

CHAPTER 14
TAX & THE FAMILY

We hear a lot of rhetoric about families, especially "hard working" ones, but the UK tax system is just as chaotic and unplanned in the way it deals with family relationships as in everything else. If you're looking for planning, and a logical situation, this is something you have to provide yourself: the system gives you very little help.

The aim of this chapter, as of the whole book, is to look at specific situations that taxpayers find themselves in, so that they can guard against the capricious unfairness of the system, and arrange things sensibly with a view to the tax impact of those arrangements.

Spreading the Income Tax Burden

I've already mentioned, once or twice, the way Income Tax works in the context of the household. One high earner in a household will pay more tax than two earners, whose total income is the same between them. This is because of the way Income Tax rates increase over a certain threshold (in fact, currently, they double when you go over the £50,000 threshold). So, it makes sense, if you have the ability to do so, to spread that income over as many members of the family, who may not be fully utilised their allowances and lower tax thresholds, as possible.

A straightforward way to do this, if you are talking about income coming from ownership of assets, like property or shares in a company, is to transfer an interest in the asset concerned to one's spouse or partner. This interest need not be equal necessarily, as shown in my following example.

Monty has a full-time job, and earns a salary of £40,000 a year. His wife Mary has no income. In addition to his job, Monty owns a house in London which is let to tenants, realising £30,000 net rental profits each year.

Monty transfers a two thirds interest in the London house to Mary (a CGT-free transfer, as they are married), so she henceforth receives £20,000 property income, and Monty's goes down to £10,000. Hence the couple are both within their basic rate Income Tax thresholds, and Mary's personal allowance is utilised, which it wasn't before the transfer. This simple action has saved the couple over £6,000 a year in Income Tax.

What this example conveniently ignores, though, is the fact that couples are very often not married these days. If Monty and Mary had not been husband and wife, an immediate tax problem would have arisen with the idea: which is that Monty would be treated as realising a chargeable capital gain on his disposal of a two thirds interest in the house. As this is an investment asset not a trading asset, there would be no "Hold Over" Relief available against Capital Gains Tax, and hence tax would become chargeable – no doubt exceeding the amount of Income Tax that was likely to be saved in the near future.

So, what can you do in this sort of situation, where members of a household are not married to each other (the same would apply, for example, to siblings living together, or parents and children) and the income producing asset is not a trading asset, so that Capital Gains Tax applies to any transfer between individuals?

I'll be talking further, in the Chapter on Inheritance Tax planning, about the family investment LLP. This is potentially a very powerful tool of Inheritance Tax planning, which is why it's mentioned in that chapter: however, it's also potentially a very powerful tool of Income Tax planning.

Miss Milton lives with her nephew and the nephew's unmarried partner, Susan. Miss Milton receives her income in a form of a small pension and a large rent roll, from a property portfolio she inherited many years ago from her late father. Miss Milton is a firm adherent of the view that "blood is thicker than water", and it doesn't bother her that her income is supporting the younger people, who are too bone idle, to put it frankly, to get a job. In fact, she makes a thing of the nephew being her heir when she goes – an event, which, to judge from her conversation, she sees as imminent.

What does rankle is not so much the money which the nephew and his partner cost, but the share that HMRC get out of the total family income. With total income at £150,000, Miss Milton's personal allowance is denied completely, and the majority of her income bears tax at 40%.

She realises that the straightforward expedient of giving a share in the property portfolio to the young people would be very expensive in terms of capital gains tax, because the properties are now worth an awful lot more than they were when she inherited them, and CGT is based on the difference between these two values. In addition to this unwillingness to make a free gift to the taxman, a certain native shrewdness tells Miss Milton that it would be a bad idea to make over substantial assets to these two. The first thing that would happen would be that she would come down one day to a "goodbye" letter from them – until they returned a year or so later having spent the money. Blood might be thicker than water, but it doesn't blind Miss Milton to the reality of their characters.

Having taken advice from an accountant, she sees that a family investment LLP is the absolutely ideal answer for her situation. She introduces the property portfolio into this LLP (treated as a partnership for tax purposes), and by careful wording of the LLP agreement this transfer avoids any charge to Capital Gains Tax or Stamp Duty Land Tax.

The income received by the LLP can now be shared out in accordance with the terms of the agreement, and, taking a say equal split of the income, the result is that each individual is taxed on £50,000 each year, rather than the whole £150,000 being taxed on the old lady. In consequence, the tax is dramatically reduced: from about £52,000 a year to about £22,000 – a saving of about £30,000 a year.

What the family investment LLP also does for this situation is enable Miss Milton to retain complete control over the whole situation, including the drawing of money out of the LLP, and the question of whether properties are bought and sold.

Jobs For The Boys

In the case of actively conducted businesses, particularly trading businesses, it's been common practice for a long time to employ members of one's family. It's an obvious way to spread income to reduce the overall tax burden. But this way of spreading your income comes with possible issues. Clearly if you are paying a wage to your teenager daughter, you will want to get tax relief, against your business profits, for the wage paid: HMRC will certainly want their tax and National Insurance on her income (assuming it's over the threshold). But HMRC have got a valid argument where the amount you're paying your relation is more than you would pay an unconnected third party to do the same job. Some or all of the wage might get disallowed, and this is a favourite source of contention between tax inspectors and their "customers".

In principle, a preferable alternative to paying wages, with all the PAYE paraphernalia and possible attacks on allowability that this brings, is to make the individual concerned a partner in the business. There isn't the same pressure on partnerships to demonstrate that amounts received by partners are truly "earned" by them in the work that they do for the business. In essence, this is because a partnership profit share is not treated as an expense, but an appropriation of profit, and therefore the "wholly and exclusively" rule applying for business expenses doesn't apply to partnership profit shares.

Children Under 18

It's reasonably well known that, if you arrange things such that your minor children (children under 18) receive an income, that income is taxable on you as the parents. This is a good example of a situation which is arguably unfair, which taxpayers have tried to make fairer, and have had their efforts stamped on in return. Very arguably, in a "fair" tax system, a household with lots of individuals in it would have higher tax allowances than a household with few: but try telling HMRC that!

Interestingly, the Anti-Settlements on minor rules have been made less effective by circumstances. When the rules were first introduced, a minor was anyone under the age of 21. Also, children very rarely remained in education beyond their minority in those days, with university education being limited to a small percentage of the population, and the rest leaving school in their teens.

Now the situation is very different, with the age of majority having been brought down to 18 and a veritable explosion in higher education. So, it's now very frequent to find children who are still completely dependent on their parents, but who are over 18 and to whom these tax rules therefore don't apply. If you have a child at university, and you are helping them financially, there is absolutely no bar, now, to arranging things such that they receive a share of the income from your investments (using an LLP is one way of doing this) and thereby using the young people's personal allowances and lower rate bands.

Another interesting feature of the rules against diverting income to minors is that it only applies where it is the parents themselves who do this.

Darby and Joan have reached a very comfortable old age, financially speaking, and, when they look back on their own struggles in earlier years, they decide that they want things to be easier for their own child, Gordon, who is married and struggling to pay the bills whilst educating his and his wife's three children privately. The three children are aged 9, 11 and 13. Darby and Joan have an investment property worth £600,000, whose income they don't need, because they are so well provided for in other ways. So, they set up a trust for their child and grandchildren, and transfer the property to this.

The transfer can take place without Capital Gains Tax, because it is a transfer into trust, and such transfers are always eligible for CGT "Hold Over Relief". The rental income from the property comes to £30,000 a year, and the trustees, exercising their discretion, pay one third of this amount for the benefit of each of the children every year (in practice it goes straight to the schools in payment of fees). Though the children are minors, the arrangement has been put in place by their grandparents, not their parents, and so the Anti-Settlements on minors rules don't apply. Each child, having no other income, has a full personal allowance available to offset against their £10,000 trust income, meaning that the effective rate of tax on this income is nil. How much more effective a way of helping Gordon than making gifts to himself!

In the above example, a trust was used, and this makes sense where the overall value being put on trust doesn't go over the inheritance tax threshold of £325,000 per person every seven years. Where it does, an investment LLP might be a better way of bringing about a mechanism under which the children can be awarded shares of the income.

Gifts

Whether or not gifts are for the purpose of spreading income, and thereby saving Income Tax, it's obviously a common thing to happen within the family context, especially now when there is such an imbalance between the generations in terms of how financially comfortable they are at different ages. Unfortunately Capital Gains Tax, as I've already said, can be a major impediment to making such gifts. Any gift of an asset subject to Capital Gains Tax (such as property, shares, or other investments) will trigger a disposal of that asset for CGT, and therefore there can be a nasty surprise in the form of a tax bill unless one of the following "get outs" applies:

- Where the asset is shares in a trading company, or a capital asset used for the purposes of a trade, where "Business Asset" Hold Over Relief is available;
- Where losses are available to offset against the gain;
- Where the asset was acquired, perhaps relatively recently, and has a current value of a similar amount to the tax base cost; or
- Where the gift is to a trust rather than directly to the individuals concerned, and therefore Hold Over Relief is available as in the example of Darby and Joan above.

There are also interesting possibilities using LLP's, where income producing assets are introduced into the LLP and capital is transferred from one member (usually the older generation) to another.

But the following example is of a situation where making a gift is actually not the best thing to do from the tax planning point of view.

George has built up a very successful engineering company, Stephenson Limited. His son Robert gives every appearance of carrying on the family business and family line with distinction, and so George decides to gift the shares to him, and retire himself. The company was formed many years ago with a nominal share capital only, and at a conservative estimate the shares are now worth £10 million.

The "gain" of £10 million on the shares, which is triggered by the gift to Robert, can be "held over" because this is the shares in a trading company. The effect of Hold Over Relief is that Robert takes on the shares at a value equivalent to George's original base cost (which was £100), and no gain is treated as being crystallised.

The years pass, and George dies. Robert himself nears retirement age, and decides to sell the company. It's now worth £15 million.

Selling the business, he makes a gain of £15 million as near as dammit, because the base cost that he's inherited from George, via the Hold Over Relief claim, is only £100.

If George had retained the shares and left them to Robert in his will, there would have been no Inheritance Tax to pay in any event, because Stephenson Limited is a trading company. But the effect for Capital Gains Tax purposes would have been that Robert was treated as receiving the shares at the value on the date of George's death. If we assume this value was £12 million by then, Robert would be paying tax now, on selling the company to a third party, on a gain of only £3 million rather than the £15 million he is actually paying tax on.

It would be hard to find a better example of a situation where you need to think beyond rules of thumb and at the actual likely tax effect of your actions.

Sharing the Tax Burden: The Capital Gains Tax Version

In the same way that you can reduce your overall Income Tax burden by spreading ownership of income producing assets amongst the family, you can do the same with capital gains. Here, there is one difference in that there is no equivalent to the "Settlements on Minors" rules in the context of Capital Gains Tax. So, you can bring into joint ownership of investment assets your children aged 1, 3 and 5 if you want, and their annual exemptions and lower tax bands will still be available against any gain.

One convenient way of doing this, again, is using the good old family investment LLP. Gains can be attributed between family members, using their annual exemptions etc, without necessarily giving those family members any control over the investment assets concerned.

Be very careful when introducing new members, or changing capital profit sharing arrangements, where the assets in the LLP have already accrued a gain, however. This is a good example of a situation where detailed professional advice is almost certainly essential.

Marriage – A Much Maligned Institution

Far be it from me to suggest that tax should form an important part of anyone's decision on whether to marry someone else (or enter a civil partnership with them). There are obviously much more important considerations to take into account than tax. However, if you are wavering, do consider the fact that you are playing with a loaded gun here. The tax system introduces some significant benefits, but also some significant disadvantages, of the married state (I will leave out continual references to civil partnerships, but the rules are the same).

Here is a potted summary of some of the more important pluses and minuses of getting married, from the tax point of view:

- Transfers of assets between spouses are Capital Gains Tax neutral, whereas transfers between unmarried partners give rise to disposals on which tax will fall due if there is a gain and "Hold Over Relief" isn't available;

- On the other hand, a married couple can only have one exempt main residence for Capital Gains Tax purposes. An unmarried couple, on the other hand, can have one main residence each, therefore potentially doubling the available CGT relief;

- Also, the Anti Settlements rules are more likely to apply where one spouse transfers income to another. Take the example of non voting, non capital shares in a company. Fred transfers these, or arranges for them to be issued, to Angelique, who is his "live in" girlfriend. The income she receives from these shares might be a pure example of tax driven structuring of the company's share and dividend arrangements. But the Anti Settlements rules, which in the context of a husband and wife would almost certainly apply to treat the dividends on these "funny shares" as the income of Fred, will not apply if they are not married;

- In favour of marriage, though, is the Inheritance Tax exemption which normally applies (where both parties are UK domiciled or "deemed domiciled") to transfers of assets during life or on death between spouses, and is an immensely valuable relief.

The following example is inspired by a very recent case involving a celebrity.

Albert, aged 90, has total assets of £25 million. He lives with Fifi, aged 30, and, as time goes on, he gets more and more concerned about the way Inheritance Tax is going to take a huge slice out of what he can leave her. So, when he realises the end is imminent, he enters into a "death bed" wedding ceremony, and finally "makes an honest woman" of Fifi. As a result, his £25 million estate, instead of bearing £10 million Inheritance Tax, bears precisely none. This gives Fifi plentiful opportunity to plan for Inheritance Tax if she wishes – either by making gifts to her nearest and dearest when she gets old enough to worry about the tax, or simply by spending the inheritance!

CHAPTER 15
PROVIDING FOR RETIREMENT

If you're a young entrepreneur starting out in business, you might be inclined to skip this chapter. But I can tell you, from experience, that the need to think about retirement creeps up on you suddenly. Particularly when you reach that magic age of 40, and you realise that lots of people retire in their fifties, working life doesn't seem so interminable after all, and the need to think about how you're going to live when you stop working becomes just a little urgent.

What this chapter definitely isn't, though, is a sermon telling you you need to pay money into pensions. I'm very ambivalent about pensions, for the reasons I'll come on to give, and there are other things you can and should be considering to provide you with a permanent passive income.

Revenue Registered Pensions

But let's have a look at pensions first. They are, after all, a multi-billion pound industry, and the vast majority of people who work, and pay tax, are involved in some way in a government approved pension scheme.

On first sight, these seem like an unbeatable deal. Making a contribution to your pension scheme, if it's officially recognised (and the "unapproved" sort are pretty much dead in the water these days) gives you immediate relief against your Income Tax for the year. Once your money is in the scheme, the income and gains arising are completely exempt from tax. The ability to get effective tax relief, in a business context, for the acquisition of capital assets really is quite exciting, and here's an example to illustrate it.

Mr & Mrs Brown run Puce Limited, which makes knitted baby wear. The opportunity arises to buy the building that the business operates from, for £500,000. Fortunately, Mr & Mrs Brown are not the sort of business people who spend every pound of profit as soon as they earn it, and they have managed to accumulate half of this sum, £250,000, in the bank account of Puce Limited. So, with the aid of a pensions adviser and finance broker, they put together the following scheme.

The company contributes its £250,000 into a newly formed pension scheme (SSAS) for Mr & Mrs Brown, and this scheme then goes on to acquire the building with the aid of a loan of the other £250,000 from a bank.

The pension scheme enters into a formal lease with the company, which pays rent of £35,000 per annum for occupying the property. The company makes a further five annual contributions of £50,000 out of its profits, and thereby the pension fund is enabled to pay off the bank loan in that period.

One of the beauties of this arrangement is that the company is getting tax relief for paying rent into Mr & Mrs Brown's own pension scheme: on the other side of the picture, the pension scheme, being tax exempt, isn't paying any income tax on the rent. So, there's a one sided advantage for the taxpayers here, as against HMRC – and all with the sanction and approval of the legislation. By the end of the period, the company will have received full tax relief, against its annual profits, for the effective cost of buying the building. As if this wasn't enough, if the building is ultimately sold (as it is likely to be at the end of the day in order to fund Mr & Mrs Brown's pensions) the capital gain accruing to the pension scheme will be exempt from tax as well.

Add to that the fact that pension schemes put value outside your estate for Inheritance Tax purposes, and what's not to like about pensions?

The Cons

Well, quite a lot actually. For one thing, politicians seem to be so obsessed with the tax breaks which have traditionally been given to pension schemes, that they are continually tinkering with the rules, and almost always in a way that's unfavourable to the pensioners. The latest assault on pension schemes, as I write, is the extra tax imposed by George Osborne on those whose pension income, together with other income, is more than £240,000. But there's been a long process of reducing the amount that can be held within a tax exempt pension scheme for each person.

Because the politicians keep changing things, pensions are actually, in my view, quite a dodgy thing to build your whole future financial plans on. You never know when they're going to kick the stool from under you. I would stress that this is a personal view, and is one of the factors (amongst many) which puts me personally off investing a lot of money in a Revenue approved pension scheme. To a large extent it depends on where your own personal emphasis is in your financial planning.

But you've also got to consider what the fundamental purpose of a pension is, and what alternatives there are for achieving the same purpose. Basically, they're a way of saving up money for your future, and you can, of course, do this without any kind of formal arrangement merely by saving up your funds and investing them in income and gain producing assets.

Looked at in this light, one of the more glaring disadvantages of approved pension arrangements is the loss of control over your wealth. For example, supposing you were looking to raise finance against this accumulated wealth in order to improve your home, or buy a bigger one. This is something you have prevented yourself from doing by tying up the funds in an approved pension scheme: and that's just one example of the disadvantages of loss of control, of course.

Furthermore, funds within the scheme can only be invested in certain specific types of investment. The main exclusion is residential property, which Revenue approved pensions aren't allowed to touch with a barge pole. If you happen to be, like me, a devotee of this form of investment, the inability to use your pension monies to build up a buy-to-let property portfolio is a very serious drawback. You might even say: what's the point of having your capital gains tax free, in a Revenue approved pension scheme, if those gains are likely to be significantly less because you can't invest the money how you wish?

Residential property, incidentally, is a good example of the way our rulers play fast and loose with our financial plans. Gordon Brown was on the point, when he was Chancellor, of extending the investment scope of pension schemes to include residential property, and a lot of people made a lot of expensive preparations for the transition. At the last minute, the plug was pulled on this idea: apparently because somebody hinted that pension schemes might then be used for "tax avoidance".

Hidden Charges

As well as not being able to invest in arguably more lucrative investments, the growth of your pension scheme is obviously impeded by the not insignificant charges which the pensions professionals levy. In order to run a Revenue approved pension scheme, you have to have a lot of financial muscle behind you, in order to pass all of the stringent criteria laid down by our legislators. So, stringent requirements laid down by law, as always, translate themselves into high costs for you, the poor individual, to meet. And these charges aren't always visible.

Another dampener to the enthusiasm for approved pension schemes is the fact that, when you take the pension at the end of the day, you are fully chargeable to Income Tax on it, except for a (normally) 25% tax free lump sum that you're allowed to take. So, to a large extent, the tax relief for putting money into a scheme can be seen as no more than a deferral, with the tax becoming payable when the money comes out.

Even the Inheritance Tax advantages come with a "catch". If you live to be over 75, and then die without having taken all of your pension benefits out, your beneficiaries are chargeable to Income Tax (note: not Inheritance Tax) on the amounts they take.

Alternative Strategies

The above very real drawbacks to approved pension schemes mean that it's obviously sensible to consider alternative strategies.

The simple strategy is simply to draw money out of your business year on year as it makes profits, and put this money aside. Sensible investment (for example in property or quoted shares) will hopefully build up a large and golden nest egg.

The obvious drawback to this simple strategy for providing for retirement is that the funds have borne your top rate of Income Tax. If, say, you're carrying on a business through a limited company, the amount you take out, perhaps by way of dividend, will have borne both Corporation Tax and Income Tax (the latter at the enhanced "dividend" rate). Of course, as I say, if you're going to be taking income in the end it's all going to pay tax eventually: but if you can invest an amount net of a comparatively low tax rate, the compounding effect (and this is an argument for approved pension schemes too, of course) can mean that you have a significantly greater fund at the end of the day.

So, consider the following more complex investment strategy, undertaken by a business run through the medium of a limited company.

Janus runs a successful gym business. The company makes cash profits of something like £200,000 a year over and above Janus's immediate needs, and his plan is to save this up in order to buy a residential property portfolio, to provide a passive rental income for him in retirement.

If he takes the £200,000 out each year as a dividend, in order to invest the money personally, he will have a substantial tax liability at his marginal Income Tax rate for dividends, which is 38.1%. So, out of the £200,000 dividend, £76,200 is creamed off by the government leaving only £123,800 to invest.

Instead of doing this he sets up a parallel investment company, Janus Investments Limited, to which the trading company lends its surplus cash. This company then invests the funds in a growing buy-to-let property portfolio. If Janus is good at investing, and the portfolio doubles in value over ten years, this means that he has properties worth something like £1 million more by the end of that period, simply because of the way he has structured things.

The investment company is, effectively, his pension fund.

Parallel Investment LLP's

But there's a further refinement on the above idea. The reason tax doesn't fall due on the £200,000 loans to the parallel investment company, in our above example, is because they are just loans. They sit around as an ever growing asset on the balance sheet of the trading company, but aren't formalised as income, and therefore aren't chargeable to tax. The reason, incidentally, why a parallel investment company is generally regarded as a better way of doing things than simply investing within the trading company is because of Capital Gains Tax Business Asset Disposal Relief.

I've been through the rules of this relief in another chapter but let's just summarise them here by saying that, if you start building up too much of an investment activity within your trading company, it can lose its trading status and hence your ability to claim BAD Relief on eventual sale or winding up of the trading company.

In my view (which, admittedly, hasn't been tested) a simple inter company balance owed by a parallel investment company is much less likely to be treated as an investment activity which fouls up BAD Relief in the circumstances.

But I think you can go one better than this, even. If your parallel investment company, which receives periodic loans from the trading company, becomes a member of an LLP, the investment company can then introduce capital into the LLP, with the LLP being the vehicle through which the investments are purchased. You could illustrate the structure diagrammatically as follows:

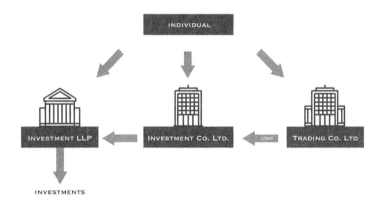

This structure is obviously more complicated than the simple parallel investment company structure. But why is it better?

Basically, it's because of the ability, on the part of the individual member (partner) in the LLP to be allocated with the benefit of all increases in value of the investments in the future: even though the funds to invest in the LLP have ultimately come from the trading company. Unlike the position with the parallel investment company, this means that, on any sale of an investment, there is a single charge to Capital Gains Tax, and the resultant gain is then entirely at the disposal of the individual post tax. By contrast, if the investment company makes a gain, it pays Corporation Tax on that gain (albeit at a lower rate than individual Capital Gains Tax) but then further tax falls due as and when the individual takes the funds out of the company to spend personally. Ultimately, it's likely that capital gains, in an LLP where an individual is entitled to them, will bear a lower rate of tax than gains made by investment companies.

In addition to this, there's actually a fairly interesting, even exciting, facility for the individual to draw down on unrealised increases in value of the investments, which get credited to his capital in the event of revaluation for accounting purposes.

VIMBO

Finally, one very good way of providing for retirement, of course, is to build up your business to a substantial value and then sell it. Apart from making sure that your company continues to qualify for BAD Relief (see above, and Chapter 13), this is probably a point which doesn't need labouring from the pure tax planning point of view. But there is one particular device, invented by a clever firm of tax advisers, which I think is worth bringing forward into the spotlight in a book about tax planning. This is a Vendor Initiated Management Buy Out or VIMBO.

Often the problem with realising the value of your business, which is valuable because of its ongoing ability to make profits, is that there are really no suitable external purchasers. It may be that the business has relied heavily on one or two individuals, and the next tier of management have never had any experience of running a business. Asking them simply to make you an offer for the company is likely to frighten them off. So, consider VIMBO instead.

What VIMBO is is a structured method of the current management buying the current shareholders out, in instalments, out of the anticipated continuing profits of the business. Rather than expecting your managers, who may be completely inexperienced in these matters, to put together a plan for acquisition, you put it together yourself.

In outline, a new holding company is formed which is the vehicle through which the company is to be acquired. This enters into a contract to purchase the target company, and issues paper in exchange for the shares. This paper is then gradually redeemed by way of the payment of dividends up from the trading company to the holding company.

VIMBO has a built in safety mechanism, designed to guard against the possibility, always very real, of the new owners of the business making a hash of it. If the instalment payments aren't continued, the original owners have a lien over the shares which enables them to take them back.

Crucially, from the tax planning point of view, the structure is arranged in such a way, if possible, as to ensure that each redemption of the holding company's paper qualifies for Capital Gains Tax Business Asset Disposal Relief.

This is often a severe disadvantage to the sort of purchase where the acquiring company issues paper, which is gradually redeemed over a period. It has the big advantage, from the point of view of CGT cashflow, that the vendors don't have to pay the tax until they get the money. But normally the countervailing disadvantage is that, having sold their company in exchange for paper, they no longer qualify for BAD Relief on the subsequent disposal of that paper. VIMBO is designed, amongst other things, to get round this problem.

CHAPTER 16
LOSS RELIEF

Nobody in business deliberately sets out to lose money: but sometimes a loss is inevitable, and sometimes a result which is actually profit commercially can be treated as if it were a loss for tax purposes.

So the main thrust of this chapter is far from being an negative one. My aim is to point out ways in which you can use our rather convoluted tax loss relief rules to your advantage; and in a way which, far from being "unfair" in your favour as the taxpayer, acts to redress the real and unjustifiable unfairness of the rules as they stand. And it is not necessarily the case that you can pass over this chapter with an airy "I haven't made a loss and don't anticipate one". Sometimes loss relief planning is a way of sensible structuring, to create a relievable "loss" that otherwise wouldn't have existed. I'll make good this cryptic comment shortly!

The usual rules apply: this doesn't aim to be like a text book setting out the rules in a dry and encyclopaedic manner. Instead, what I look to do is pick out certain situations where planning can make a real difference, and which are not immediately obvious to the lay person.

Types of Losses

Essentially there are two types of loss from the tax planning point of view: the useful sort and the not so useful sort. But the rules actually have a tripartite division:

- Capital losses
- Rental losses; and
- Trading losses

Capital losses are arguably the least useful category out of the three, because they can only be used against capital gains, and capital gains tend to be charged at lower rates of tax, generally, than income. A capital loss is where you sell an asset within the scope of CGT, such as a property, shares in a company, or assets of a business, for less than you paid for it. If you have losses in excess of your capital gains for a tax year (ended 5 April) the excess is carried forward against gains in future years.

The worst case scenario, with capital losses, is where losses are offset against gains that were within a person's annual CGT exemption in any case, as the following example shows.

Stuart has realised capital gains, from selling shares, in the year ended 5 April 2020 amounting to £10,000. In the same year, he also sells an unsuccessful investment which realises a loss of £10,000.

The £10,000 loss is offset automatically against the £10,000 gain, and therefore the loss relief is effectively wasted, because the £10,000 gains would not have borne tax in any event, being covered by Stuart's annual exemption.

Depending on what then happens in the 2020/21 tax year, Stuart might well have been better advised to make the disposal realising the £10,000 loss after 5 April 2020. In the absence of other gains in 2020/21, the £10,000 loss would have been carried forward, and offset against gains made in excess of the annual exemption in future years (in the case of brought forward losses, they are not "wasted" against gains in the same way).

Alternatively, if Stuart had made gains of say £30,000 in the 2020/21 year, the £10,000 losses would have had a real effect in reducing the amount of CGT payable.

Rental Losses

If you have an excess of expenses over income from your property business in a year, this loss is also available to carry forward, against income from the same property business in future years. Unlike trading losses (see below) rental losses can't be offset against income from other sources; and I've also pointed out, in a previous chapter, the restrictive – perhaps over restrictive – attitude of HMRC towards losses from different areas of the same person's property investment activities. But there is one exception to this rule against offset against general income, which is where capital allowances are available.

The big block on claiming capital allowances against rental businesses is that you can't claim these for plant or equipment in a "dwelling house". But if you are letting commercial property, the picture can be very different.

> Mary buys a run down old warehouse which she refurbishes and fits out as a building for serviced offices. An element of her expenditure qualifies as "plant", and she duly claims capital allowances for the first year in which the property is let. Because the first tenants only move in later on in the year, the capital allowances generate an effective tax "loss". This loss is available against Mary's other income in the same tax year.

Trading Losses

Now we come on to the big one, and the type of loss relief which arguably, you could say, has "caused all the trouble". Until recently, a trading loss could be offset against your other income (and indeed capital gains) without limit. What's more, the relief isn't just against the income for the same period in which the loss arose: you can carry it back one year and even, in the first four years of a new trade, carry it back up to three years.

And trading losses aren't just available against a person's other income. They can also be offset against capital gains, and I'll come on to give an example of how that could be really useful in practice.

Trading losses are particularly useful because, not only are they "amphibious" (that is they can cross over the border into relief against capital gains) but also, being a loss available against income, can of course end up getting relief at rates as high as 45%.

Because trading loss relief is so useful, almost inevitably an industry built up, which became particularly vigorous in the early years of this century, consisting in "engineering" trading losses as a way of producing particularly glamorous reductions in the tax liabilities of the wealthy. (Note the approved modern use of the word "wealthy" as a kind of insult.)

In the heyday of the "schemes" you could get away with a scenario such as the following – or at least, the promoters of the schemes said you could.

Hopeless Films exist, according to their glossy manifesto, to put new life into this country's flagging film industry. They do this using tax reliefs provided specifically in the law for this end, and so at first sight, you would have thought, should have the taxman's unqualified approval. Certain types of expenditure on film production were eligible for 100% relief as a loss in the year incurred, which could then be offset against the income. (In this way, film loss relief is the same, effectively, as any other trading loss relief in practical terms.)

Nothing, you might say, could be fairer than that. However the commercial and common sense reality is that most investors are not going to be interested in a dodgy investment like making films. The relief had to be "sexed up" in order to attract real investment, and the following instance shows the sort of way they did this.

Beverley is a banker is who has just received a particularly juicy bonus, of £1 million. Terrified by the size of the tax bill on this, she looks around for ways to shelter it, and her Independent Financial Adviser puts her on to Hopeless Films. Hopeless Films set out their stall. If Beverley invests £200,000 in one of their film schemes, they will "lend" her another £800,000, on a non-recourse basis, to be repaid only in the event that the film is successful. At a time when the top rate of tax was 40%, what this effectively meant was that Beverley got tax relief for a £1 million investment, when she only actually shelled out £200,000. So the effect of claiming the relief was (or should have been) that, in return for her £200,000 cheque, Beverley received a £400,000 tax refund. Everyone wins except the taxman.

By various means it was made clear to Beverley that she would never actually have to repay the £800,000 "loan": except in the unlikely event that the film was a success.

I mustn't give the impression that film schemes were the only way of getting a perversely favourable result for taxpayers by "loss amplification". All kinds of trading activities, including trading in investments, were set up for the purpose of getting juicy tax refunds arising from contrived arrangements of this sort.

The Backlash

Most people would say that spending £200,000 in real terms and getting tax relief for £1 million isn't exactly playing the game, and I'd be inclined to agree with them. But the way HMRC fought back against this kind of arrangement is instructive.

Firstly, they took as many of the schemes as they could to court on technicalities. If you hadn't really incurred a trading loss, this is something that the court would agree with HMRC you shouldn't get tax relief for. In addition to this, we had the inevitable legislation. Under the General Anti Abuse Rule (GAAR) a "loss" which isn't a real commercial loss is barred in any event. If HMRC had stuck to refining the rules, and taking court action, such that people only got relief for true commercial losses, I think nobody could seriously have objected to this.

What they did, though, typically, was go much further and introduce swingeing new restrictions which punished the innocent alongside the guilty. We now have two blanket restrictions on loss relief:

- Where you aren't carrying on the trade actively yourself, your loss relief is limited to £25,000;
- There is an overall limit of £50,000 or 25% of your income for the year, whichever is higher.

The key point is to note is that these limits apply just as much to genuine losses that you have incurred in the real trade as they do to contrived tax avoidance schemes. Can anyone possibly maintain that all the unethical behaviour, in the area of taxation, is confined to the taxpayer's side of the fence? Rather than take the trouble to sift through the false from the true, HMRC prefer to deny much needed loss relief to entrepreneurs who have incurred real, often crushing losses. It's all about HMRC's convenience, not fairness.

How to Maximise your Claimable Losses

But I'll spend the rest of this chapter giving a series of real life situations where people have been able massively to increase the tax benefit of losses and expenditure by sensible planning. These are in no particular order, but give, at the very least, a flavour of the sort of thing you should do, and what you should be thinking about.

I'll start with the common situation of a business person who sets up new line of trade.

Regnezals Limited has built up a thriving and profitable business manufacturing left handed tennis balls, under the capable management of its 100% shareholder Mr Crisp. He decides to diversify the company's business, or rather depart from it completely, by setting up a new manufacturing business, making left handed vacuum cleaners. The market for the new product will, of course, be completely different from the old, except for the fact that all of the customers will presumably be left handed. So he doesn't need to use the current brand name or goodwill of the company.

Clearly setting up a new plant to manufacture a completely different sort of product is going to involve a lot of capital expenditure, including on plant and machinery which is available for 100% capital allowances (see Chapter 4).

The "knee jerk" reaction to this new situation would be to set up the new factory under the aegis of the existing company: But Mr Crisp is smarter than that. He sets it up as a sole trader, with himself as the name on the business. All of the costs of buying plant etc create a substantial upfront tax "loss", which is available for Mr Crisp to offset against his personal income (from the company) for the year of loss and, indeed, because it is a new trade, for the three years previously. HMRC helps out the new venture, therefore, with a large tax refund.

You'll note that the purpose behind giving the "early year's loss" relief, which Mr Crisp makes use of in the above example, is precisely to assist entrepreneurs to get new businesses off the ground, and therefore it's completely in accordance with the spirit of the rules, as well as their letter, that he should have this relief.

Now let's look at some planning based on the ability to offset trading losses against capital gains.

Priti sells one of the properties in her buy to let property portfolio on 30 April 2020, realising a capital gain of £200,000. The proceeds are used by her in setting up a new trading business, which involves buying three commercial vehicles at a total cost of £150,000. The commercial vehicles are all acquired (or firmly contracted for) prior to the end of the tax year 2020/21, and Priti, rather than carrying on this business through a limited company, forms an LLP with her husband Rajeev to carry it on. 100% capital allowances are granted on the commercial vehicles, and the new business shows a start up "loss" of £175,000 (after allowing for other costs not matched by income in the first period). The £175,000 is offsetable against the capital gain on the buy to let property, meaning that Priti pays almost no tax on it. Note, in particular, that there is no restriction in the loss relief, in this situation, to £50,000 or 25% of the income.

A point I have made before, but is worth making again, is that the availability of capital losses isn't always obvious, or is sometimes forgotten about.

Roderick foresees a "planning blight" affecting the value of one of his let properties, and so he's keen to sell. The problem, which is universal for property investors, is that there is a substantial capital gain on the property, which is worth something like four times as much as it cost him: and so the CGT on such a sale would be a substantial charge, preventing him from being able to buy any replacement property of comparable value. CGT is acting, as it so often does, as a tax on inflation – in this case property price inflation – rather than on genuine increases in value.

Very sensibly, Rod goes to see a tax adviser. (This is an unashamed plug for my profession.)

After carefully running through his financial life history, the adviser uncovers one vital event which has occurred in his past.

In 1990, Rod loaned money to a friend of his with a view to that friend setting up a brewery. The brewery needed continual further injections of capital, which Rod felt bound to give rather than lose the whole of the value of his investment, and by the time the company finally folded, a couple of years later, he was owed an irrecoverable £250,000. He had always seen this as being a complete dead loss, because loaning money to your friends doesn't give rise to any trading loss relief for tax purposes.

However, as the tax adviser pointed out, it was still not too late (because the gain arose prior to 1996, when you had to put in a formal claim within time limits) to establish this as an allowable capital loss.

The evidence was therefore gathered together and a claim formally put in, and a £250,000 loss was accepted by HMRC – meaning that Rod could dispose of his property with little or no capital gains tax.

My final example here is less high flown than that, perhaps, but is the sort of situation which is frequently met with in real life.

Felicity is one of those rare beasts: a person who invests both in property and quoted shares, and is generally speaking very successful at both. The one exception, which she always jokes about, is her shareholding in Consolidated Coconuts Inc, a US company which she bought in large quantities when it had just suffered a slump in value, expecting that the share price would bounce back. Actually what it did was slump still further until the company filed for Chapter 11 shortly afterwards. She still holds the shares today, but they are effectively worthless.

Seeing an opportunity on the investment side of her investment business, she looks to raise finance by selling one of her old buy to let properties. The gain on this is £500,000, on which she is looking down the barrel of 28% tax charge, that is £140,000. By entering into a CGT loss claim, on the basis that the Consolidated Coconuts shares have become of "negligible value" – even though she hasn't disposed of them – she establishes a massive CGT loss in the same year which nullifies the tax on the disposal of her buy to let property.

I could multiply examples such as these, derived from real life situations, almost endlessly. But hopefully you get the idea.

CHAPTER 17
PROPERTY:
THE £1 MILLION QUESTION

Let's take a scenario which, although imaginary, is very true to life. A sells a small industrial unit, for £100,000 more than he paid for it. His tax bill on this profit is about £19,000.

Simultaneously B sells an exactly similar industrial unit, also realising a profit of £100,000. His tax bill is £47,000. Both A and B have identical financial affairs apart from this one issue. How can this be?

Well, my purpose here isn't to keep you guessing at the answer to this riddle. The whole point of this chapter is to emphasise, as strongly as I can, the importance of one fundamental question as it affects all those who own property by way of business.

Put briefly, A's liability to tax is so much less than B's because A is paying capital gains tax on his profit, whereas B is paying income tax. And of course this isn't down to personal choice or individual perversity. It reflects the different intentions of the two men at the time they first acquired their properties. When A – the man who is paying CGT – bought his industrial unit it was with a view to holding it long term as a source of rent, and the hope of future capital growth was a secondary consideration in his mind. B, by contrast, bought the property with a view to giving it a lick of paint and some minor refurbishment, and then selling it on to realise a "fast buck". B acquired his property, in fact, as stock of a property trade, whereas A acquired his as a fixed asset investment. Profits of a trade are chargeable to tax as income, whereas profits from selling fixed investment assets are within the CGT net. The two taxes are subject to very different rates, with CGT on commercial property topping out at 20%; whereas the highest rate of income tax (which the unhappy B was subject to in the year in question) is 45%, with an additional 2% effective "tax" in the form of self employed National Insurance contributions.

On the surface, the situation may have looked identical, and A could even have held his property for as short a time as B. The way you tell the difference between trading and investing in property is by looking at a whole range of circumstances, and I'll sum these up in a table. In the left hand column are the features of somebody who is trading in property, and the right those which characterise a property investor. Normally speaking it's true to say that not a single one of these factors is necessarily decisive on its own: but you have to look at the totality of the situation in deciding which side of the line your property activity falls.

Trading	Investing
1. Frequent transactions	1. Infrequent transactions
2. Short period of ownership	2. Long period of ownership
3. Major conversion work undertaken	3. Periodical maintenance carried out
4. Short term finance	4. Long term loans or mortgages
5. Advertisement for sale at an early stage of ownership	5. Letting to long term tenants
6. Business plan prepared showing projected profit on sale	6. Long term cashflow forecasts prepared
7. Other evidence of the intention to sell in the short term	7. Other evidence of intention to retain long term.

This isn't necessarily an exhaustive list, of course, because circumstances differ widely from case to case. What all of the points have in common though, is that they are fundamentally about a person's intention. Yes: it's literally true to say that the huge difference in the tax treatment of property activities, such as the one I have illustrated and several more that I'll come on to describe, are about what is going on in your mind.

That's important point number 1. Important point number 2, if it's not too obvious to make it, is that your intentions with regard to a property are completely within your own control; and there's no reason at all why your intention shouldn't be influenced by the ultimate tax effect.

The Impact on Tax

I've already given an example of the huge difference of the amount of tax you can pay on profits from selling properties, according to whether you are trading or investing. But that's just one of the ways in which the distinction between the two types of activity is crucial. Here are some others:

1. CGT Reliefs

If you're investing, and therefore subject to capital gains tax, you've got the possibility of claiming the various reliefs which exist for CGT purposes but not for income tax purposes. I've said a lot more about capital gains tax reliefs in Chapter 13, but in the context of selling property, possibly the two most important are main residence relief and business asset disposal relief. Main residence relief applies where a property has been your home at any time in your period of ownership, and in the context of property businesses a frequent instance of the importance of this relief is where a person fences off part of his garden and builds a new house on it. The increase in value of that part of the property up until the commencement of the development trade may well be fully relieved from CGT, with only the development profit falling to be taxed.

A frequent, although theoretically at least, a dangerous strategy is for a builder to acquire a beaten up old house, live in it, do it up, sell it, and then move to the next one, and so on. The aim is to run what is effectively a very nice lucrative little trade of refurbishing houses, but to do so completely tax free. I've called this a dangerous strategy because if you do it too often, and with too little gap between each property, HMRC could conclude that you are actually carrying on a trade rather than holding each house in turn as a fixed home. In practical terms, it's a case of everything in due degree: don't overexploit main residence relief, and you will be left in peace, it is to be hoped, to continue to enjoy it.

Another way in which you can massively reduce your tax on the profit from selling a property is if you can bring it within the description of furnished holiday accommodation. Again, I've talked about this in another chapter, and would just sum up here by saying that, if you own a property as a capital asset (rather than as trading stock of a property trade), and you bring about the position that that property qualifies under the criteria as furnished holiday accommodation, then BAD relief should be available (within its limits) on your sale of the property, reducing the tax rate to an almost acceptable 10%.

2. Establishing Trading Losses

My next example is of a situation where it's better to be trading than investing. Not all of us get our property purchase decisions right, and there are times when the property market in different parts of the world undergoes what the papers call a "crash". Where this happens, property which is held as trading stock can (indeed must) be written down in the accounts of the property trade to its net realisable value, and hence an unrealised loss is actually effectively treated as thought it was realised for tax purposes. Here's an example to illustrate how this situation can work hugely to your advantage.

Silvester is a dynamic individual who seems able to hold down two jobs simultaneously. He is a high ranking director in a city financial institution, and therefore is paying income tax on his salary at the top rate of 45%. Simultaneously though, he has a finger in the property pie, with a small business in which he has acquired three properties for development. Properties 1 and 2 have been held for two or three years, while Silvester goes through the hoops of getting planning permission for major redevelopment. Property 3 has only recently been acquired. Unfortunately, for Silvester, Property 3 was acquired just on the brink of a property "crash" and is now worth less than he paid for it. In fact, the relative cost and current market value figures for the three properties are as follows:

	Cost £'000	Market Value £'000
Property 1	250	275
Property 2	300	400
Property 3	250	200

In doing the accounts for this property development activity, the stock needs to be shown at the lower of cost and net realisable value. So in the case of Properties 1 and 2, the stock valuation figure is the one in the left hand column, under "Cost". For Property 3, by contrast, whose net realisable value is less than its cost, the figure that goes into the stock valuation is the £200,000 market value. What this translates into in profit and loss terms is that the activity shows a gross loss for the period of £50,000, which Silvester can claim for relief against his highly taxed employment income.

Note the interesting feature of the above, which is that the taxpayer wins both ways. He gets relief for the loss in value of Property 3, even though this loss hasn't been realised: but he doesn't have to offset against this the unrealised gain on the other two properties. Accounting rules are rules.

3. The "Osborne Tax"

This infamous tax, named after the chancellor who introduced it not long before being kicked out of government, consists in a disallowance of the loan interest paid on buy to let property portfolios. This disallowance, which is for higher rate income tax purposes only, has sent shockwaves through the whole property industry, with the more highly geared landlords out there ending up with a more than 100% rate of tax on their commercial profits.

In another example of trading being treated more favourably by the tax system than investing, though, this Osborne Tax disallowance doesn't apply to trading activities, that is the activities of property developers who hold residential property as trading stock.

4. Property Companies and Capital Gains Tax

If a company is set up to hold a property portfolio as an investment, the company will obviously itself be treated as an investment company rather than a trading company. By contrast, a company set up to trade in property will qualify as a trading company, including for the purposes of capital gains tax holdover relief and business asset disposal relief. So taking the example of someone who sells their property development company to as purchaser who wants to acquire a ready made portfolio in this way (and these purchasers certainly exist), this person will be liable to tax at only 10% to the extent that BAD relief is available to him. Someone selling a property investment company's shares will pay tax at twice the rate, that is 20%.

5. Inheritance Tax

Here is another example of a major difference between the tax treatment of trading and investment, with trading winning hands down this time. A business of holding property as an investment is fully chargeable to inheritance tax, in the event of the person owning it dying or making a gift of it into a trust. A business which consists entirely, or mostly, of trading in property, by contrast, gets 100% business property relief. In some circumstances, this huge difference will more than make up for the direct tax penalty of being treated as trading, which is that profits are liable to income tax not capital gains tax. And I'd like to make a further point in this connection, which is that, the difference between trading and investing being one of intention, there's no reason at all why that intention shouldn't change. Let's take an example of this.

Grandpa was a very successful builder in his time, and, like most successful builders, he has retained a proportion of the properties he has developed as long term investments, finally building up a portfolio of properties worth £10 million, on the rents from which he comfortably lives in his retirement. Grandpa decides that his only child (a daughter) is very well provided for already, and therefore changes his will so that his only grandson, Johnny, becomes the sole beneficiary of his estate.

Fortunately, Johnny isn't one of those people who are spoilt by inherited money, and indeed as far as he can see it looks as though Grandpa is going to survive for a very long time to come. But Johnny is concerned about the potential inheritance tax exposure on Grandpa's estate. If you take into account Grandpa's own home, the property portfolio is facing the prospect of a 40% tax charge, or £4 million inheritance tax based on current values. He immediately sets to thinking of ways in which something can be done about this.

An obvious way, I suppose, would be for Johnny to ask Grandpa to make him gifts of properties, but there are two problems with this. Firstly, all of the properties are worth considerably more than they cost the old man to build some years ago, and therefore a gift to him of the properties would trigger a capital gains tax charge. Secondly, despite Johnny's prognostication of a long life for Grandpa, actually he isn't likely, unfortunately, to survive the necessary seven years to make the gifts completely IHT exempt. So there's a real danger of the dreaded "double whammy": capital gains tax being payable on the gift, and then inheritance being retrospectively charged on the same gift as well, because the donor has failed to survive the necessary seven year period.

But Johnny isn't the sort of person that takes situations lying down. Of the ten properties which make up Grandpa's portfolio, he selects six, and decides to develop them for sale – with Grandpa's approval. Johnny sets up a limited company in his own name which therefore takes on all the burden and expense of developing these properties. A business plan is set out, and bank finance obtained on that basis. The plan shows each of the six properties in turn being converted into much more valuable units, and sold on the open market. Johnny's company, which is taking all of the active role in this process, will charge Grandpa for its services, thereby ensuring that most of the development profits will actually end up in Johnny's company.

What has actually happened here? The answer is that more than half of Grandpa's portfolio has effectively been converted into trading stock of a property development trade – and this is duly reflected as such in the accounts. On Grandpa's demise shortly after, he leaves to Johnny a business which is predominantly, though not wholly, trading in nature, and the whole business is therefore eligible for 100% business property relief – wiping out the feared £4 million inheritance tax bill at a stroke.

The Structural Decision

As a tax adviser one of the questions I'm asked most frequently is: how should I structure my forthcoming planned business property acquisition?

The answer, as so often with questions posed to tax advisers, is "it depends". All circumstances are different, of course, but as a general rule of thumb it makes sense, with the tax system we currently have, for properties which are acquired as part of a development trade to be acquired by a limited company. The simple reason for this is that limited companies pay a flat rate of tax (currently 19%) on both income and gains: so the profits when they are realised, and taxed as income, are taxed at what tends to be a massively lower rate than would be charged if the business was being carried on in non limited company form (for example as sole trader, partnership, or LLP).

On the other hand if the property to be acquired is planned to be held as an investment, the sole ownership/joint ownership/LLP structure is arguably preferable. This is because the ultimate gain on disposal is then going to be charged at personal capital gains tax rates. Although these are actually slightly more than the corporate tax rate, the difference, of course, is that a gain which accrues directly to an individual belongs to that individual absolutely free of any further tax: whereas a gain made in a limited company can often only be extracted and enjoyed personally by the individuals behind the company, at the cost of incurring a further charge to tax. This is normally income tax on the company paying out a dividend.

Very often in practice of course, my clients are engaged in both sorts of property related activity, in relation to the different properties that they own. So a structure along the lines of what I illustrated in the previous chapter, with a trading company (being the company undertaking property developments) and an investment company and LLP existing alongside each other can be very flexible and tax efficient. In this way money can flow freely, subject to only a few constraints, between the trading and investment sides of the same person's overall property business.

Chapter 18
VAT:
Should I Join the Club?

Sometimes, when you're on or near water, you see a large sign which says something like "Danger! submerged obstruction!" This indicates that anyone in the vicinity should look out in case they hurt themselves on a concealed hazard of some kind. In many ways VAT is like that. It's more a trap for the unwary, you might say, than a tax in the classic sense.

What's more, we have to admit that VAT is one of the dullest taxes in existence: even compared with the rest of the motley collection of government levies by which we are assailed. Somewhere the late lamented Miles Kington refers to someone doing something "with all the enthusiasm of a man sitting down to do his VAT return", and you might say that that just about sums up the subject.

VAT isn't a tax, generally speaking, where clever planning can save you huge amounts of money (although there are exceptions to this generalisation), but it's more a case of making sure that you know enough about the way VAT works to avoid it damaging you and your business's finances. Hopefully, this Chapter will help bring about this result.

One thing everybody in business should do, and the majority unfortunately don't do, is take VAT seriously. It tends to be relegated to the lowest level of employee on the finance side, usually the book-keeper that prepares the prime records. Quite hair raising decisions are made by people in this position with regard to how transactions should be treated for VAT purposes, and these aren't always checked by anyone else. In a way, you can see why this is the case: the people at the top of the business, particularly if it's other than a very small scale one, simply haven't the time to look at every financial transaction. If VAT impinges on your business finances at all (and it does, in one way or another, on most) consider having a "mock VAT audit" done. The way this works is that you ask your accountant, or a specialist VAT adviser, to come along and inspect the books in the same way HMRC would do if they were coming on a control visit. Hopefully, such a mock audit is equally likely to find out anything wrong in the way your system deals with VAT: but without the painful result, potentially, of a demand for tax.

Something else which makes this Chapter, in my humble submission, essential reading for anyone in business is the fact that, while there are very few opportunities to save spectacular amounts of VAT by careful planning, there are undoubtedly choices which fall to be made affecting this tax, where the right choice could make a quite noticeable difference to your financial health.

Do I Need To Register For VAT?

Not every business needs to be registered for VAT by any means. If all, or all but a small amount, of the business's income is VAT exempt, there's no need to register. Indeed, if you aren't making any vatable supplies at all as a business you can't register.

So, the first thing to be sure of is whether your business's turnover is VAT exempt or not. This depends on what sort of services or goods you are supplying, and there is a list, in the Appendix to this book, of different types of business supply and whether these are exempt, standard rated (that is taxable at the current 20% rate), subject to tax at the reduced (5%) rate, or zero rated (technically taxable, but at a zero percent rate).

If your supplies fall within the exempt category, then they don't count towards the turnover threshold, which is currently £85,000, above which your business needs to register. For example, most of those whose business consists in holding, improving, selling and/or letting old residential property have no business dealing with the VAT man. Sales and rents of residential property are VAT exempt. (The one exception to this is the sale of newly constructed or converted residential property, which is zero rated.)

Voluntary Registration

But sometimes people in business whose vatable turnover doesn't go over the £85,000 limit will nevertheless register for VAT on a voluntary basis. This may sound crazy, but there are various reasons why it could be to your advantage to do this. To be specific, it may be to your advantage to register because being VAT registered enables you to reclaim the tax on your expenses and on the purchase of capital assets. The flipside of this, of course, is that your turnover will become vatable whereas, without voluntary registration, or the necessity for compulsory registration, it wouldn't have been. But this isn't a disadvantage, and doesn't counterbalance the advantage of being able to claim VAT back on your costs, in two specific situations:

- Where all of your customers or clients are themselves VAT registered businesses, who can reclaim the VAT that you add to your bill, and for whom therefore VAT registration doesn't make you any more expensive, effectively; and
- Where your turnover ("outputs") is zero rated.

Zero rated traders have the best of both worlds, because they don't have to charge any VAT on their turnover, but the VAT on their costs is all reclaimable. Two common examples of businesses of this type are farmers (who produce zero rated food) and house builders, whose product, being new dwellings, is zero rated.

Humphrey is a window cleaner who has most of the shops in the High Street on his books as customers. He works hard, and manages to earn a gross income of somewhere in the £60,000 to £70,000 region. By registering for VAT, he can claim back the VAT not only on his general overhead expenses, but also on the new van which he plans to purchase.

Humphrey's customers aren't at all bothered by receiving his invoice with the addition of VAT. Being retail shops, they're all VAT registered and can reclaim the tax. So, Humphrey is better off to the tune of several thousand pounds by registering voluntarily.

Pre-Registration Input Tax

The situation would be the same, in fact, for Humphrey in the above example, if he had acquired the van at any time in the four years prior to registering. This is because pre-registration input tax can be reclaimed when a business registers, providing, in the case of goods, the asset purchased is still owned at the time of registration, and the purchase was less than four years previously; and in the case of services received, that these services were supplied to the business no more than six months prior to registration. So, timing of registration can be important in some circumstances.

For this reason, amongst others, it's obviously very important to keep VAT invoices for costs you incur: even if you aren't VAT registered at the time you incur them.

Business Splitting

Now we come to an area where decent (although not huge) amounts of tax can be saved by careful structuring of the business. The technique known as "business splitting" makes use of the fact that each individual business has its own separate turnover threshold, for registration, of £85,000 (currently). In theory, if you had a business with a £400,000 turnover, you could split it into five separate businesses where each one only has a £80,000 turnover – none of which, therefore, have to be registered.

It won't surprise you, though, to be told that things aren't quite as simple as that. HMRC have two powers in the way of counteracting business splitting, one basically fair, and the other a real sledgehammer.

The "fair" approach, which HMRC take, more often than not, to counter business splitting, is a single business direction. Where there is a sufficient linkage between the "split" businesses, (as by definition there is going to be in the situation we are talking about) HMRC can direct that the various businesses be treated for VAT purposes as if they were one, with effect from the date of the direction.

And it's the timing of this direction which makes it a comparatively benign piece of legislation in the taxman's favour. Under the single business direction, there's no question of going back over several years and claiming tax for those years on the basis that the various businesses should have been treated as a single business throughout the period. The direction only applies from the current time onwards.

Socrates takes on the lease of the Frog and Wasp, a flourishing town centre pub. He has some fairly ambitious plans for the pub, including refurbishing the previously disused kitchen so as to be able to provide bar snacks. The "wet" sales are provided by Socrates in his capacity as sole trader, and his wife, Xanthippe, runs the dry sales, or food side of the business.

Unless or until Xanthippe's sales go over the £85,000 VAT threshold, the food side of the business doesn't need to be VAT registered, and this is a good thing because customers will only very rarely be in a position of reclaiming VAT charged on the pub food they eat at the Frog and Wasp, and commercial market considerations indicate that you can only charge so much for a sausage sandwich, regardless of whether you're VAT registered or not.

The sledgehammer approach, which the VAT man uses from time to time, consists in arguing that the purported split of businesses wasn't effective. In the case of Socrates and Xanthippe, the approach would be to say that the Frog and Wasp was "really" a single business and presenting it as if it were two is a "sham". That is, Socrates and his wife are only pretending that they have two businesses of wet sales and dry sales. If HMRC manage to make this argument stick, the results can be very painful, with arrears of tax being sought, normally for a four year period, together with penalties and interest. The rules are nothing like so benign as those relating to the single business direction.

A good example of a "sham" splitting of business follows.

> A number of glazing "businesses" are carried on under the same roof. One of these, Woodlands Glass, is a sole tradership run by the main man, Dave Geezer. A second, Three Oaks Glazing, is a partnership between Dave and his wife Suzie. A third business, again, is run as a partnership between Dave and his old mum (who doesn't actually even know the way to the workshop).
>
> This and various other "businesses" are all run from the same premises, and make use of the same advertising in the local paper and on the internet. The advertisements, and the website, certainly don't go to any great pains to differentiate the businesses from each other, and there is a single phone number to call, and a single email address to use to contact Dave (because it's always him that deals with enquiries for all the various businesses).
>
> What's more, Mr Geezer is fairly cavalier about record keeping. We're not saying that any of the cash jobs don't find their way into the business books, but it's undoubtedly true to say that the books are somewhat sketchy, and there's only one set of records for all the purported businesses. Basically what Dave does, at the end of each year, is fairly randomly split the business sales between the various separate purported entities, making sure that the total turnover of each is less than the VAT registration threshold.

The visiting VAT inspector Herbert Peebles makes short work of the situation. He throws the book at Dave with an all out "sham" argument. The tribunal agrees: these different "businesses" are really just one business, dressed up to look as though there were several of them. VAT, with interest and penalties, is due going back four years.

How Not To Do It

The above example gives you a pretty good summary of the various features which you should make sure are absent from the situation if at all possible. If you want to go in for business splitting to avoid registering your business (or some of it) for VAT, you have got to do the job properly. Ideally, you would make sure that:

- The different business names are clearly marketed separately to the outside world;
- If possible, the type of supplies made should be different between the different businesses;
- The businesses should have separate bank accounts, and should have their transactions recorded in completely separate sets of books;
- There should be a clear rationale behind which business a given supply is made through.

And so on.

Partial Exemption

Where VAT accounting can get really fun (code for potentially an absolute nightmare) is where different supplies that the business makes are taxable at different rates, and/or some of those supplies are exempt from VAT. Where some of the supplies are exempt and some taxable, the business is referred to, for obvious reasons, as "partially exempt", and this has an impact on how much VAT you can claim back on your costs and capital asset acquisitions.

Clearly in an overall scheme of a tax where exempt traders can't claim any "input" VAT back, and taxable traders can claim all of their input VAT back, there needs to be some system for deciding how much can be claimed back where some of the supplies are taxable and some exempt. What the standard method of calculating input VAT recovery does, in summary, is allocate first of all those costs which are directly related to the onward taxable supplies, and those which are directly related to the onward exempt supplies. The input VAT that can't be so easily categorised (including on most overheads) is then divided up on the basis of the separate proportions of turnover. In a rough and ready way, this will often give a reasonably "fair" result.

In other cases, though, it doesn't give a fair result, and you can apply to HMRC to use a special method. There can be quite a lot of money involved in framing the special method correctly, and it may be necessary to do some lateral thinking, as illustrated in the following example.

Mature Builders Limited is a longstanding property development business which builds new houses, each time retaining one or two of the completed units as an ongoing investment and selling the rest. This has been going on for a great many years, and the company now has a very large investment property portfolio, made up of residential properties. It still does developments, but the gross turnover from selling newly built dwellings is now about the same as the rents received from the investment portfolio.

The standard method of input tax recovery, in the case of Mature Builders Limited, would basically give a roughly 50:50 split of "residual" (i.e. overhead) input tax. But the company's accountant successfully argues that the floor space in the company's HQ building (which includes workshops and storage rooms for materials) is actually 90% used for the construction of the new dwellings rather than administering the rental property portfolio. A "special method" is therefore agreed with HMRC under which the company reclaims not 50%, but 90% of its residual input tax.

In that example, the business was partially exempt because the rental on existing residential properties is VAT exempt, whereas sales of newly built dwellings are zero rated. But that's clearly just one instance out of very many of partially exempt situations.

In this Chapter I've tried to set out some of the key points that every entrepreneur and investor should be aware of in relation to the basics of VAT, and VAT registration. In my next Chapter I focus in on the one industry, or business area, where very substantial and serious VAT mistakes can be made, which is the area of land and property. I strongly advise those who have any dealings in this industry at all to pay careful attention!

CHAPTER 19
AVOIDING VAT DISASTER ON PROPERTY

This heading may seem a little bit negative, but VAT planning does so often consist of avoiding problems, and capricious liabilities, rather than securing startling reductions to some kind of "normal" liability. In fact, VAT planning is mostly about making sure that you can get back the VAT on your costs ("Input Tax") without forfeiting that right due to careless action or inaction of one sort or another. It seems to me that we're certainly on very solid ethical ground here: the VAT regime isn't designed to catch people out (although sometimes it seems as if it is) – it's simply a question of knowing your way round the system and claiming what is your rightful due.

As I've already commented in the previous chapter, those who own, do up, and sell residential property (other than new residential property) don't generally have to worry about VAT too much, or at all. But there is one important exception to this, which I've highlighted in the section on "conversions" towards the end of this chapter.

The Option to Tax

This has got to be one of the strangest ideas in the whole tax code. It's actually the case that a taxpayer (or perhaps more accurately, an unpaid tax collector) has the choice whether to levy the tax or not. It's probably easiest to explain what the option to tax is by way of a series of examples, starting with a simple one.

George is planning to buy a shop in the High Street, which has a couple of flats above it. Once purchased, he will be letting the shop and the flats (separately) to tenants. At a fairly late stage in the legal process (which so often seems to be the case) it becomes apparent that the seller will be charging VAT on the property (as he has the option to do).

So George, in his turn, opts to tax as well. The effect of this is that the rents on the commercial part of the property have VAT on them; but also, more importantly, he can claim back the VAT charged to him by the outgoing owner. Neither the vendor nor George have any VAT liability on the residential part of the property, because the sale of a "second hand" dwelling, and its renting out, are both VAT exempt even if you have made an option to tax the building.

If George had been intending to occupy the shop himself to carry on a trade which was vatable (for example retailing) he wouldn't have needed to opt to tax the property. This is because the Input VAT on the cost of the commercial part is "attributable" to his onward taxable supplies of retail goods, and since these are taxable in any event, there's no need to put an option to tax on the property as well. This is a point which is often misunderstood, and properties are opted for tax unnecessarily.

Please note that an option to tax applies only to a given property in a given ownership. Where the property changes hands, the option lapses unless the new owner also opts. Furthermore, an option to tax a given property by someone like George in our example doesn't affect any of the other properties that that person may own.

Going Concern Transfers

For reasons which aren't particularly germane to this issue, a transfer of a business as a going concern from one person to another is a supply which is outside the scope of VAT. So VAT can never apply to such a transfer, regardless of whether there are things being supplied (for example trading stock) that would normally have VAT on them when they are "supplied" from one person to another. In the context of commercial property and the option to tax, recognising the application of this can save you a lot of money, as in the example below.

I C Crax & Co is a firm of chartered surveyors. After occupying their office premises at number 30, High Street, for some years, the opportunity arises to buy these offices from the landlord, using money which two of the five partners have managed to save up. The agreed purchase price is £400,000, and Arthur and Bob, the two partners concerned, have fortunately saved up exactly this amount.

At a late stage of the conveyancing process, a hitch occurs. Without much thinking about it, I C Crax & Co has been paying rent for many years to the landlord with the addition of VAT, in latter years at 20%. This hasn't really mattered to them, of course, because surveyors provide a fully taxable service and, as a taxable business, they are able to reclaim all the VAT that has been charged to them on these rents. But what they hadn't thought through, on agreeing the purchase, was the fact that this must mean that the landlord has "opted to tax" the premises.

The effect of this is not just that the VAT is added to the rent, but also that it is added to any sale proceeds on disposal of the property itself, and at the eleventh hour, so to speak, it therefore transpires that I C Crax have got to find £480,000 (that is the agreed purchase price of £400,000 with the addition of 20% VAT) rather than the £400,000 they've actually got the money for.

Moreover, to add insult to injury, the Stamp Duty Land Tax (SDLT) on the purchase is worked out on a figure of £480,000 not £400,000. In other words, there is SDLT on VAT: tax on tax.

Fortunately the firm's accountant, when consulted on this problem, has a neat solution. If Arthur and Bob actually acquire the property, rather than the I C Crax firm as a whole, and then rent the offices to the firm, they will be acquiring as landlords rather than as traders, and by opting to tax the rents they are in exactly the same position, formally speaking, as the landlord they are buying from.

Result: The acquisition is of a going concern, and is therefore outside the scope of VAT. No VAT is even charged (no need to charge it and then reclaim it) and therefore Arthur and Bob only have to come up with £400,000, not £480,000. Plus, the SDLT is less because it's calculated on the £400,000 figure and not on the £480,000. A neat solution.

Timing of the Option

It isn't just the question of whether you opt to tax the property that's important. It's also important when you opt. In the example of the firm of chartered surveyors, the option was entered prior to exchange of contracts, meaning that there was no VAT on the deposit payment or, of course, on the completion payment. If you postpone opting to tax until after completion, then VAT has to be charged and paid over on the whole amount: even if you can then subsequently reclaim it. If you opt after paying your deposit and before completion, there's VAT on the deposit but not on the completion monies. In short, the option to tax only has effect from the time it has been made.

The perhaps surprising result of this is that it's often a good idea to opt to tax a property before you own it. I've even seen it suggested that somebody going off to an auction of commercial properties should opt to tax the whole catalogue before they arrive at the auction house, regardless of whether they are going to buy any of the properties or not!

To sum up planning using the option to tax, whilst in principle it's an option, you are effectively forced to opt in situations where you are incurring a lot of vatable cost on a commercial building – whether on buying it, building it, or improving it. Unless you are occupying the property yourself for the purposes of a vatable trade (in which case, as we've seen, you can reclaim the VAT in any event on basic principles) the only way you will be able to get the VAT back on this possibly substantial expenditure is by opting to charge VAT on the rents you get from letting it. If a property passes through a series of different landlords' ownerships, the effect of one of those landlords opting to tax the property is usually going to be that all subsequent landlords also have to opt to tax. The chain is only broken by somebody buying the property who means to occupy it themselves for the purpose of a vatable trade. Or, just occasionally, a landlord may find himself having to "swallow" a substantial amount of input vat because his intended tenant is running an exempt business. Let's look at a case study explaining this.

Restholme is a large purpose built day nursery. It comes on the market as a result of the unfortunate insolvency of the previous owner, which was precipitated by losing his tenant in the day nursery and there being a long "void period" during which he was having to pay large bank interest and repayments. When this previous owner built the property, he was effectively forced to "opt to tax" the rents he would be receiving, because he couldn't afford to forego claiming back the VAT on the builder's invoice for the work on the property. This was eventually what led the tenants to move out, because being a day nursery business, and therefore exempt from VAT, they weren't able to reclaim the VAT charged to them by the landlord, and this simply made Restholme too expensive for them.

The new owner decides that he will have to "swallow" the irrecoverable VAT on buying the property for £2 million. That's a whacking £400,000 extra Restholme is effectively costing the new owner: but the alternative would be to lose 20% VAT on the £200,000 a year rent he is expecting to receive from a prospective tenant. Better to suffer the £400,000 irrecoverable VAT upfront, he reasons, than effectively lose £40,000 a year for anything up to 25 years.

So, the new owner refrains from opting to tax Restholme, suffers the £400,000, and charges rent without VAT to the incoming tenant.

Developing New Dwellings

If you build a new dwelling, whether a house or a flat, your sale of that new dwelling will be "zero rated". This is very good news indeed, because it means that you can claim back all the Input Tax on the costs you've incurred in building the new dwelling, but don't have to charge any VAT to the person that buys it from you. Rule one.

Rule two is that renting a dwelling to someone, even a brand new dwelling, is not zero rated but exempt from VAT. Rule three: it isn't just the property owner, who develops it as a new dwelling, that can zero rate the result. A building contractor, involved in a project of building new dwellings for someone else, also zero rates his services.

On the face of it being VAT exempt (as residential rents are) seems just as good as being zero rated. But it's not at all the case in many situations, as the following example brings out.

Crown Dwellings Limited is a company set up to build a small development of "executive homes" on land it has purchased and obtained planning permission for. The development takes a couple of years in total, and during that period the bottom drops out of the property market. Nobody is buying or selling any properties because of externally caused economic uncertainty. Crown Dwellings Limited therefore has six empty properties on its hands after they have been completed. In order to fend off the bank manager, they've no real choice but to rent out the properties to tenants on short term leases.

From the VAT point of view, this is an absolute disaster. All of the VAT incurred on building the new houses, which will have been reclaimed by the company in the course of the development on the basis of their plan to sell on "zero rated", becomes potentially recoverable by HMRC. Why? Because, having intended initially to sell the new dwellings (a zero rated, and therefore "taxable" supply) they are now changing so as to use the houses for renting to tenants – an exempt supply. Input Tax attributable to onward exempt supplies is not recoverable and, if it has been reclaimed, can be assessed back by HMRC.

If the letting to tenants is only temporary, it seems that HMRC are content to restrict themselves to clawing back a proportion of the Input Tax. But this whole situation could have been avoided, quite simply, in the following way.

Crown Dwellings Limited is the owner of the development described in the previous example, but instead of developing the properties itself, it forms a 100% subsidiary, Three Crowns Construction Limited, which acts as a kind of inhouse or "captive" building contractor. Because Three Crowns Construction Limited is providing a service of building new dwellings, it can zero rate the bills it sends to its parent company for the construction work, and can reclaim all the VAT on its own costs, including all of the materials.

Because Crown Dwellings has now received only zero rated costs, there simply isn't any VAT for HMRC to claw back in the event that Crown needs to let the properties rather than selling them.

DIY Builders

It was recognised very early on that VAT could cause a serious imbalance between professional builders and those building their own homes. Whereas a professional builder can get all the VAT back on the building materials, a Do It Yourself builder can't, because he isn't in business. In order to address this perceived unfairness, the DIY Builders Scheme was introduced.

If you are building a new dwelling (or converting a non residential building into a dwelling) and this is not by way of business but for private occupation (including occupation by friends and relatives where appropriate) you can go in for the scheme and receive a repayment from HMRC of the VAT you've incurred on the materials.

But do watch out for the very stringent requirements of the scheme. You need to complete a very bureaucratic set of forms, with full proof of the tax incurred, and, importantly, this all has to be done within three months of completion of the work – otherwise HMRC will throw your claim out.

Just a word about what's meant by converting from commercial to residential. What this means is that the property must not have been lived in as a residence before the conversion, although there is a relaxation of this rule where the property used to be lived in as a dwelling, but hasn't been for at least the previous ten years.

Conversions

As I've mentioned, this is one area where even businesses whose subject matter is "old" residential property should be thinking about VAT. A few years ago, presumably to encourage the provision of more housing, the government introduced a reduced rate of VAT, which is 5%, for various types of conversion of property, of which the most common one to find in practice is the not particularly elegantly titled "changed number of dwellings conversion".

This means exactly what it says on the tin. If you have a conversion where there is any number of dwellings in the building beforehand (including nought) and a different number of dwellings after the conversion (again, including nought) the rate of VAT to be charged in the course of this conversion is 5% and not the normal 20%.

Tin Tin Developments Limited has various conversions on hand, which it is using Bob the Builder to carry out on its behalf. In property one, a large house is being converted into four flats. Property two consists in the conversion of an old print works into a flat and a maisonette. Property three is the reverse of property one, effectively, with a building which had previously been in three flats being knocked together to form a single large house. Bob the Builder should be charging 5% VAT on his invoices for all of these developments.

The reason anyone involved in such conversions needs to be aware of the availability of this reduced VAT rate is because it doesn't necessarily always happen automatically. Builders are by no means all thoroughly au fait with these "new" rules, even though they have actually been around for a few years now, and their default tends to be to charge 20% VAT on everything except building brand new dwellings.

Sometimes a considerable amount of persuasion needs to be applied, in order for you, as their customer, to get your rights. In a way, you can see why this is, because the onus is on the builder to charge the right amount of VAT, and if he doesn't charge you enough, he's likely to have to meet the difference out of his own pocket, because of the way the VAT rules work. Whoever loses, it isn't HMRC.

CHAPTER 20
FURNISHED HOLIDAY LETTINGS

Nathaniel sells a cottage by the sea, that he has been letting to holidaymakers for the last 23 months, and realises a capital gain of £100,000. His friend Siegmund sells another cottage near the same town, also realising a gain of £100,000, but he has owned and let the cottage as holiday accommodation for just over 24 months. Nathaniel's "fair share" of tax, that we are told he has a moral obligation to pay, is £28,000. His friend's fair share, which an equal moral obligation rests with him to pay, is £10,000.

The history of the way furnished holiday lettings have been treated for tax over the years is a good example of the way our tax system surges to and fro meaninglessly like the waters of a river swept from side to side by the passing of boats. Politicians come and go, and the ones who exercise any power over taxation can't resist the temptation to be constantly fiddling with the rules: including, or even especially, those rules which involve people's long term financial planning.

The story starts a great many years ago when the government of the day decided to encourage the provision of holiday accommodation in this country by making a rule that it would be treated as a trade for tax purposes. This has a great many advantages, which I'll come on to itemise. What the government that made this law completely forgot, though, was that the UK had signed a treaty with what's now called the European Union, which made giving a tax relief for purely UK based accommodation illegal. Members of the EU can't favour their own countries in this way over other member states, and so it was duly announced that the relief would henceforth be available for such properties situated anywhere in the European Economic Area. At around the same time, the abolition of the relief was announced! Due to a change in government in 2010, though, the incoming Coalition decided to keep the relief. Then much more recently, the government woke up with horror to the realisation that people had been using this tax relief to reduce their tax! So, the rules were changed again and some (but not all) of the benefits of owning furnished holiday accommodation were curtailed.

If you could somehow draw a graph of the "right amount of tax" as it relates to dealings in holiday accommodation, the graph would look like a demented ECG printout.

What I'm going to be doing in this Chapter, though, is not give some kind of academic history lesson on furnished holiday lettings (FHL), but illustrate some of the ways in which this is still a highly tax favoured type of business activity. But it undoubtedly does help, in understanding where we are now, to consider in outline how we got here.

Income Tax

There were two big plus points from the Income Tax point of view in FHL being treated as a trade. Firstly, capital allowances could be claimed on "plant" included within FHL properties (there's more about this in Chapter 4). Secondly, if you made a loss on letting FHL for a year, it was freely available to offset against your other income for the same and some other years. Again the details of how Trading Loss Relief works have been referred to elsewhere, in Chapter 16.

It appears, however, that some people were using this loss relief to "avoid tax". Hence one of the recent changes, clipping the tax wings of FHL, has been to abolish this ability to claim FHL losses against your other income.

But the other relief, comprising the ability to claim capital allowances (think about the advantage of being able to claim 100% write off on a new boiler, for example) is still something which differentiates FHL from ordinary letting, and can obviously be a huge tax advantage.

Inheritance Tax

Frankly, the treatment of FHL for Inheritance Tax isn't something which reflects a huge amount of credit on HMRC. To start with, when the new rules came in establishing that FHL was a trade for the purposes of Income Tax and Capital Gains Tax, IHT wasn't included in the list. So, was FHL to be treated as a trade, giving rise to the immensely valuable Business Property Relief (currently 100%, so Business Property doesn't pay any Inheritance Tax at all), or was it to be treated the same as ordinary letting, that is fully chargeable to the tax?

HMRC (or the Inland Revenue, as they then were) came up with a statement, to be found in their published Manuals for Inspectors, to the effect that FHL would be treated as a trade for IHT purposes, thus bringing it in line with the treatment for the other two taxes. So far, so good – and a lot of people, including people I know, undertook their long term planning for Inheritance Tax on that basis, acquiring holiday property with a view (amongst other things) to securing freedom from Inheritance Tax.

The next stage was that this paragraph quietly, and without any announcement, disappeared from the Revenue manuals. HMRC then started pursuing a lot of cases where Inheritance Tax relief had been claimed in the courts; and it has to be said, they have had some fairly substantial successes in this area.

So, you see the sequence of events: you announce a relief publicly, wait for a lot of people to plan on the basis of that relief, then quietly remove the relief and enter into a long drawn out and expensive (funded by taxpayers on both sides) litigation to attack those who've planned on the basis of your announcement.

Where are we now? Well, unfortunately, it has to be said that any kind of normal FHL is dead in the water as IHT planning now. A series of quite unassailable decisions on appeal has seen to that. You would have to be doing an awful lot more than the bog standard holiday accommodation landlord in order to get IHT relief in the new climate. If, for example, you provided regular meals for your guests, so that the service you were providing was more like that of a hotel, then you might get relief. But simply sweeping and garnishing the property between guests is no longer regarded as enough under the current orthodoxy.

Capital Gains Tax

It's when you come to Capital Gains Tax that the reliefs for FHL are still preserved in their pristine glory. Let's look at the principal ones, and hopefully you'll be able to see what exciting tax advantages you can get by going in for this sort of business.

First of all, Gifts Relief. If you make a gift of an FHL property to someone else, "Hold Over Relief" is available for the gift. This relief is described in more detail in Chapter 13, but put briefly the effect of claiming it is that Capital Gains Tax does not arise on a gift, by reference to the market value of the asset gifted, as it does in the "normal" situation, where the relief is not available.

Elias Roos has been talked by his daughter, Christina, into buying an apartment overlooking the sea in a popular resort, and the initial spur behind this was Inheritance Tax planning, based on the old understanding of the rules that FHL qualified for 100% relief. That was in 2005, and the property has increased in value by a considerable amount since then.

Now it seems as though IHT relief isn't available after all, Christina applies further persuasion to her father, who makes a gift of the property to her. On the basis that he then goes on to live for at least another seven years, this will have solved the Inheritance Tax problem by taking the property out of his estate. Elias' tax return for next year includes a computation of the gain and makes reference to a claim to hold it over, signed by both Elias and Christina. The property, which cost £250,000 in 2005, is now worth £600,000, and the computation shows the "gain" of £350,000 being deducted against Christina's base cost to carry forward: effectively meaning that she has a base cost not of £600,000, but of £250,000. And no tax falls due now at all.

Now let's have a look at Roll Over Relief. If you read Chapter 13, you'll be aware that the ability to "roll over" gains depends on those assets being assets used for the purposes of a trade. So, if you sell an ordinary let property and buy another one, you've still got to pay the full tax on the sale of the old property – meaning that you've got less, in effect, to reinvest in the new one. Where Roll Over Relief is available, the gain is deducted from the base cost of the new asset, and no tax falls due.

Louise owns a large and comfortable house, with a superb scenic view over Wigan Pier. For the first two years of her ownership, it was let to ordinary tenants on six month shorthold leases, but after that the touristic potential of the property was pointed out to Louise, and she decided to let it actively as holiday accommodation, qualifying under the FHL criteria (which I'll set out below).

After two years of this, Louise sells the property, realising a capital gain of £100,000, and reinvests the proceeds in an even more attractive property in Rotherham, which she immediately advertises for letting as FHL.

On a claim to roll over the gain, £50,000 is available for relief, because, during Louise's ownership of the old property, it was a trading property (FHL) for half the time and a non trading property for the other half. So, £50,000 is deducted from the cost of the Rotherham property for the purpose of future CGT disposal calculations, and the other £50,000 becomes taxable now.

Business Asset Disposal Relief

Now I come on to what I suspect is by far the most interesting of all of the reliefs available for FHL. BAD Relief is the relief which reduces the tax on disposal of trading businesses from the full rate (28% or 20%) to 10%. Because FHL is treated as a trade for CGT purposes, it follows that this relief can therefore be claimed.

Hugh has owned a flat in Central London for a great many years. Initially, it was his home, but he moved out in around 1981 and started letting the property to tenants, which were on a long term basis from then until recently. In December 2016, he decided to make the flat available for short term lettings under the FHL rules, duly appointed agents and the short term lettings to holidaymakers began. In January 2020, he then sold the property, realising a capital gain of £500,000. (That's what properties in Central London are like.)

Even though the property has only been FHL for just over two years, BAD Relief, because of the way the rules work, applies to the whole gain. Hence the tax which Hugh pays on his £500,000 gain is only £50,000 – rather than the £140,000 that would have been payable if he had sold it as a straightforward "ordinary" let property.

The point to note here is that the relief only requires the assets sold to have been a "business" for a two year period prior to sale, in order for the relief to be available.

To complete our roster of CGT reliefs which are available for trading businesses, and therefore apply to FHL, I will just briefly mention the "Losses on Loans to Traders" relief. If you've made a loan to an individual or a company for the purpose of the borrower running an FHL business, and the loan becomes irrecoverable, you can claim a capital loss, to be offset against gains in the same tax year or future tax years. This contrasts with ordinary loans, for which there is no CGT relief if they go bad.

How to Qualify

So, having set out my stall (largely consisting of tempting CGT reliefs) how do you qualify for a let property to be treated as FHL? Here are the criteria:

1. The accommodation has to be "available" for letting as holiday accommodation for at least 210 days in the year (that is, for 30 weeks out of the 52). Note that HMRC consider that the property is not so "available" if you are staying in it yourself. There are two possible interpretations of this, but obviously it's wise to go along with HMRC's view if you want a quiet life!

2. The property must be not only available, but actually so let, for at least 105 days (15 weeks).

3. No single letting should exceed 31 days, in calculating whether the above criteria are met.

> David occupies his villa in Portugal from the beginning of November till the end of March each year. For the rest of the period, it is let out on short term lets of less than 31 days each to visitors. Occasionally, the villa is unoccupied, but this is for less than half of the period from 1 April to 31 October. The villa qualifies as FHL because it is in the European Economic Area, and meets the criteria of number of days available and let.

"Get Out of Jail Free" Cards

Because these rules are fairly exacting, and in principle one day's shortfall in either the availability or "actually let" conditions can wipe out your tax advantages at a stroke, there are a couple of elections which provide, appropriately enough, for a relaxation of the rules for furnished holiday accommodation.

One of these is the "averaging election". If you have a number of FHL properties in the same business, and some of these meet the daily criteria and others don't, you can elect to have the days averaged so that, if the average figure is more than the 105 day requirement, your whole business will qualify.

Another potentially useful relaxation of the rules is the "period of grace" election. If (and only if) you had the genuine intention to let the property for the requisite number of days in the year, and you simply failed to meet this, you can elect for the year to count anyway: providing the preceding year counted. There's even the ability to elect again in the second year of failing to make up the requisite number of days, providing you made the election in the first year of failure. So, all things considered, this is a very generous relief. And you can use both the averaging and period of grace elections at the same time if this will get you "past the post".

The Catch?

So, all in all, it's still well worthwhile, in a great many cases, going to some trouble to let your property as furnished holiday accommodation rather than on the normal type of tenancy. What you have to take into account, of course, is the fact that tax isn't everything! It may be that you actually make more of an income from letting your property on normal six month type tenancies, and it is very likely that you'll have less hassle if you do so. So, it's obviously sensible to balance out the contending considerations and count the cost of the tax reliefs which you are achieving. Of course, this may be a pessimistic view, and FHL may turn out both more profitable and more fun. It all depends on your circumstances and your point of view.

CHAPTER 21
PRACTICAL INHERITANCE TAX PLANNING

I'm now going to attempt to compress into one chapter a subject that really deserves a whole book: both because there are a large number of valid Inheritance Tax planning strategies out there, and also because Inheritance Tax (referred to as IHT from now on in this chapter) has the potential to be the biggest tax liability you'll ever be hit with.

The basics first, though. What is IHT?

When you read in old novels about Death Duties, and their disastrous results in leading the old home to be sold up etc, you are reading about a predecessor of IHT called Estate Duty. This no longer exists, but IHT has taken its place. When it was first introduced in 1974, it was actually a considerably more dangerous tax even than it is now, with lifetime gifts being fully chargeable to the tax (albeit at a lower rate than bequests on death). Under Mrs Thatcher in the 1980's this lifetime gift charge was basically removed, and the only exceptions to this are gifts made within the seven years prior to death and gifts into trust – of which more later.

Basically, then, what IHT does is take a 40% chunk out of the estate of somebody on death. Any gifts made within the seven years prior to death are effectively added back to that estate and tax charged on the resultant number. This 40% charge is mitigated in various ways, and in certain circumstances, including:

- Bequests to a surviving spouse or civil partner, or to a charity, are exempt.
- The first £325,000 of the estate is within the so called "Nil Rate Band" (extended in certain limited circumstances by the "Residential Nil Rate Band").
- Certain types of asset are relieved from the tax, such as "business property" (basically an interest in a private trading business) and agricultural property.

Gifts & The Capital Gains Tax "Menace"

Making gifts of your assets to others, typically the younger generation or generations, is clearly therefore the most basic and effective form of IHT planning. Even if you don't survive the full seven years after making a gift, there is a kind of "Taper Relief" if you manage to last at least three years, with the tax on the gift being reduced by 20% for each year after the third. (But do look out for the trap here: a gift wholly within the nil band isn't tapered, because there isn't any tax on this gift in itself.)

Gifts of cash are perfectly straightforward from the tax point of view, but where you are giving away assets that you have held for some time, a problem immediately raises its ugly head: which I have referred to as the Capital Gains Tax (CGT) "menace". The problem is that a gift of an asset is treated for the purposes of CGT, goodness knows on what rational basis, as if it were a sale of the asset for its full market value. So, you can end up paying tax in order to save tax: that is paying CGT in order to save IHT. In the worst case, you can end up paying both: the so-called "Double Whammy":

Adam is an old man who has built up a substantially valuable personal estate over his life. He's hung on to it for many years, ignoring suggestions made to him that he should give it away to save IHT, and has now reached an advanced age with a significant potential IHT exposure.

In a belated attempt to make amends, he transfers one of his investment properties, worth £1 million, to his son Abel. This is a valuable house, let to tenants for many years, which originally cost him as little as £200,000 very many years ago. CGT on the £800,000 gain is duly paid: a £224,000 tax charge. Adam reckons that this is better than paying £400,000 Inheritance Tax on his death (or rather his executors paying it), and he's probably right in thinking this. Unfortunately, however, Adam dies two years after making the gift. The full value of the gift is therefore brought back into his estate, and Inheritance Tax is payable on this value in addition to the CGT that's already been paid: a double whammy.

If you read the Chapter on CGT Reliefs, and were paying attention, you'll know that this harsh picture is softened somewhat by the availability of "Hold Over Relief" in some circumstances. Where the asset given away is an interest in a trading business, or an asset used for the purposes of trade, the gain can be held over, which means effectively deferred, so that no tax is payable until the recipient goes on to sell the asset for hard cash (or give it away in circumstances where Hold Over Relief isn't available). And another situation in which this relief can be claimed is where the gift you are making is into trust – regardless of whether it's a business asset or not. So, if you're giving away an asset like a let property, which doesn't qualify for Business Hold Over Relief, it might seem obvious to make it a gift to a trust for the relevant beneficiary or beneficiaries, rather than an absolute gift. Why didn't Adam, in the example above, give the property to a trust?

The answer, quite simply, is that gifts into trust give rise to an IHT charge: at 20%, to the extent that the transfers into trust made by the same person over a seven year period exceed the nil rate band of currently £325,000. Of course, this would have meant Adam paying £135,000 IHT rather than the £224,000 CGT, but he didn't know he wasn't going to survive the seven year period, and the CGT saving is, at the end of the day, only a deferral and not a permanent reduction.

So, we have a problem here which doesn't always have a solution. One possible get out, at least in theory, would be to borrow against the asset rather than giving it away, and then give away the cash you had borrowed. This has the effect of reducing the value of your estate, and the practical difficulty of paying the loan back, and paying interest on it, can sometimes be avoided if you can find a reasonable "equity release" deal from a specialist provider. Equity release is a kind of loan (typically against your own home) which doesn't have to be paid back during your lifetime, but only out of the proceeds of selling the property after your death. Worth considering where the CGT menace is too overwhelming, but do make sure you shop around to find the best deal (if there is any deal out there which is sufficiently attractive to you).

Investing In Relievable Assets

Moving away from lifetime gifts to a completely different sort of planning, it clearly makes sense, at least from the IHT point of view, to invest your wealth in the sort of assets which qualify for 100% IHT relief, that is in agricultural property or business property. Let's look at agricultural property first.

APR, or Agricultural Property Relief, is unique in that it provides full relief, in some circumstances, for a "pure" investment business. You don't have to be a working farmer to get the relief, and can get it even if you are simply a land owner letting out the property to someone who is. And it isn't just the fields that qualify: farm buildings, and even the farmhouse itself (providing it's of a character suitable to the property) will all get relief.

This sounds good. But what are the drawbacks? Well, first there's the difficulty of finding suitable land to buy. It's got to be the case that the IHT advantages of agricultural land are already factored into the price you pay per acre, and the result is that agricultural property tends to give you a very low rental return in comparison with the capital value. You need to know what you're doing when you're investing in agricultural property.

With business property, the fact that it is basically only investment in private trading enterprises (not blue chip companies) inevitably means that these investments will be riskier than other repositories for your money. Interestingly, investments on AIM (the alternative investment market – a kind of junior stock market) do qualify for IHT relief at 100%; but of course AIM companies are correspondingly riskier than fully quoted ones, as a general rule.

Sometimes, though, there's some interesting lateral thinking available using business property relief (BPR). Consider the following example.

Sarastro is an old man, whose life savings, invested in cash, near cash, and quoted securities, amount to about £5 million. So, without Inheritance Tax planning, his estate is facing an Inheritance Tax exposure not much less than £2 million.

His daughter, Pamina, is running a successful fashion business. An opportunity has come up for Pamina to buy the West End premises from which her fashion business is conducted, at a price of £1.5 million. The banks don't want to know, because Pamina has no cash to put up as a deposit. But her father, Sarastro, comes to the rescue with a £1.5 million injection of capital into her business, in return for which he's made a sleeping partner.

£1.5 million of his estate is now invested in a fully relievable asset, which is his interest in the partnership. After a two year qualifying period, this is set fair to save £600,000 Inheritance Tax on Sarastro's subsequent death.

"Mixing" Investment & Trading Businesses

An interesting feature of Business Property Relief derives from the way it's worded in the legislation. The rule starts off by saying that this 100% relief is available for an interest in a business (including a business carried on by a private company). It then goes on to say, as if as an afterthought, that relief isn't given after all if the "business" consists wholly or mainly of making or holding investments. If you follow this carefully, what this means is that a business which is partly investment, and partly trading, will qualify for the relief providing the proportions are 50:50 trading: investment, or a higher proportion of trading than that.

There can be situations where the awkward question arises: "50% of what?" But the following example illustrates a way in which this feature of BPR can be used to reduce your IHT exposure.

Macdonalds Farms is a partnership between Angus and his son Hamish. The partnership currently owns 400 acres of pastureland, some agricultural buildings, and the house in which Angus lives. In addition to his interest in the partnership, Angus also owns, outside the partnership balance sheet, a collection of cottages which were originally (in the old days of labour intensive farming) cottages for farm workers to live in. They are now let out to television producers and advertising executives.

It's the way of the world, but the cottages are actually worth almost as much as the farm itself, and Angus and his accountant are anticipating a fairly hefty IHT liability on these when Angus passes on. They have ruled out the idea of his giving the cottages to Hamish, because the CGT bill that would arise is just too big to contemplate (irrational though this might be).

Instead of giving the cottages away, though, Angus decides to introduce them into the partnership, so that they are held as partnership property in common with Hamish. As a result, Angus now has a larger interest in a composite business which consists partly of trading activities (the farm) and partly of investment activities (the letting of the cottages). But the whole interest qualifies for 100% BPR, because the composite "business" is at least 50% trading in nature.

Incidentally, you might have thought that Angus would be incurring Capital Gains Tax after all, in putting those cottages into the farm partnership: at least on the half of them which Hamish is treated as acquiring as a partner with his father. However, this CGT can be avoided, if the partnership agreement makes it clear that Angus, the farmer, who is introducing the property, retains 100% of the right to capital profits on those cottages. Under the HMRC Statement of Practice regarding Capital Gains Tax on Partnerships, it is therefore treated as if he had not made any disposal of those cottages on introducing them into the partnership.

Unconventional Wisdom

This is my name for an IHT planning technique which involves just a little thinking outside the box. See what you think of the following case study.

Father has liquid assets of £1 million, all of which are facing a 40% Inheritance Tax charge on his anticipated death, because the available "nil rate band" is used up completely by the value of father's house.

Son is running a successful trading company, in which father isn't involved in any way.

Following a careful process of valuation, it's decided that a 50% interest in the shares of this company is worth £1 million. So son sells this to his father for its market value of £1 million. After the two year qualifying holding period for BPR, father has his converted £1 million worth of his estate from fully taxable assets to fully relievable: thereby saving an anticipated £400,000.

This is unconventional wisdom because the conventional sort is to the effect that the old should pass businesses on to the young, rather than the other way about. And the example of Father and Son is simply one out of countless ways in which this important principle can be put into effect.

Family Investment LLP's

Now I come on to a big subject, which has received almost no attention in publications of any kind up to now. Limited Liability Partnerships (LLP's) are a form of business vehicle most commonly associated with lawyers and accountants; but there's no reason at all why they shouldn't be used to run investment businesses as well. And I think that the advantages of Family Investment LLP's as a vehicle for doing this are almost completely unknown to the general business public and their advisers.

You would most often see these used, I would suggest, in the context of an Investment Property Portfolio. So I'll take a case study involving such an investment portfolio to try and highlight the very significant advantages (not all related directly to tax) that Family Investment LLP's have.

Albert and Bertha are "generation one" in a three generation family. Their children are Charles and Diana, and their grandchildren are Edward and Frances. Albert and Bertha have built up a large and valuable property portfolio, worth about £10 million. They introduce this into the ABCDEF LLP, set up as a vehicle to hold the family's wealth.

They then make not only their children, generation two, members of this LLP (partners), but also their grandchildren (generation three).

They are careful to avoid giving generations two or three an interest in the future capital gains on the existing properties, because doing this would trigger taxable disposals by Albert and Bertha. However, the next generations are given an interest in new properties acquired after the LLP has been set up. The interests are spread over as many people as possible because, if a property is sold (one of the ones acquired after the establishment of the LLP), this means that there will be several annual exemptions, and possibly lower tax bands, to offset against the gains: thus potentially making the tax bill much smaller.

CHAPTER 22
PASSING THE BUSINESS ON

Tax planning – particularly planning for inheritance tax – is often the main driver for wishing to pass the business on to other, younger, people to carry on. But it's by no means the only reason. All of us are getting older at exactly a rate of 60 minutes per hour, and the time inevitably comes when someone younger needs to take over the reins, barring a simple shut down or sale of the business. They do say, also, that things are much harder for younger people starting out in the world of work than they used to be: hence parents and elder relatives may well wish to give the youngsters a helping hand by bringing them in on the family business.

This book is explicitly aimed at both those running trading businesses, and those holding investment portfolios which are sufficiently large or complex to benefit from sensible tax structuring. But in the context of passing the business on, the distinction between a trading activity on the one hand, and an investing activity on the other, is exceptionally important. So, I'll say a few words about this distinction here. (It also can make a considerable tax difference precisely whom you are passing the business on to – as will transpire, I hope, from what follows.)

So, what is this essential difference between trading and investing, which is of such importance for tax purposes? I include within the term "trading" the provision of all kinds of services, as well as a straightforward trade in goods. The provision of services will always be "trading" in nature, for these purposes. It's when you come to exploiting assets for gain that the distinction can sometimes be a little bit harder to draw. The same assets, particularly properties or shares in companies, can be the subject matter of both trading and investing type businesses. In essence, an investing business is where you are holding the asset in order to derive income, rather than with a view to selling the asset at a profit. As I've pointed out in Chapter 17 in respect of property, it's all about intention: and you'll find some useful pointers to making the distinction, in the context of property, in that chapter. But the same essential distinction applies with regard to any other type of assets.

Passing a Family Trading Business Down the Generations

The most straightforward scenario, from the taxation point of view, is where you are running a trading business and are looking to pass the ownership of that business down to close family members. This is where the perverse rule, that I've alluded to before, to the effect that a gift of an asset is treated for capital gains tax purposes as if it were a sale of that asset for market value, comes in. Quite how the "fair share" or "right amount of tax" brigade justify taxing someone as if he had made a capital gain when actually the reverse has happened, because he has lost something valuable, I've no idea. But it's a fact of tax and business planning life that we have to work round as best we can. In the case of a trading business, there is a "relief" against this rather bogus tax charge, in the form of Hold Over Relief, the importance of which is so great that it has come up a number of times in the course of this book. What Hold Over Relief does, to sum up briefly for the present purposes, is enable a donor of a trading type asset to pass that on without CGT, such that the recipient effectively takes over the donor's original base cost for future CGT purposes.

Father gives the shares in a trading company to Son. The shares in the company were originally acquired by him for par value, which is £100. Because the business has been successful, the shares in the company are now worth £100,000, so without Hold Over "Relief" a gain of £99,900 would be treated as accruing to Father on the gift, with Son taking over the shares at a value of £100,000 to offset against any future disposals he makes. But, providing both Father and Son jointly elect to claim Hold Over Relief, the gain doesn't become taxable and Son is treated as effectively inheriting Father's base cost for the shares in the company, which is £100.

In order to qualify as a trading business, in the context of a limited company, one has to be sure that there are no non trading activities within the company, or if there are, that they are not "substantial". (This is the same test that applies for Business Asset Disposal Relief – see Chapter 13.) So, a company which was predominantly trading, but which also owned, say, a buy-to-let property portfolio, could fail to qualify for Hold Over Relief on a gift of its shares. What "substantial" means is actually a mystery, although HMRC have made their own guess, which is that it means "20%". So, a company 20% of whose value comprised its buy-to-let property portfolio (an investment, not trading activity), and which also derived more than 20% of its income, and involved 20% of management time, in the investment business, would not qualify. Where you exceed the 20% criterion on one of these three factors, or two, but not all three, goodness only knows whether your company is a trading one or not. You can try asking HMRC, and see if they will volunteer an opinion, and good luck.

So, here, in fact, is an important planning point. If you can avoid getting anywhere near the point at which your company ceases to be a trading one, you will enable a gift of the shares in the company to be made without incurring tax; just as this is also desirable from the point of view of achieving the 10% "Entrepreneurs' Relief" rate on any sale of the company. Rather than buying investment assets in the company, take the money out of the company (by way of dividend, or, perhaps, loan to another freestanding investment company) rather than involving your trading company in undertaking the investment activities.

The Position of the Recipient

Where you give shares in your trading business to close family members, such as your adult children, It's likely that you will also be able to avoid the recipients being chargeable to tax. There's no general tax on the receipt of gifts in this country (despite proposals by the current Labour opposition to introduce such a tax), and the only danger area is where HMRC could regard the gift as having been made by reason of the recipient's employment. Generally speaking, although each case turns on its own circumstances, HMRC seem to accept that a gift to a close family member derives from love and affection rather than being a taxable "perk" of the recipient's employment.

Coming back for a minute to the motivation of passing the whole of the business, or an interest in the business to younger members of the family, you might, at first glance, consider that Inheritance Tax planning is likely to be a major driver. This would certainly be the case, but for the fact that trading businesses are in any event relieved 100% from Inheritance Tax by "Business Property Relief". So, on the face of it, you're not going to save any Inheritance Tax by making the gift as you won't be paying any tax if you die owning the trading business in any event. You may, though, fear for the continued availability of Business Property Relief given successive governments' tendency to play around with these long term capital planning rules. Or, you may have a problem with excepted assets, as in this very typical example.

Where a company qualifies for Business Property Relief, it's sometimes the case that not all of the value of that company is relieved, because there are "excepted assets" in the business balance sheet. These are assets which, whilst they are a part of the business, are not actually needed for the purpose of carrying on the business. With Teulon Wallpapers Limited, it's a large cash balance, which has built up over many years of profitable trading, and which far exceeds any cash requirements that the business has. If Samuel Sanders, the managing director, put hand on heart, he would say that he would never really need to put his hand on more than £100,000 of the company's £1 million cash deposit, even in highly adverse trading conditions. So, of the total value of the company shares of £2 million, about £900,000 is an "excepted asset", and would not be taken out of the Inheritance Tax picture by Business Property Relief. On the death of the 100% shareholder in Teulon Wallpaper Limited, there would therefore be a taxable value of £900,000.

Fortunately, in this case as in a great many similar cases, the existence of the cash asset is not such as to deny the company trading status. Hence a gift of shares can be made during a person's life which can be made the subject of a Capital Gains Tax Hold Over Relief claim, and if the shareholder does this in the case of Teulon Wallpapers, the taxable exposure can in principle be reduced from £900,000 to nil, by way of a complete gift of all of the company, providing the donor lives the necessary seven years after making the gift.

But the overall moral of this story is: don't assume that a trading company will escape IHT altogether, and therefore doesn't need to be made the subject of lifetime gifts to save Inheritance Tax.

Passing on the Trading Business to Senior Staff

This is where we come to a very important practical difference between businesses which are set up in limited companies on the one hand, or in unincorporated or partnership form on the other. If you pass the shares in a trading company to senior staff who aren't also very close family members, you are likely to be in all kinds of difficulties with the Employment Related Securities (ERS) rules. For unincorporated businesses and LLP's, on the other hand, the question of a tax charge arising on a new partner receiving some kind of "benefit", in the form of an interest in the business, rarely, if ever, comes up in practice.

But the ERS rules are a real headache in the case of limited companies, and are one reason why running a business through a company can be less tax efficient than running a business through the other sort of vehicle. Essentially, what ERS means is that the employee concerned, on receiving shares in the company, will pay Income Tax on the value of the shares he receives, and the employer itself will have an employer's National Insurance liability to meet on the same value. The only way of avoiding this (where the "love and affection" get out isn't in point) is for the employee concerned to pay full market value for the shares he or she receives. You can guess how often that's a practical proposition!

As I've remarked elsewhere, this problem of the ERS rules is actually a major brake on the ability to bring new talent into equity ownership of a limited company business, and hence must have a significant effect on the economic health of this country. But, rather than have rules which encourage the sharing of equity amongst staff, our legislation actually goes out of its way to make it as difficult as possible to inject new blood into an ageing company.

The following example illustrates a tentative idea for getting around this problem.

Hammer Blow Limited is a long established company in the steam riveting business. Aloysius is the 100% shareholder, but is getting on in years, and increasingly relies on his young MD, Ignatius, to drive the business forward. Ignatius is not related to Aloysius in any way, but there's really no one else to whom it would be at all suitable for Aloysius to pass the business on. The problem is, that any gift by Aloysius to Ignatius would be treated as income of Ignatius under the ERS rules.

Instead of transferring shares in the company, then, Aloysius decides to involve Ignatius in a more indirect way. A Limited Liability Partnership (LLP) is formed having the limited company as one member, and Ignatius as the other. The business of the company is "hived down" to the LLP, taking care to ensure that the company is not thereby giving up any of its capital interest in the business, and hence no capital disposal, subject to Corporation Tax, should be treated as being made by the company.

As a partner in the business, Ignatius can now feel that he has a real stake in it, and the LLP agreement enables him, within parameters, to set his own remuneration: moreover, it gives him greater assurance of continuity of involvement than would be the case if he were simply a director in a trading company.

The above example leaves unanswered the important question of what will happen to Aloysius's shares when he dies. It's likely that Ignatius will be the beneficiary of the will, but there is some hope that receiving the shares in Aloysius's will would not be treated as the same situation from the ERS tax point of view as a gift during Aloysius's lifetime.

Management Buy Outs

The only other straightforward way of avoiding a possibly crippling ERS charge, that I can think of, on passing a business down to senior staff, is by way of a management buy out, under which they pay a fair market value for the shares they receive. In a high proportion of cases, I suspect, it's going to be impossible for the management of the business simply to lay its hands on the kind of large capital sum needed to buy out a whole business. I've mentioned VIMBO (which stands for Vendor Initiated Management Buy Out) in a previous chapter, and the essential feature of this, as a way of getting around the problem that the senior staff are unlikely to have much money, is that the shares are effectively bought out gradually, out of the future profits of the business. A holding company is set up which acquires the shares in the company, and whose own shares are owned by the management buy out team. As the target company, hopefully, makes profits year on year it pays these up to the new holding company by way of dividend (not taxable because within a 100% group) and the holding company then uses the money to pay off the former shareholders. In other words, if you are willing to wait for your money, an MBO can actually bring about the position that you achieve full value for the company you have built up, whilst ensuring the continuity of the business.

Investment Businesses

Now I come on to a much more difficult proposition from the tax planning point of view, which is passing on a business which isn't trading in nature. First of all, I'll look at the example of investment businesses which are not run through limited companies. A large property portfolio is a typical example of such a business, where, typically, the older generation wants to pass on an interest in the property portfolio to the younger generation, both for the sake of saving Inheritance Tax and in order to provide the younger generations with a financial "leg up".

The problem, of course, once again, is CGT. Hold Over Relief against Capital Gains Tax is not due where you are making a gift of an investment asset to another individual. Consider the following example, though, where the main aim of the exercise is to provide the younger generation with an income (rather than Inheritance Tax planning being to the fore).

Grandfather and Grandmother have an investment property portfolio worth about £2 million. They also have many other sources of income, including pensions; such that they don't really need most of the rents from the property portfolio in order to provide for their own income needs. On the other hand their children are fairly strapped for cash, with ruinously expensive school fees to meet for their own children.

So, Grandfather and Grandmother form a Family Investment LLP into which they introduce their property portfolio, taking care with the transitional paperwork to ensure that there are no charges to Capital Gains Tax or Stamp Duty Land Tax on doing so. The grandchildren are then brought in as members of the LLP (through the medium of nominee-ships held by their parents, because the grandchildren are still minors).

A share of the rents can then be attributed, within the LLP division of profits, to the grandchildren, thus meeting their school fees (by way of direct payment from the LLP to the school) and at the same time utilising the grandchildren's personal allowances and lower rates of income tax.

In short, the LLP is a neat way, it seems to me, of splitting up the income and capital rights over the income producing assets concerned. In this way the current owners of the investments can avoid triggering a Capital Gains Tax charge (by careful wording of the LLP agreement) and at the same time confer a right to income on their grandchildren.

CGT on Gifts

What the action taken by the grandparents in the above example doesn't do, of course, is tend towards any Inheritance Tax saving. The grandparents still retain the capital rights over the assets they have introduced to the LLP.

And the basic problem of CGT applying to gifts of assets, which can't be solved by "Hold Over Relief" leads to the danger of a "double whammy", under which CGT is paid on the gift, and then Inheritance Tax is paid on the same gift if the donor fails to survive the necessary seven year period.

In some instances, it's possible, no doubt, to mitigate this problem by selecting assets on which no substantial gain has yet arisen, to be the subject matter of a gift, rather than assets, which may have been held for a longer period, on which there is a substantial gain.

Alternatively, in some cases it may be possible deliberately to trigger capital losses (see the chapter on loss relief, and also the chapter on CGT reliefs) in order to offset the tax that would otherwise be payable on the gift of the investment assets.

More ambitiously, I've also alluded, elsewhere, to the fact that, apparently, a transfer of capital in an LLP can be made without triggering Capital Gains Tax. This is an untested route, but does seem to be supported by a logical reading of the rules relating to the Capital Gains Tax treatment of LLP's and partnerships. It is difficult to say how these rules would work at all if a gain arose on simply transferring a capital interest in the LLP, without a corresponding change in the capital profit sharing arrangements at the same time. But don't try this one at home: speak to a specialist adviser.

Investment Companies

Once again, transferring shares in an investment limited company is likely to be motivated by Inheritance Tax planning, and once again the gift would not be eligible for CGT Hold Over Relief. What's more, you could even have an ERS problem (see above) if you gave away shares in an investment company to individuals who were either not close family, or where the gift seems to be linked in some way to that individual's work in the business.

So, this could even result in a triple whammy: Capital Gains Tax on transfer of the shares, Income Tax on the recipient, and Inheritance Tax on the gift if the donor dies within seven years!

Another reason why tax planning involving investment companies easily qualifies as the toughest nut of all to crack is the fact that the underlying assets, in an investment company, are never scaled up, for tax on capital gains purposes, where a person transfers the shares in the company to another person. It's easiest to bring out this potentially major tax planning disadvantage of investment companies in an example.

Mr Small is the 100% owner of an investment company, Small Co Limited, which owns a single property: a garage which the company bought many years ago for £10,000 but is now worth £100,000. Because of the value of its underlying property, the shares in the company are also therefore worth £100,000.

In order to save Inheritance Tax, Mr Small gives the shares in the company to his daughter Susan. The shares themselves originally cost Mr Small £10,000 (the capital he put in so that it could buy the garage at the time), and therefore Mr Small makes a capital gain of £90,000 on the gift which, at 20%, lands him with a CGT charge of £18,000. Susan, a year or two later, then exercises her control over the company by selling the garage, for £120,000. The gain on this sale is £110,000, on which the company has to pay Corporation Tax, and then Susan has to pay further tax on extracting the money from the company. Even though Mr Small has paid Capital Gains Tax on the uplift in value from £10,000 to £100,000, all of this tax effectively falls to be paid again, by the company, because the transfer of the shares to Susan has not resulted in the company having any uplift to its own base cost.

By contrast, if Mr Small had simply bought the garage himself, rather than through a company, the tax on its transfer to Susan would have been the same – but she would have then had a CGT base cost of £100,000, and would not have had to pay tax on the same gain all over again.

The same principle applies to the "tax free uplift on death" for CGT purposes. If an investment asset is held within a company, this asset isn't scaled up to market value on the death of a shareholder – contrasted with the position where the investment asset is held directly by the deceased.

Trusts

The exception to the rule that no Hold Over Relief is available on a gift of investment assets is where that gift is into trust. The only problem with avoiding CGT by gifting into trust, though, as I've commented elsewhere, is that you are limited to giving no more than the nil band (currently £325,000) into trust in any seven year period – because, over that figure, gifts will be charged to Inheritance Tax at the lifetime rate of 20%.

Trusts, of course, can also get around the lack of Hold Over Relief in relation to investment businesses which are not held through limited companies.

Small Gift – Big IHT Effect?

In the sphere of an investment limited company, though, one can sometimes make use of the different rules which apply, in valuing gifts of shares, for Capital Gains Tax on the one hand and Inheritance Tax on the other. Take the following example.

Henry has 51% of Family Investment Co Limited, and the total value of this company, derived from the value of its underlying investments, is £10 million. Hence, as a working hypothesis, Henry is looking at a valuation for his 51% of the company at about £5.1 million. On his death, therefore, an Inheritance Tax charge of over £2 million could arise. The other 49% of the company is owned by an unrelated former business partner.

Henry decides to gift 2% of the company to his son. This, of course, gives rise to a Capital Gains Tax charge, but the CGT is based on a valuation of a 2% holding of the company in isolation. This is subjected to a heavy discount from the pro rata value of £200,000, because, looked at in isolation, it is a fairly (although by no means totally) uninfluential minority. If one assumes that a 50% discount could apply, Henry only therefore has a CGT bill based on a value of £100,000, which may well be acceptable in the context.

The context is that he has moved from having a controlling shareholding in Family Investment Co Limited to a non controlling holding, which is usually subject to a big discount. Therefore, the value in his estate goes down from £5.1 million to (it could be) something like only half of this. A CGT sprat to catch an IHT whale.

Another approach you could take is to give away shares in a family investment company in small tranches, piecemeal. But you do need to watch, here, for the rules which apply the market value of all the shares as a whole where there is a series of linked transactions.

Finally, of course, you could try to crack this toughest of nuts by putting the shares in the investment company themselves into an investment LLP, and then give away capital (subject to all the caveats about this being untested which I have already given).

CHAPTER 23

INTANGIBLE ASSETS

It's not an accident that Intangible Assets are a powerful tax planning tool in the UK system. This situation has actually been brought about deliberately, by specific government action. In 2002, the then Chancellor Gordon Brown changed the tax landscape in an important way, by introducing what is now known as the Intangible Assets Corporation Tax regime. It may surprise some of those reading the examples that follow to see how much tax you can actually save from using this regime to your advantage; and you may even wonder, particularly in the case of some of the examples, whether Mr Brown and his Inland Revenue lackeys actually intended the system to be quite as favourable as it is. But the rules are as they are, and it's probably idle to consider how much Gordon Brown, or anyone else in his administration, actually understood about the tax relief they were introducing, or anticipated how it would be used. They may, for all I know, have fully anticipated everything that I am going to say in this chapter, about how to slash your tax bill using intangible assets.

If you're actually wondering what exactly the scope of the phrase "intangible assets" is, perhaps we need to go back to school for a mini Latin lesson. Intangible means something which can't be touched. Important examples of intangible assets are:

- The goodwill of a business;
- Computer software rights;
- Patents;
- Copyrights;
- "Know how";
- Rights given under a legal contract;
- The "image rights" of celebrities, like sports people and entertainers.

And so on. Some, but not all of these, are the rights given to the owners of these assets under the law of a civilised country. For example, if you have to taken out a patent over some invention, this is valuable because the law will protect you if someone steals your ideas. But probably the most important type of intangible asset of all, which is goodwill, isn't really a legal right at all, or at least not in its essence. Goodwill is the status of the business as a going concern, which is known to clients/customers and the possessor of which can turn it to account to make business profits. It's everything that an unknown business, or a business which hasn't yet opened up its doors, hasn't got.

And our tax system recognises that goodwill, which you might have thought was too nebulous a concept to have any significance for a highly specific discipline like taxation, can be very valuable and important. Just as one example, in the Capital Gains Tax "Roll Over Relief" regime for non incorporated businesses, goodwill is one of the categories of asset that you can roll over gains out of and into.

> Stephen has just sold his fish paste manufacturing business for £500,000, realising a gain, on the goodwill and the factory, totalling £300,000. Three years later he buys an accountancy practice from a retiring accountant for £500,000, and rolls over the gain into the newly acquired business, almost the whole of the £500,000 representing goodwill: that is the benefit of the practice's relationship with its ongoing clients.

The Intangible Assets Regime

But handy though it can be for some people that goodwill is an asset within the Roll Over Relief code, that's not the main thrust of what I'm talking about, and indeed this relief in itself long predated Gordon Brown and his Finance Act 2002 changes. The 2002 regime, to start with, only applies to limited companies: for no good reason that I've ever been able to work out. And the main point about the Corporation Tax Intangible Assets regime is that it is a tax relief, obviously aimed at encouraging companies to acquire such assets. It does this, quite simply, by allowing tax relief for the annual depreciation or, more correctly, "amortisation" of the asset after it has been acquired, which takes the form of an annual deduction in the profit and loss account of the company. This is then allowed for Corporation Tax purposes – unlike depreciation generally, which, for a similarly mysterious reason, is normally disallowed.

When Mr & Mrs Bott sell out their food manufacturing business to Mega Foods plc, what the purchaser is really particularly after is the secret recipe of a particular sauce which is extremely popular with the British public. It's true that the Botts' business has a considerable amount of goodwill too, but the accountants decide that a fair apportionment of the £25 million purchase price is to allocate £15 million to the secret recipe. This therefore becomes an acquired intangible asset for Mega Foods, who decide, on the advice of their auditors, that it is reasonable to write off or "amortise" this £15 million figure over ten years, on a straight line basis.

So, the Mega Foods profit and loss account incorporates an expense, deductible for Corporation Tax purposes under the Intangible Assets regime, of £1.5 million per year.

Related Parties

Now we come to an aspect of the rules which a lot of people find surprising. The relief isn't just given where intangible assets are acquired from unconnected third parties, as in the example of Mega Foods plc and Mr & Mrs Bott. It's also available for transactions between related parties. And it's really this which leads me to describe the Intangible Assets rules as putting a powerful tax planning tool in the hands of UK businesses. In short, you can sell something "to yourself" (actually to your limited company), and subject to the transitional rules your company can claim tax relief for this. This must be an intended feature of the rules, however surprising it may seem at first sight, because it is such an obvious consequence of giving this relief, that people will seek to bring about the availability of the Corporation Tax deduction by transactions between parties under common control. Indeed, the fact that the rules go out of their way to exclude relief, but only in certain specific cases, suggests that the legislators were well aware that relief would be given to the general run of such transactions.

Monica is a software developer with a special gift for devising popular apps for smartphones. She was at the forefront of these, before many people had even heard of smartphones, and has been developing apps since round about the year 2000. In 2019, she decides to transfer her business, which was previously carried on by her as sole trader, to her own limited company, Monica Apps Limited. A specialist valuer values all of the "intellectual property" comprised in the apps at a figure of £1 million.

Of this valuation, about £200,000 represents separate and distinct software programmes which Monica had developed before the start date of the Corporation Tax Intangible Assets regime, which was 1 April 2002. Under the transitional rules, Monica Apps Limited can therefore claim relief on amortising £800,000 of the purchase price (from Monica) of the software rights, but is not allowed to claim relief on £200,000 of it, because this represents assets which existed before 1 April 2002.

What these transitional rules are obviously aimed at stopping, is businesses turning "old assets", for which the rules don't give any relief, into "new assets" by engineering an acquisition after April 2002 of those assets by someone connected. That is, the legislators seem to care a lot about stopping us claiming relief on assets we've owned since before the start date of the new rules; but don't seem at all bothered on our engineering an acquisition by a connected company of assets which were owned for the first time after April 2002. Even these pre 2002 asset rules have been relaxed now, with effect from July 2020, but you need a degree in Chinese to understand the new legislation (as you so often do nowadays), so best leave this to your accountant!

Goodwill

In the case of goodwill, the rules said that you were treated as owning the goodwill before 1 April 2002 if you were running the business in which it arises before that date. This neatly circumvents any arguments about "goodwill" meaning customer relations, and attempts to claim relief on the value of customer relationships which can be demonstrated to have come into existence after 2002.

Goodwill is, in fact, a special case, because the taxman seems to have decided, in 2015, that it was too generous to allow companies to claim relief for this particular type of intangible asset (and closely related assets such as customer relationships). So, the relief for goodwill amortisation was abolished for goodwill acquired after July 2015. Where goodwill was acquired before July 2015, relief is still available; and in fact April 2019 saw the reintroduction of the relief in a modified, and stricter, form: it's as if the government feels it acted hastily four or five years ago, and now regrets having gone as far as totally abolishing the relief in respect of goodwill.

One reason why goodwill has been singled out for this harsh treatment is no doubt because planning of the sort given in the example below, involving Marina, was becoming just a little bit too widespread in HMRC's opinion. But this doesn't really explain why the relief was abolished for everybody, not just for transactions between related parties as in Marina's case.

Marina ran a newsagent shop as a sole trader, and it was so well established in the area that the accountant reckoned it had a goodwill value of
£100,000. "This is what we'll do", he told his client. "We'll form a company, Marina News Limited, and transfer your business to the company,
putting a value on the goodwill of £100,000. The downside is you've got
to pay CGT next January of about £10,000 on the capital gain you're
treated as making when you sell the goodwill to your company. The upside is that you get tax relief for the £100,000 in the company, over a period of years, and you can draw the £100,000 out from the company without any further tax – because the company owes you £100k as a result of
your having sold the goodwill for this amount."

At the time this was done (which was before 2015, of course) the Corporation Tax rate was 20%. So do the sums: Marina as an individual, pays
10% tax (CGT) and pays no more tax at all on £100,000 of profits arising
over the period. The company gets 20% tax relief for exactly the same
figure. This looks like a negative rate of tax of 10%!

The interesting thing is that, whilst this "negative tax" wheeze was stopped for
goodwill, it still remains in its full force for all other types of intangible assets.

Who Owns the Asset?

What this ability to transfer an intangible asset to your own connected company, and claim tax relief there, does is to make the question of who owns a
given asset crucially important. To illustrate how important this is, and to
make the practical moral of all this theorising, I've given two examples below:
one of a situation where the intangible asset concerned just happened to be
owned by the individual outside the company; and another where, let's say,
that result was carefully brought about.

Andreas is a computer programmer who, as so many programmers do, provides his services to his principal client through the medium of a limited company: Deliverable Logistic Solutions Limited. In conjunction with the day job, he's also developing software in his spare time, on his home computer, which is nothing to do with DLS Limited. So, he keeps it quite separate, so as to avoid any implication that his main client can have any ownership rights over that software.

Once this "private" software is at an advanced stage, and is ready to roll out as a product to the world, Andreas brings about a formal transfer of his "private" software to DLS Limited at a fair valuation. The limited company then immediately starts amortising it, and actually creates a loss in the first couple of years as the new business of exploiting the "private" software gets slowly off the ground. Andreas saves tax, thereby, on the income his company is deriving from the day job.

Boffins Productions Limited is a high tech company which spends most of its time on some very advanced research and development work. Professor Egghead is the 100% shareholder and principal director of the company. As part of the same way of thinking which led the politicians to introduce the Intangible Assets regime, there is also an enhanced tax relief for R&D expenditure, where incurred by limited companies, which gives Boffins Limited a highly satisfactory 230% deduction for R&D expenditure: that is, for every £1 spent on qualifying R&D, the company can claim a deduction as if it had spent £2.30.

Professor Egghead is a clever man. He also has a very clever accountant. Acting on the accountant's advice, the professor draws up a formal agreement between himself and Boffins Limited, which specifically states that the intellectual property resulting from the work he does will belong not to Boffins Limited, but to Professor Egghead personally.

If you think about it, this is fair enough. Boffins Limited isn't, actually, paying the professor much for his long hard hours spent in the laboratory, and the hard work and intelligence, genius even you could call it, is something which he is providing all himself. So, the company has no kind of "moral" right over the intellectual property: it's just something which HMRC might claim the company owned in the absence of this specific agreement to the contrary.

There's nothing stopping Egghead transferring ownership of given proportions of this intellectual property to the company once it has been fully developed, though. For example, his technique for getting stones out of a horse's hoof using sophisticated laser technology is something which he decides to transfer to the company so that it can exploit it commercially. He pays Capital Gains Tax on the sale, at a rate of 20% this time, because he isn't transferring a "business" as such to the company, and therefore can't claim Business Asset Disposal Relief. But he still enjoys the benefit of Corporation Tax relief in the company for writing off the intellectual property year by year, and pays nothing when he draws down on the credit balance he has with the limited company as a result of the transfer. All in all, the only tax paid on this element of the company's profits is the Capital Gains Tax that the professor pays on the original transfer to the company. At 20%, this seems like quite a bargain given that Income Tax rates are 40% on a person's total income over £50,000 in a year.

The Conclusion

As so often with tax planning, the moral to be drawn from all of the above is that you can get some surprisingly favourable results by thinking hard about how you arrange your business finances, and in particular who owns the assets of the business. This is particularly pertinent, for reasons which I hope are now obvious, in the case of intangible assets.

CHAPTER 24
LLP's with Company Partners

With the subject of Limited Liability Partnerships (LLP's) which have limited companies as partners, we are moving into what you might call "A Level" tax planning. The idea of being in partnership with a limited company in which you have shares isn't new: but it's very much in the nature of a minority interest as far as accountants, tax advisers, and their clients generally are concerned.

There was a moment, a few years ago, when it looked as though this structure would come into fashion; but that situation changed abruptly, for reasons I'll come on to explain.

First of all, though, let's just revise, briefly, what an LLP precisely is and how it works. LLP's are bodies corporate legally, like limited companies. In the same way as companies have to, they must produce accounts drawn up in accordance with a very specific set of rules, and a version of these accounts needs to be submitted each year to Companies House, where they are then put on public record. Legally, an LLP is a separate person like a limited company, and can therefore enter into contracts, own assets, and carry on a business. And of course, as the name implies, an LLP brings with it limited liability, in a similar way to a company.

The two main ways in which LLP's differ from limited companies are firstly that they tend to have a fluid capital structure, with capital being introduced and withdrawn with little or no formality (contrasted with the formality of issuing and redeeming shares in a company); and from the tax point of view they are treated as if they were partnerships.

For Accountants & Lawyers?

Although LLP's are suitable vehicles for carrying on any kind of business whatsoever, including investment businesses, there's still a view, which is surprisingly widespread, that LLP's are really "for" firms of accountants and lawyers.

This is actually understandable given the history of LLP's. They came about as a result of pressure, principally, in fact, from the accounting profession, on the government to introduce a business vehicle which, whilst it enabled the accountants who are partners to continue to enjoy the various benefits of self-employed taxation (of which more below), also enabled them to enjoy a limitation of their personal liability to creditors of the business, along the same lines as limited companies gave. Essentially, it was a tax driven thing, because the limited company structure had existed for a very long time, and, of recent years, the old bar on accountants providing their services through limited companies had been removed. So, it seems almost certain that it was the tax advantages of a partnership or quasi partnership structure that made the LLP idea seem so attractive. One example of the preferable nature of partnership status to that of director of a limited company is in the National Insurance contribution liability, as we've seen elsewhere. If you are taking earned income out of a limited company, this involves you in both employer's and employee's contributions which can amount, at the highest, to as much as 25.8%; and that's on top of the Income Tax liability. Self-employed individuals, on the other hand, pay a maximum rate of National Insurance, effectively, of 9%.

Limited Company Partners

Where things start getting interesting, from the tax point of view, is when limited companies become partners in the LLP. There is a misconception somewhere out there that this arrangement is in some way dubious: but in fact, the legislation makes very full provision for how such a situation is treated for tax purposes. And it's not just unconnected companies that can go into partnership. The situation I'll be talking about throughout the rest of this chapter is where the limited company is actually owned by one or more of the other partners in the partnership or LLP. Again, our tax legislation envisages this specific situation and there are some fairly prescriptive rules about how to deal with it.

A "typical" example of an LLP with a company partner is as shown in this diagram:

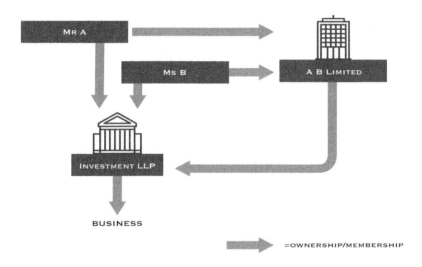

This shows a business carried on in "partnership" (that is, deemed to be so for tax purposes) by two individuals, alongside whom is a limited company in which those two individuals own all the shares. The LLP agreement will make provision for how the profits of both an income and a capital nature are to be shared out amongst the various partners. Shares of income profits allocated to the individuals are chargeable on them to Income Tax, and shares of profit allocated to the limited company member (partner) are chargeable to Corporation Tax. A nice simple concept. A key point to remember, always, when considering this sort of structure is that it differs from a limited company business structure in one very radical respect. The profits of the LLP are taxable on the members, in whatever proportions they are shared out amongst those members, regardless of whether monies are drawn out of the business by the partners or left in. With a company, it makes a lot of difference, because drawing money out from a company will be taxable, in normal circumstances, as a dividend received by the shareholders.

What is the point of this structure? Well, in answering that question it's hard to know where to begin!

The Best of Both Worlds?

Perhaps a good starting point is to recall that the benefit of a partnership or LLP generally is that the partners pay a much lower rate of National Insurance, because they're treated (if they are "genuine" partners – see below) as self-employed, and therefore pay a more favourable rate of National Insurance contributions. But in a partnership without a limited company partner, there is a potential major downside, as compared with a limited company business structure, that the tax rate applied to the profits can be much higher. A limited company cannot pay tax at a higher rate (currently) than 19%. In a partnership, by contrast, where the profits are taxable directly on individual partners, the effective rate can be as high as 45%.

This is where the existence of the limited company brings about the possibility of enjoying "the best of both worlds". Let's have a look at a mini case study.

Mr A and Ms B, as in the diagram above, are in partnership, through an LLP, with their own company (which they own 50% each), A B Limited. The business of the LLP is wholesaling electrical equipment, which involves holding a large stock.

In the accounting year just ended, the LLP has made a profit of £300,000, of which £50,000 has been paid to each of Mr A and Ms B as drawings, with the other £200,000 being represented by an increase in the stock held by the business of that amount.

The LLP agreement allows them to allocate the profits as follows:

	£
Mr A	50,000
Ms B	50,000
A B Limited	200,000
	300,000

So, the £200,000 of profits which are retained in the business as increased stock, whilst they are still liable to tax because they are profits which the business has made, are liable only at the Corporation Tax rate of 19%. Without A B Limited, all of the profits would have been chargeable on the two individuals, at high Income Tax rates.

Benefits in Kind

Now let's look at another major potential advantage of the LLP structure. As well as enabling individuals to receive income which is treated under the more benign self-employed regime for National Insurance contributions, the LLP structure also gives you a better result, normally speaking, in the way of the taxation of the private use of business assets: especially cars.

There's actually an astonishingly large divergence between the way partnerships deal with benefits in kind and the way companies do. If you are a company director or employee driving a car owned by the business, you are taxed as if you had received an "income" equivalent to a given percentage (which can be as high as 35%) of the list price of the car when new. This is regardless of whether the car is worth anything like that now; and it is also regardless of how much business motoring you do in the car. If you do any private driving at all (and HMRC will be very slow indeed to believe that you do none) you are hit by the full whack in terms of the benefit in kind scale charge. So, for example, if you are driving a beaten up old Rover which had a list price of £30,000 when it was new very many years ago, you can end up paying tax on a notional income of over £10,000 in a year even if you only do a few hundred business miles.

Moving from this punitive regime (Gordon Brown, who introduced it, must have had a real thing against car drivers) into the partnership regime is like moving from a stuffy room out into the fresh air. Quite simply, there is no separate Income Tax charge on an individual partner who makes use of the partnership assets for private purposes. Instead, the way the tax system recognises the private use is to apply a disallowance to a proportion of the partnership's costs in owning and running the car, meaning that the partners as a whole pay tax on a marginally higher profit than has been realised for accounting purposes.

So, the LLP with company partner structure enables you to enjoy this usually much more benign regime for benefits in kind in combination with a tax rate on the element of profits allocated to the company which is likely to be much lower.

Fresh Blood

I've bewailed, elsewhere, the harsh regime applying to employees of a business when they are brought into a share in the equity ownership of that business. Where the business is conducted through a limited company, any kind of shareholding bestowed on an employee of the company is a major event in tax terms, with the full value of those shares (except to the extent, if any, that the employee pays anything to acquire them) is treated as income chargeable to tax and Employer's National Insurance contributions.

With a partnership or LLP business structure, there is no claim by HMRC that an individual being brought into equity partnership should pay tax on the value of some kind of "receipt". Traditionally, this makes the promotion to equity of senior employees of professional firms, such as accountants, lawyers, surveyors etc, which have generally been carried out through partnerships, very much easier. The limited company structure, by contrast, almost seems as if it were devised to prevent the business introducing fresh blood into its top tier of management.

Once again, you can combine these advantages of the partnership structure, of being able to introduce individuals into equity without a tax headache, with both limited liability and a corporate tax rate on the business profits: by using an LLP with a company partner.

HMRC Fight Back

Unfortunately, with what might be termed the "shadier" side of the tax advisory profession, it can be a case of "give them an inch and they'll take a mile". Sometime around the year 2010 HMRC seemed to wake up to the idea that LLP's with company partners were being used for tax planning which verged on the aggressive. So, we saw two years' Finance Acts (2013 and 2014) with a lot of legislation aimed at clipping the wings of this "tax avoidance". Amongst the changes were the following:

- A new tax charge was introduced where companies left their profits invested in the LLP but the individuals drew out more than they had ever invested, becoming thereby "overdrawn" on their capital accounts with the LLP;
- LLP members who had no influence over the business, no capital in the business, and no variable profit shares were taken out of the favourable self-employed tax and NI regime, and put back into the bad old employment regime; and
- The amount of profits that could be allocated to the company member in a "mixed" partnership such as that shown in the diagram with A B Limited, was restricted to a fair return on the capital, or separate provision of services, that the company "brought to the party".

The whole thing did look quite alarming at the time, and it seems that the result has been to put a lot of accountants and tax advisers completely off the idea of an LLP with a company partner.

Actually, my view is that the widespread conversion of such LLP's back into limited companies, which was the general response of taxpayers and their advisers, was a massive overreaction: but ignorance engenders fear.

The upside, from the point of view of those of us who still see tremendous benefits in this structure, is that, being very much a minority interest, it's less likely to incur HMRC's ire in the future. The new rules by no means abolish LLP's with company partners: they merely provide a framework within which we now work.

Property LLP's With Company Partners

As I say, LLP's aren't just for accountants and lawyers. They're also not confined by any means to trading businesses, but can be extremely useful and flexible vehicles for carrying on investment businesses. And there are some tax planning features of the structure which are arguably particularly favourable to holding an investment portfolio within an LLP with a company partner.

I think the best way to bring out some of these advantages is to have a look at a hypothetical (or possibly not so hypothetical) case study:

> John and Edwina are by no means property magnates, but they do have enough of a property investment portfolio to make sensible tax planning well worthwhile. They have a limited company, Pickled Egg Limited, which owns £1 million of investment property, free of mortgage. They have recently sold a personally owned property, and also inherited some money, and now have another £1 million to invest. They find a large block of flats which is on the market for £2 million, and arrange bank borrowing of £1 million to make up the shortfall.
>
> The way this is structured is by setting up an LLP with John, Edwina, and Pickled Egg Limited as partners. Picked Egg Limited introduces its £1 million property portfolio into the LLP (taking care to arrange the constitution in such a way that this does not trigger charges to tax on chargeable gains or Stamp Duty Land Tax). In phase two, they arrange the £1 million bank borrowing as a loan to Pickled Egg Limited, and loan their own £1 million cash to the same company. The company therefore has £2 million, which it introduces as capital into the LLP, and it is the LLP which then buys the new property.

The result of these manoeuvres is that the LLP now owns property worth £3 million, and all of the capital in the LLP belongs to the company member, Pickled Egg Limited. Pickled Egg's balance sheet shows a £3 million investment in the LLP on the assets side, and £1 million owed to the bank, £1 million owed to John and Edwina, and £1 million reserves to balance it on the other side. Now the tax planning fun begins.

First of all, it's possible to allocate all of the rental profits from the enlarged portfolio to the limited company, because, even after the new rules introduced in 2014, it has perfectly ample capital (brought to the party) to justify an allocation to it of all the rents. In year one, in fact, these rents are £150,000, and therefore all of this bears tax, subject to the interest deduction, at 19%.

After the company has paid Corporation Tax, the net amount of cash left can be paid out to John and Edwina completely tax free – because the company owes them £1 million on director's loan account. This is useful, because John and Edwina both have their own other sources of income which would make them higher rate Income Tax payers on any share of rents, or on any dividends paid to them by the company.

The "Osborne Tax"

There's more about this elsewhere, but briefly summarising, with residential property portfolios nowadays there is a restriction on the relief you can get for paying loan interest. In fact from the beginning of the 2020/21 year, none of the interest paid on such loans will be allowable for higher rate Income Tax at all. So, you can see the immediate advantage of the LLP/company partner structure in this example. The loan has actually been taken out in the name of the limited company, and the limited company is therefore paying all of the interest out of its share of the rents received from the LLP. (In this example, of course, it's a 100% "share".) The disallowance of interest which I've labelled the "Osborne Tax", after its introducer, doesn't affect John and Edwina's portfolio at all because it doesn't apply to interest paid by limited companies.

There's also an interesting Inheritance Tax planning angle here. I forgot to mention it before, but John and Edwina have put the shares in Pickled Egg Limited into the names of their two children, who are aged 16 and 18. Sharp eyed accountants amongst my readers will have spotted that the arrangements are likely to involve significant profits being allocated to the company from year to year, which the company then uses to pay off its liability in the form of the director's loan. The effect of this is that the company gradually increases in value over the years. By putting the shares in the company into the children's names, this means that this gradual increase in value happens outside John and Edwina's estate, and therefore reduces, effectively, the amount of Inheritance Tax they are ultimately likely to pay by 40% of the amount concerned.

As an alternative to having the shares in the company partner (or a proportion of them) being owned by your children, you could if you chose put those shares into trust for your children and remoter issue. This combines the benefit of effectively reducing your own inheritance taxable estate with the benefit of asset protection that holding valuable assets in trust brings. And if you set up the trust at an early stage, perhaps at the outset when the company may have no value at all, it is easy to put these shares in trust without any danger of an Inheritance Tax "lifetime charge". See the chapter on Inheritance Tax Planning for more details.

Ethical Planning?

Some might be thinking that I have gone off piste rather in this chapter. The book is meant to be, after all, a guide on how to save tax legally and ethically. Subject to the caveat that applies to all tax planning (to the effect that it's all a matter of interpretation) there should be very little doubt that the attractive tax savings that you can potentially get from an LLP with a company partner are perfectly legal. But is this complex and, an unsympathetic person might say, contrived structure straying over the "ethical" line?

In my view, the answer is, not at all. In the HMRC backlash which I talked about, in 2013 and 2014, there was a certain amount of very self-righteous comment on the part of those producing the relevant press releases, to the effect that people were getting the benefit of company tax rates without being treated as employees of a company, by using precisely this structure. However, this is a completely topsy turvy view of what is right and natural. The partnership tax regime is in many ways an older and more straightforward system of charging tax, and the company structure, by contrast, seems to be contrived in such a way as artificially to increase peoples liabilities, particularly to National Insurance contributions. If you are Mr A running A Limited, the tax system actually treats you, quite perversely in my view, as if you were employing yourself. Hence remuneration you take out of A Limited is subject to the much higher rates of employment NI. Similarly with benefits in kind, if you own the shares in a company which owns a car, why should you pay tax as if someone else was providing you with a benefit? Actually it all belongs to you, ultimately, and avoiding a tax charge by using a partnership structure seems to be nothing more, I would say, than redressing the perverse imbalance introduced by the company tax system as it applies.

CHAPTER 25
BUY-TO-LET PROPERTY PORTFOLIOS IN THE WAKE OF THE "OSBORNE TAX"

In my Chapter on Tax Planning for Landlords, I promised to give more detail, of the most up to date kind, on the impact of the so called "Osborne Tax" on buy-to-let landlords. This is the nickname for a truly vicious tax change introduced by the Chancellor of that name not long before he "retired" from politics – and it's also sometimes given the nickname "Clause 24" or "Section 24", after the provisions of the Act that brought it in. What it consists in is the disallowance of interest on loans taken out by residential property landlords, and I'll come on to describe it more fully shortly. It deserves a chapter to itself because it's certainly the hottest tax planning topic there is out there at the moment.

The "Moral" Argument

When George Osborne stood up in the House of Commons to deliver his Budget for that year (the changes first came into effect from 6 April 2017) he brought forward what can only be described as an attempt to justify the new tax imposition morally. What most people suspect is that the changes were actually a "blunt instrument" aimed at cooling the residential property market – particularly in London – but there was no whiff of this in the Budget speech. Instead he claimed that it was somehow "unfair" for landlords to get tax relief for the interest they were paying when individual homeowners didn't. What this fatuous argument ignores is the fact that homeowners have no income against which to claim tax relief for their mortgage interest. Landlords are obviously in a completely different situation.

The effect is that loan interest is disallowed for higher rate income tax purposes, although it is still allowed for basic rate purposes, thus, incidentally, adding yet another layer of complication to our tax system. So, landlords end up paying tax on a higher profit than they have actually made.

Claude is a buy-to-let landlord who bought property at a "boom" time, and borrowed heavily to do so. If the truth were known, he's probably in negative equity at the moment – a distressingly familiar situation. All in all, he makes very little profit from his rental portfolio after expenses and, in particular, interest: so it's a good thing that he has a "day job": as a hospital porter. His summarised rental profit and loss account, in a year fully affected by the Osborne Tax (which is being phased in over four years) looks like this:

	£'000
Rentals after repairs & other expenses	150
Interest paid on loans	130
Therefore net rental profit	20

Because of his other income, the £20,000 profit uses up his whole basic rate allowance for the year. The profit for higher rate purposes is £150,000, rather than the "actual" profit of £20,000, and the higher rate tax on the £130,000 disallowed interest is £26,000. (That is, at 40% minus 20%).

So, Claude ends up paying tax of £26,000 on £20,000 income: an effective tax rate of 130%.

In the above example, Claude is in a terrible situation, financially. He can't even get out of this tax prison by selling the properties: because they're in negative equity. He would end up with residual loans to pay back with no money to pay them back. His only way out of this situation, which he's in thanks to the capricious actions of power mad politicians, is to go bankrupt.

So, how does the ethical position sit here between the government and the taxpayer? Has the buy-to-let landlord got a moral duty to pay tax of over 100%? If he does anything, like restructuring his arrangements, to reduce this intolerable burden, is he a "tax dodger?"

The Limited Company Escape Route

Limited companies aren't affected by the Osborne Tax, and still receive full tax relief for loan interest paid on residential property loans. So, there has understandably been a lot of attention recently given to ways of rearranging landlords' financial affairs to bring about the position that the rental income, and the loan interest expense, are shown within the profit and loss account of a company rather than an individual. I'll come on to the various ways of doing that in a minute, but before considering these options in detail, how about some more straightforward ideas for improving the position of Claude and others like him? I think there are three main such "straightforward" ideas:

1. Accept the hike in your tax bill, and put up rents to your tenants to compensate.
2. If you have any cash available on deposit, use this to pay off as much of the loans as you practically can. There's already a huge difference between the interest you receive on bank deposits and the rate you pay on loans, and the loss of tax relief on the loan interest is tantamount to an effective huge increase in the interest rate.
3. Sell some properties to pay off loans.

"Non Company" Solutions

None of these non company solutions are without problems, of course. My own suspicion is that most of the "do nothing" brigade will have recourse to the first "solution" – of increasing rents. It may or may not be easy for them to put the rents up enough to compensate them for the extra tax cost, but without any doubt at all the result of this government tax "raid" will be inflationary. Ironically, considering the probable purpose of the tax hit was to cool down the property market, general increases in rents could even have the effect of increasing the attractiveness of buy-to-let properties to buyers who don't have to borrow money: thereby leading to further property price increases.

It's hard to know what George Osborne exactly expected landlords to do. In business, if your costs increase, you have to put your prices up. Only a profound ignorance of business could lead anyone to suppose otherwise.

The idea of paying off loans with spare cash is fine – providing you've got the spare cash.

And we've already seen that selling off properties, in order to reduce your loan exposure, isn't necessarily as easy as it sounds. Even if you're not in negative equity, it takes two people to make a sale, and the residential property market is not always easy for sellers, particularly, at the time of writing, due to another gift to us from the government – known as the "Brexit crisis". Remember, too, that selling properties is likely to give rise to liabilities to Capital Gains Tax: a crystallisation of this tax on "property price inflation".

Less Ambitious Limited Company Planning

Companies don't just have the advantage that they aren't affected by the "Osborne Tax" loan interest disallowance. They also have the advantage of paying tax at a flat rate of 19%. So is there a way of making use of this fact short of the more heavy duty, structural solution of transferring the properties themselves to a company or a structure involving a company?

One idea you could consider is to set up a company which charges you, and the property owner(s), a fee for managing the property portfolio. This doesn't have any direct effect on the Osborne Tax as such, because you're still paying interest and still getting that disallowed; but it can have the effect of reducing the overall profits on which you are paying tax, and maybe, in some cases, could have the effect of reducing your income below the level at which you are a higher rate taxpayer, and the Osborne Tax bites.

So, a captive service providing company could be an answer in a minority of cases. Even so, you've got to consider some drawbacks to this idea, as follows:

- Running a company costs money. You have to do accounts according to a set format, and there is inevitably an irreducible minimum of "red tape";
- If you pay the company's income back out to yourself as dividend, of course, it reverses any benefit of reducing your marginal tax rate. So, you either have to find someone else that you don't mind paying the dividends to, or you have to accumulate the money in the company: which isn't going to suit most people;
- If the company charges more than the VAT threshold in a year (£85,000 currently) it has to register for VAT and charge 20% on its fees. This pretty much nullifies any advantage of reducing the Income Tax; and
- There has to be a worry that HMRC will query the allowability of the fees as a genuine expense against the rental profits.

The Two Structural Options

So having considered a number of ideas which have significant problems, and are likely only to work in a minority of cases, let's come on to the structural solutions to the Osborne Tax that are being propounded. These are the limited company option and the LLP option.

The limited company option consists, quite simply, in transferring the property portfolio to a limited company, so that henceforth the company receives the rents and pays the interest. Ergo the company gets full relief and you effectively get full relief.

An immediate problem, before we come on to the tax issues, with transferring a property portfolio to another ownership vehicle like this is the attitude of the mortgage lender. Is the lender going to want to transfer the borrowing, effectively, to another person? If they do, it's likely they'll use this as an opportunity to charge fairly chunky arrangement fees and valuation fees etc, and it is also likely that they will want to put your interest rates up. Some proponents of structural solutions therefore suggest that you should move the portfolio across beneficially only, and not legally. That is, the legal ownership on the land registry stays the same, and the identity of the borrower vis a vis the loan company stays the same: but the legal owner is now holding as nominee or "bare trustee" for the new entity.

There are some heavy weight legal considerations to take into account when doing this sort of thing, and so I would never suggest doing it without the benefit of proper legal advice. But there does seem to be some kind of consensus out there that the legalities can be dealt with effectively along these lines.

The LLP option is a little more complex, and it's probably easiest to explain it in a diagram:

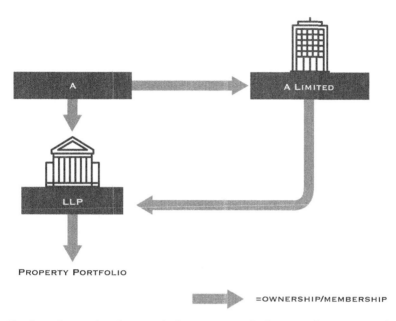

PROPERTY PORTFOLIO

→ =OWNERSHIP/MEMBERSHIP

I've bored you elsewhere with descriptions of what exactly an LLP is, but in summary it's a corporate entity which is taxed as if it were a partnership. In the LLP option the owner of the property portfolio is the LLP, and the limited company is just a partner in the LLP, with no separate activity of its own. Subject to some conditions which I'll come on to, the idea is that the income of the LLP is allocated, in the annual division of profits, to some extent to the company member, with the result that the Osborne Tax doesn't apply to that portion of the income.

So, both structures have in common the fact that the Osborne Tax is avoided by bringing about the position that the income is received by a company rather than by an individual. Both options therefore potentially involve income "rolling up" in a limited company's balance sheet, in the form of ever increasing reserves. How you eventually unwind this situation is a complex matter, but as the purpose of the rest of this chapter is to consider the respective pros and cons of the company option and the LLP option, I won't be going into this aspect in any detail, because it is common to both options. Suffice it to say here that this apparent mere "deferral" of tax can in some circumstances become effectively a permanent saving, depending on your long term "end game".

Which to Choose?

How, then, do you decide between the company option and the LLP option? It's time to run through those pros and cons in detail. (These are then summed up below in a table.)

1. The company option has the advantage of relative simplicity. The company owns the properties, and therefore receives the income and pays the interest, and that's that. The company structure has a long track record and is understood by most people. The LLP option, by contrast, is more complex and has a very short track record. It's a kind of "hybrid" between a company ownership and individual ownership, and involves creative allocation of profits to be as tax efficient as possible. In the case of a company, it's obvious that it's the company which has to pay the tax on the whole profits.

2. On the face of it, there's a Capital Gains Tax problem when you put your property portfolio into a limited company. This is because you're treated as if you'd sold that portfolio into the company for its market value, and any gains inherent in the properties come home to roost. Fortunately there's a relief known as "Incorporation Relief" which applies in all cases where a person transfers a "business" to a limited company, and the company issues shares to that person in exchange. So, is your property portfolio a "business"? The answer is it might be or it might not be. At one extreme you've got a single flat owned by an old lady which she receives rents from. At the other extreme you've got a huge portfolio managed by an office full of full-time workers. Clearly the latter is a business, but is the former? If you're somewhere in the spectrum in between, are you on the business side of the line or not? In short, relief from CGT, when you're transferring to a limited company, depends on the interpretation of an undefined, and very vague word, which is the word "business". Turning to

the LLP structure, CGT can also apply when you transfer into this: but it's much more straightforward and black and white to avoid this. You don't claim Incorporation Relief as with a company, but you make sure you write the LLP agreement in such a way as to avoid there being any deemed disposal of the properties – using the "transparent" nature of the LLP. So, the LLP structure has the advantage, over the company option, that freedom from CGT doesn't involve tricky questions of interpretation.

3. Now we come on to the even trickier question of Stamp Duty Land Tax (SDLT). In the "vanilla" situation, the transfer of one or more properties to a company is chargeable to SDLT as if it were a purchase by that company at market value. The exception to this, which is what proponents of the company option use, is where the transfer is going from a partnership to a company connected with that partnership. For SDLT, then, we have a different question: "is the transferor a "partnership"?" This is generally a more difficult question of interpretation than the "business" issue that applies for CGT. If husband and wife, say, own three or four properties jointly, are they in "partnership"? Personally, I would say no. The word partnership generally connotes some kind of trade. Those promoting the company option often, ironically, have recourse to LLP's to get around this issue. They recommend to clients that the portfolio should go into an LLP first, and remain there for say two or three years. It's then transferred from the LLP to a company, and because an LLP is automatically treated as a partnership in all circumstances, you've ticked the SDLT relief box.

But what about the old anti-tax avoidance case, which holds that, where you have a series of transactions which are preordained, and it has steps inserted which have no purpose other than to avoid tax, the government can ignore the inserted steps? Surely the two or three years whilst the portfolio is owned by an LLP is an inserted step, which should get ignored? The result for SDLT then would be the same as a straightforward transfer straight to a company: i.e. SDLT on the market value. The proponents of limited companies say they get around this by avoiding the series of transactions being "preordained". At the time you put the properties into the LLP, you're not sure whether you're actually going to go on to the next stage, which is a transfer to a company. But I'm not convinced. I think in hindsight it's going to look very much, to the taxman, as though you always meant to do it.

4. Income drawdown, after you've transferred the property portfolio, is much easier in an LLP. To the extent that you've put value into the LLP, you can draw this value out again tax free, because it's just a return of your capital. With the company option, the normal situation, under Incorporation Relief, is that you haven't got any amount owed to you by the company that you can then draw on tax free – because the company has issued you shares in exchange for your properties. It's true that you can then redeem these shares, but the cost of doing this is that the capital gain you deferred under Incorporation Relief becomes chargeable. Some proponents of the company option have come up with a "clever" way around this, which involves carving out a liability in your favour prior to the transfer. But you have to take this with the caveat that it's a scheme designed simply to flout the clear intentions of Incorporation Relief, and this, to me, is always a danger signal.

5. Under the LLP route, if the property portfolio increases in value as the years go by, this results in more credit available for you, as the LLP member, to draw down. Revaluation surpluses are credited to the members' capital accounts, and, unlike the situation with limited companies, revaluation surpluses can be drawn down in LLP's. Turning to the company option, this ability to draw down future increases in value doesn't, as far as I know, exist. You are stuck with the value of the properties on the date they went into the company (if you can even draw down on this) and once that's gone, you can only take mon-

ey out of the company in the form of taxable income. A major plus for the LLP option and minus for the company option, in my view.

6. Within an LLP, because it is "transparent" there's only one charge to capital gains taxation when a property is sold. Under the normal form of the LLP structure, all capital gains arise to the individual. So, given that we're talking about residential property here, that's a 28% tax charge, levied directly on the LLP member, whenever a property is sold. In the company structure, it's the company which pays tax on the gain, of course: and that's at the lesser rate of 19%. So is the capital gains treatment an advantage for the company option?

My answer to this would be "not really". The problem with gains accruing to companies, of course, is that if you want to draw that money out personally, you're likely to have to pay tax, either as income or, if it is on final winding up of the company, as a capital gain. So, you have the notorious "double charge to tax" when a company sells an appreciating asset like a property. Of course, if you are looking to keep the money within the company for ever, this isn't a problem, and indeed the company gives you a better outcome. But you might ask the question, what is the use of money, if you have to keep it in the company for ever?

In summary, this is a much more ambivalent issue, and really depends on what your long term plans are, both for holding the property, reinvesting the proceeds in more property, and for winding up or retaining the structure long term.

7. There's no CGT free uplift on death for properties owned in a limited company. With an LLP there is, because, again, of its "transparent" nature. Let's give an example to show what a huge difference this can make:

Mrs X inherits a property on her husband's death, at a time when it has a value of £200,000. It originally cost the husband £50,000 many years ago. She sells the property shortly afterwards for the same value, and pays no Capital Gains Tax, because £200,000 is the sum she's deemed to have acquired it for. Mrs Y's situation is identical except for the fact that what she has inherited, strictly speaking, is the shares in a property company which acquired the property for £50,000 many years ago, and which is now worth £200,000 because the property that the company owns is worth that. Mrs Y arranges for the company to sell the property for £200,000 shortly afterwards. Commercially this is an identical situation to that Mrs X found herself in. But the difference is that the company has to pay Corporation Tax on a chargeable gain of £150,000, because its base cost is the same as it always was. The company hasn't died. To add insult to injury, Mrs Y then has a tax bill of about £50,000 personally on drawing the gain out of the company.

This lack of CGT uplift on death, in the context of a property investment company, is a very major problem with property investment companies in my view, and I've touched on this problem elsewhere, in the chapter on property. Where, as often happens, a property company passes down through many generations of a family, some quite bizarre results can come about. I've known a company which has luxurious flats in High Street, Kensington which have a tax value of £5,000: meaning that on any sale, virtually the whole proceeds will be subject to tax as a capital gain.

8. When we come on to Inheritance Tax planning the situation is again markedly different between the two options. If you want to give away some of the value of your property portfolio, and it is held through a company, usually the only way to do this is to transfer shares in the company to the intended recipient. The lion Capital Gains Tax is in the path, when you come to planning along

these lines. Any transfer of shares in an investment company to another individual will trigger a capital gain, on the difference between the current value of those shares and their original cost to you.

I've explained elsewhere why, in my view, transferring the capital in an LLP, which is the equivalent under the LLP option, can be done without Capital Gains Tax. The proponents of the company option have actually got quite clever here, and sometimes advocate the use of "funny shares" which have a low value initially but which enjoy all the benefit of the increase in value of the underlying portfolio. I've no doubt these arrangements, as well as being clever, can sometimes work if put in place properly. But you've still got the disadvantage of a lack of flexibility, because usually this sort of structure will have to be put in place at the outset, and to do that you've got to know exactly who you want to benefit and by how much. Changes in the capital structure of a limited company later on in its life are difficult to bring about without triggering Capital Gains Tax disposals. An overall summary would be that the LLP structure is much more flexible from the point of view of future Inheritance Tax planning, for this and certain other reasons.

It may help if I set out the above list of pros and cons in a table, as follows:

Limited Company	LLP
1. Straightforward and long "track record"	More complex
2. CGT on the way in depends on the interpretation of "business"	CGT avoided by wording of LLP agreement
3. SDLT on the way in depends on the interpretation of "partnership"	SDLT avoided by wording of the LLP agreement
4. Drawings from the property portfolio normally taxed as income	Drawings from the LLP can be captial, and therefore not taxable
5. Increases in value "trapped" in the company	Increases in value can be drawn down.
6. Potential double Captial Gains Tax charge	Single CGT charge
7. No uplift in CGT value on death	Uplift on death
8. IHT planning hampered by inflexibility of structure and CGT on investment company shares	IHT planning more flexible

CHAPTER 26
SAVING TAX OFFSHORE

I was down at my local the other day enjoying a quiet pint of the "Lewes nectar" – Harveys' Best Bitter – when I overheard the following conversation between a man in a suit with open necked shirt and a young woman who seemed to be hanging on his every word:

Man: Shocking the price of the beer in here. Of course, most of it's tax
Young Woman: Is it?
Man: Yes, 98% of the price of every pint goes to the Government
YW: That's an awful lot!
Man: Yes...still, I'm glad to say it's just about the only tax I do pay that bunch of s***s. They only give it to one armed black lesbian single mothers.
YW: Well, how d'you manage that then? You told me only yesterday about the hundred grand you made on that property deal in Hastings, and your tyre place is always busy. And it's very kind of you to let me come and swim in your pool – don't get me wrong – but that house and everything must cost money. Another pint?
Man: how many have I had?
YW: I think that was your sixth.
Man: Oh, well, just one more then.[Drinks] Yes, I do Ok, but I don't see why this Government should help themselves out my pockets. I've got it all offshore.
YW: Offshore?
Man: Yeah, it's a bit complex, but my tyre business is set up in a Bermuda company, and I get paid all in Swiss Francs into a Panamanian bank account.
YW: Wow!
Man: And that property deal was actually done in a Jersey trust set up by a non domicile, and the money was paid in Iraqi Dinars into a US Dollar account

in Hong Kong.

YW: Wow! Could I do that with my nail bar in West Street?

Man: Yes, it's simple. You just set up an offshore company...

And at this point they got up for a cigarette break outside, and I heard no more of this fascinating conversation. I began to see, though, why HMRC officers sometimes drink "undercover" in bars with their ears flapping to pick up this sort of boasting. I certainly wasn't going to be a busybody and interrupt, but as a tax adviser I could have pointed out a number of reasons why offshore tax planning wasn't as simple as he was making out. So, Moral Number 1: don't listen to what people tell you in bars!

And yet, despite the mystique and glamour of offshore arrangements generally, summoning up mental images of palm trees, swimming pools, and men in suits and sunglasses sipping pina coladas under parasols with other men similarly attired, the principles involved aren't actually all that complex. Personally I only claim specialist expertise in UK tax matters, but the fundamentals of international taxation are fairly universal, and you only need to have a grasp of five or six straightforward rules to know what works and what doesn't.

1. A UK resident person pays UK tax on his worldwide income and gains
2. A person who isn't UK resident pays UK tax only on UK income and gains
3. Non UK residents don't pay tax here on all UK income, with dividends from UK companies escaping tax for example, and they also don't pay tax on all UK gains (only, in fact on gains on UK property)
4. Connected persons are effectively forced to deal with each other at commercial prices cross border
5. Someone who is non UK resident for less than five years will pay tax on his return on income and gains made offshore but that he was basically already entitled to when he left, and
6. Beware of the "transfer of assets abroad" rules! (More of this below.)

I hope it goes without saying that this book isn't really aimed at the non UK resident person with income and gains from sources which are all outside this country. And at the other extreme I hope it will also become clear, from what follows, that the UK resident with an exclusively UK-based business or investment portfolio is wasting their time and money trying to save tax using any kind of offshore arrangement. The barriers stacked up against planning in this situation are quite simply too formidable to get over, as I'll explain. But there are a number of situations, which are illustrated below in a series of short but I hope dramatically satisfying scenarios, where we can avoid UK tax becoming payable unnecessarily by careful planning.

The Three Hurdles

If you start from the standpoint of someone seeking to put any particular income source outside the grasp of the UK tax authorities, you have basically three hurdles to get over. The first is the "fixed base" or "permanent establishment" hurdle. Where you have premises of any kind in this country, the basic rule is that income derived in any way from those premises, like business profits or rent, will be taxable here. But my first example will point to the importance of how you measure the profits that are actually being made in that fixed UK base – which may be a lower number than the accounts initially suggest.

The second hurdle is that of residence. If you can establish that a certain source of income arises outside the UK, because it wasn't dependent in any way on UK premises, you'll still be paying UK tax on it if the recipient is resident here. Where one is talking about an individual, the rules for deciding whether that individual is UK resident or not for tax purposes are quite complex and prescriptive. They are so complex, in fact, that it's probably easiest to use a form of flowchart: like the excellent one that, at the time of writing, appears on the KPMG website (google KPMG Statutory Residence Test Flowchart).

That flowchart basically enables you to decide where an individual is resident in the eyes of HMRC, by reference to periods of physical presence combined with a number of "ties" that the individual has with the UK. But if you're going to be doing things like setting up companies in Caribbean tax havens, as the bloke in the pub suggested, you also have to consider the question of where companies are resident.

You may think the concept of a company living somewhere is an odd one, and I would agree with you. However the lawyers needed to apply the pre-set regime of residence to companies somehow, to decide where they should be paying tax, and so the idea they dreamed up, no doubt on some warm and drowsy afternoon in a dusty court room, was that a company should be treated as resident where its "central management and control" is exercised. So that test, or one very like it, is the one that now applies for nearly all international taxation purposes. This is a hurdle that can be difficult for the would be avoider of UK tax to get over, as the following example shows.

George sets up a business of making tent poles in a remote corner of Nigeria, and establishes a Nigerian company to do so. He knows (because his accountant has told him) that if he had formed a UK incorporated company, this would be treated as resident in this country for UK tax purposes, because this is the default position which overrides the normal place of control rules. UK residence is the last thing he wants, because this would mean paying 19% UK corporation tax on the company's profits, rather than the nil tax which is due for various reasons in the local tax code.

Unfortunately UK residence is what he gets, despite the company being incorporated and carrying out its business in the African country. This is because HMRC argue successfully that, George being the only "real" or effective director of the company, the fundamental decisions relating to its conduct are made by George in his office in the City of London or at his home in Surbiton.

Part of the saloon bar mythology is that you can avoid George's problem by flying out of the UK and physically holding a board meeting, some say once a year, some say twice a year, in that non UK location. That might have cut some ice once, but HMRC are certainly not so easily convinced these days. Quite rightly they now tend to concentrate on the reality of where important decisions are made, rather than where some elaborate charade would have you believe they are made.

So the corporate residence hurdle can be a high one to surmount; but very often the real killer is the third one: the Transfer of Assets Abroad rules. These apply basically where you are UK resident yourself and any arrangements are made, with tax avoidance in mind, which result in a non UK person (usually a company) receiving income, the benefit of which might accrue to you in the future. So it's very widely worded, as anti-avoidance legislation tends to be, and would certainly catch that bloke in the pub's Bermuda company and Jersey trust. And the effect of the rules applying is that the income is taxable directly on you, the UK resident – whether it actually gets paid to you or not. In many cases it would be better simply to put the income through a UK company, and pay 19% corporation tax on it, than risk being stung for income tax personally at rates up to 45%.

So What Can You Do?

I've spent most of this chapter so far on what might be called negative advice, warning of the difficulties that lie in the path of those who look to save UK tax by using any kind of offshore arrangements. This seems to me necessary because of the amount of naïve and wishful thinking I've come across amongst clients and prospective clients on this subject; but it strikes me that a mere list of "don'ts", beside being depressing reading, falls short of the truth about the exciting possibilities which do actually exist in the fascinating world of international finance and taxation. So I'm now going to modulate from the minor key to the major. There follows a number of scenarios, some based on real life situations, where I think planning is both legitimate and potentially very lucrative.

Example 1: Management from offshore

Interfusion Plastics Ltd is a wholesaler that buys in goods from all around the world, but principally from the Far East. These are held in warehouses in various parts of the UK and sold on, mostly in bulk to other UK wholesalers but sometimes to customers in the United States. It's good business, with the draft trading accounts showing profits of £1 million a year.

Now there's no doubt that the profits of this company are taxable in the UK: for a start it's a UK incorporated company, which means that HMRC will also treat it as resident here. And its profits are in any event closely linked to the UK premises, which are warehouses with offices attached. But what are the true profits of the company?

The company's sole shareholder, Henry, was originally a UK resident, but now lives in Guernsey full time, setting foot in this country only occasionally. He's not only the sole shareholder, in fact: he's also the driving force behind the whole business, having set it up from nothing when he left school. All the most lucrative deals and contacts are looked after by Henry from his home office on the island, or, often using his laptop or mobile phone in Airport departure lounges and hotels where he stays on his many business trips. It's no exaggeration to say that the company wouldn't be viable without Henry's input. He bills for this input from a Seychelles company, and after his substantial management charge the UK company's profits are more like £250,000 a year.

Of course, using a company set up in a tax haven like the Seychelles is a red rag to the HMRC bull, but they have to concede, after an investigation, that the level of the management charge is a fair one given the importance of Henry's input to the business.

In a similar vein, if a UK company is making use of money loaned to it by a non resident, the interest paid on that loan will be an allowable deduction, reducing the profits chargeable here, provided that the interest is charged at a fair commercial rate.

Example 2: The Commercial Get Out

> Isolde is UK born, bred, and resident, and proud of it. But she is also very enterprising, and has decided to set up a company in a North African country, Gomboolia, to manage a frankincense plantation, together with locally based plant which packages the incense, and also manufactures charcoal and clay burners. Under Gomboolian rules, any company based in the country needs to be incorporated there and have a locally resident director, so she teams up with Abdul who manages the company and all the day to day running of the business "on the ground". Gomboolia has a rudimentary or even effectively non existent tax system, although Isolde doesn't know this when these arrangements are all set up.
>
> The profits after Abdul's salary are mostly ploughed back into extending the company's crop, land holdings, and manufacturing capacity. Isolde has basically got a profitable, but tax free business.

Note how Isolde gets over all three hurdles for a UK resident person to run a business whose profits are outside the scope of UK tax. Firstly the fixed establishment of the business is outside the UK, secondly the company, with care, can avoid accidentally acquiring UK residence by making sure its "central management and control" is in the African country, and thirdly Isolde should be able to show that the reason for forming a non UK company was not to avoid tax but as a result of impeccably commercial motives – in this case, the legal requirement that a Gomboolian company be used. Bear in mind, though, that if Isolde takes dividends from the company these will bear tax in the UK.

Example 3: Outsourcing

Rajiv runs a successful accountancy practice from the UK, where he lives, but he also has an interest in an office in Mumbai, which does a lot of the "number crunching" on the UK clients. This is set up as an Indian company which Raj owns 50:50 with an Indian resident, Mukesh. A lot of profits flow into this joint venture (JV) company from the UK practice, although the charges made by the JV are set at the same level as the Indian office would charge unconnected practices, to avoid possible HMRC attack. Again the three hurdles for escaping UK tax (even though Rajiv is UK resident) have been surmounted. The business is both based and controlled in Mumbai, and commercial considerations dictate that an Indian, rather than a UK company be used (thus rendering the "Transfer of Assets Abroad" rules inapplicable). Not only is India the natural country for the JV company to be incorporated in, but it can also be argued that any purchaser would be very unwilling to buy a UK company for a number of commercial reasons.

Example 4: Short Term Non-UK Residence

Brian is a property professional with a large number of good contacts in this arena. He has been chasing a major deal for some months, under which he hopes to bring together a land owner with a major developer. This is dependent on a number of contingencies, including planning permission, and it's definitely a case of not counting your chickens until they're hatched. However things are now looking as though they are going to come together at last, and Brian stands to receive a commission on the deal, if it goes through, of as much as £1 million.

Fortunately with modern technology Brian decides that he can see through the final stages of the negotiations "from home", and he decides to migrate for a time to his villa in Portugal, leaving the UK on 31 March 2020 and taking his laptop computer with him. The deal is duly signed on 1 June 2020 and Brian receives his money a few days later. He carefully avoids any but the most minimal return visits to this country until after 5 April 2021, and thus qualifies as non UK resident for tax purposes for the year 2020/21.

The commission is outside the scope of UK tax because it all accrued to Brian in a year in which he was non resident.

Example 5: Longer Term Non-UK Residence

Mysterious Barricades Ltd is a successful manufacturer of equipment used by riot police for defence against violent demonstrations: a thriving growth area. Francis is the 100% shareholder. Over the years a healthy balance has built up in the company bank account because Francis doesn't believe in paying any more income tax than absolutely necessary, and so has kept the profits in the company rather than paying dividends.

Eventually the time comes when Francis decides that the company's senior management can get on perfectly well without him, and he emigrates to a tax-favoured canton of Switzerland on 31st July 2020. About a year later, having ascertained the tax position in his new home jurisdiction, Francis votes himself a dividend of all the spare cash in the company, which by now amounts to several million pounds. This is tax free as far as the UK is concerned, because Francis has carefully ensured that he is out of this country for long enough periods to count as non UK resident.

To avoid the temporary non residence rules, which would treat that multi-million pound dividend as taxable here on his return, Francis avoids reacquiring UK residence until after five years have passed, on 31 July 2025. The tax deferral resulting from keeping the money in the company over the years has turned into a permanent saving.

Note the difference between this situation and Brian's, in Example 4. The value had accrued in Francis' company when he was UK resident: so, to realise the value tax free, he had to be outside this country for five years.

Example 6: Tax Free Capital Gains

As the above examples illustrate, leaving the UK, even only for a finite period, can be an effective way of avoiding tax on substantial lumps of income. Very broadly speaking this entails a one year absence if the income first arises after you've become non resident, and a five year absence otherwise.

The same used to be true about all capital gains, including gains from selling UK assets. This country had an unusually friendly attitude to inward investment by non residents, who enjoyed more or less complete freedom from CGT. Too friendly, a recent Chancellor obviously decided - step forward our friend George Osborne - and capital gains tax has recently been extended to UK situated buildings and land disposed of by offshore owners. But other types of asset can still be sold tax free from offshore, as the following scenario shows.

Pippa has always believed in ploughing her profits from specialist heavy steel construction back into the business, rather than frittering them away on holidays and fast cars, or simply allowing cash to build up in the company bank account. So when the time comes for her to retire, she has a very valuable asset in the form of the shares in Pipsteel Limited, but precious little liquidity. The company's value is all held in the form of property, stock and goodwill. So she's spent the last few years grooming her "team" for a management buyout, in which she hopes to be paid out in annual cash instalments from the future profits that the business makes under the new ownership. (A VIMBO - see chapter 15)

When everything has been agreed and the paperwork is in draft, Pippa buys a one-way ticket to a sunny island where they haven't got a capital gains tax, and flies out there shortly before 5 April. The sale happens on 6 April, in a tax year where Pippa has established non UK residence, and she won't pay any tax on the gain provided she is careful not to spend too much time back in the UK over the next five years.

The examples I've given here are no more than a taster of the sort of planning that is feasible. But my more zealous readers might ask how ethical I think all these offshore shenanigans are? Certainly a lot of offshore planning in the real world would be likely to elicit pursed lips from the average reader of the Guardian, and much of what goes on is probably downright illegitimate. But I think that the international tax laws are the way they are generally for a reason. The fundamental rule that you shouldn't have to pay tax in a country where you aren't enjoying any of the benefits of citizenship, whilst it can no doubt be manipulated, seems basically to be a fair one.

CHAPTER 27

AFTERWORD: THE ETHICS OF TAX

Which of the following statements most closely aligns with your views?

1. It is everyone's duty to pay the maximum possible tax.
2. Everyone should pay their fair share of tax.
3. People should pay tax in accordance with the spirit, not just the letter, of the law.
4. No one is under any moral obligation to pay more tax than the law requires. Everyone can arrange their affairs to minimise tax, and ethics don't come into it.
5. Taxation is theft, and people are entitled morally to reduce what they pay by legal and illegal means, including lying to the gang of robbers known as HMRC.

The subtitle of this book is "how to save tax legally and ethically". If you're concerned about questions of right and wrong (and most people are) you'll form your own view on what is ethical, but it's obviously important that that view should be based on reason. My qualifications for setting out my own thoughts on this subject, such as they are, are firstly that I am a tax adviser with a third of a century's knowledge and experience of the reality of taxation; and secondly that the question of right and wrong, as far as it applies to tax, is one that I have given a great deal of thought to. I don't claim to be a professional philosopher. But the views of those who actually shape tax policy, and prompt behaviour, are also not those of profound philosophers. The law gets made, and the practical business of the world is carried on, not by philosophers but by politicians, journalists, lawyers, bureaucrats and entrepreneurs. Almost all of these, in my experience, have very ill thought out ideas about taxation, based on a kind of tunnel vision which only sees the reality that is right in front of their eyes.

You might say that the same accusation could be levelled at me: I am not objective, as someone whose job is to make sure people don't pay too much tax. I have, however, tried to be as objective as possible in what follows, and at worst my point of view surely deserves to be listened to, as someone who actually knows something, technically, about the subject? Too few tax advisers speak out about the ethical side of their job, probably because most of them are too busy trying to keep up to date with the constant change and proliferation in tax law.

Shades of Opinion

No doubt there are as many different shades of opinion on the subject as there are people who've thought about it, but the above five statements are aimed at being typical expressions of what a substantial number of people really think. So, my aim, in this chapter, is to consider each one and see which appears to be the most reasonable.

Few readers of this book, I think, are likely to subscribe to opinion number one. Personally I don't know anybody who has expressed this view in my hearing. But it wouldn't surprise me to hear that there are some people, for example the Guardian reader who wrote to that paper a few years back suggesting that there should be a "UK taxpayer of the year" award, who do feel that this is a reasonable moral statement.

But surely there are two considerations which rule this out of court? Firstly, the law itself gives us a number of choices, which have different tax effects: such as the choice between running a business through a limited company or as a sole trader/LLP. Even the law, and therefore those who make the law, recognise the perfect validity of a choice which gives the lower tax result, particularly if that choice is actuated not by tax saving motives but by commercial motives.

Another example is the ability to nominate one of two or more residences to be treated as your main residence for Capital Gains Tax, and therefore exempt from the tax on any sale. Those who introduced this rule not only envisaged it would be used in order to reduce tax, but can only have put the provision into the statute book so that people could reduce their tax from what it would have been.

My second reason for thinking that number one isn't right is because I can't see where this moral principle comes from. It isn't part of traditional morality, as far as I can see, and I can't see this principle in the sayings of any of the great moral teachers of the past. So, let's move on from view number one.

Is Taxation Theft?

Going straight to the other extreme, and considering point of view number five, I'm quite sure that this has a not completely insignificant number of adherents in real life: even though very few people would own up to thinking this out loud. And actually, though I am fearful to say it, the idea isn't totally without its intellectual credentials. None of us chose to be governed and taxed, and the real world explanation (as opposed to theoretical jabbering about a "social contract") is that the government takes money from us not because we think it right, but because they are stronger than us.

But I don't adhere to this view myself, because I think it's wrong to equate constituted authority with a gang of criminals. It also seems to me to be wrong to equate taxation with stealing, because those who tax us do so not for their own enrichment (at least such is the theory) but for the common good.

Finally, there's the old fashioned prohibition which we should have learned at our mother's knee, against lying. Tax evasion, which is what attitude number five would condone, is probably best defined by saying that it involves deliberate deception: suppressing some of the income and therefore putting the wrong figure on your tax return, for example. It's true that some moralists say that it's sometimes permissible to lie in a good cause, but society would be unworkable if everyone were freely allowed to decide whether depriving the government of the money it needs to run the country is a "good cause".

The "Fair Share of Tax"

Number two is a much more widespread view, at least to judge from pronouncements by HMRC and the politicians. It seems obviously reasonable to say that everybody should pay their fair share of tax.

But this view depends on there being some kind of consensus of agreement on what a fair share of tax is. A lot of government pronouncements suggest that we should pay tax because of the benefits we receive from the government – such things as law and order, street lighting, and defence. But the implication of this is that it is "fair" for you to pay for what you are getting. Why, then, do people on low incomes pay nothing for what they are getting, whereas those on high incomes pay a lot more than the actual cost of what they are getting? What would you think of a shop where a Mars Bar was given away to a poor person, but cost £10,000 for a millionaire to buy?

For the life of me, I can't see why it is "fair" for those with more money to pay more than those with little money. The much overused word "fairness" is very emotive, of course, and its use tends to generate more heat than light. Surely the reality behind all of this debate and argument is this. The government needs a certain amount of money to run the country. It can't get that money from people who haven't got it, and therefore it gets the money from those who have got it. It does this not because it is "fair" to tax the rich more than the poor, but because it's the only practicable way of achieving the result they are looking for in the real world.

Perhaps those with more left wing leaning political views will feel that I have dismissed too easily the concept of it being fair for the rich to pay more. I have a strong suspicion, though, that if you held a referendum on the question, the more uncompromising socialistic view would be defeated.

Finally on this subject, all of the above argument, when it is used as a battering ram against "tax avoidance", is assuming, of course, that our tax system actually has the result of achieving a "fair" amount of tax for each person. The nitty gritty reality, as I know from all my years in practising in tax, is that the tax system is more like a juggernaut without a driver, or an unexploded bomb, than a carefully worked out system aimed at achieving a fair result. Therefore actions taken to reduce your tax bill (which is what this whole book is about) don't even necessarily militate against the achievement of number two. A person could easily be in for paying an "unfair" share (if there were any such valid concept) unless they took action to reduce the tax bill.

The Legal View

Perhaps surprisingly, given the current climate of opinion, it seems that the law is still that number four is the correct approach. Our law is a strange mixture of acts of parliament made up by MP's, and legal decisions where the law is effectively made up by judges. When a judge says something, that is the law until another judge says he was wrong, and no one, I think, has yet said explicitly that Lord Clyde was wrong in 1929 when he said (in the famous case of Ayrshire Pullman Motor Services and Richie v IRC):

> *"No man in this country is under the smallest obligation, moral or other, so to arrange his legal relations to his business or to his property as to enable the Inland Revenue to put the largest possible shovel into his stores. The Inland Revenue is not slow – and quite rightly – to take every advantage which is open to it under the taxing statutes for the purpose of depleting the taxpayer's pocket. And the taxpayer is, in like manner, entitled to be astute to prevent, so far as he honestly can, the depletion of his means by the Inland Revenue".*

The view I have summed up under number four is, in fact, no more than a paraphrase of what Lord Clyde said. What it comes down to, under this view, is that anything legal is fine morally, because there's no moral obligation as such behind paying tax (except the obligation of "honesty"): merely a legal obligation. It is essential to be able to distinguish between these two kinds of obligation, and more modern thinking arguably confuses the two.

This confusion is made worse, rather than helped, in my view, by the highly tendentious use of words such as "avoidance", "tax dodging", or "contrived" in relation to tax saving schemes. When, for example, does a careful rearrangement of your affairs to minimise tax (which Lord Clyde would have said you are perfectly entitled to do) become "contrived"?

The Spirit of the Law

As far as I can see most people – or perhaps it's just most people who air their opinions on the subject – would probably fall in with statements numbers two or three, or perhaps both combined. I've already explained why I think idea number two is completely untenable logically; but this still leaves view number three to be considered. This is that you should obey the spirit of the tax law, and not just the letter.

But I have two problems with this point of view. Firstly, it seems to me that the idea of there being a "spirit" of the tax law is a fantasy. Another judge famously once stated "there is no equity in taxation". Whether or not it's true to say that there is no "spirit of law" as far as tax is concerned, I know from personal experience in my profession that, if there is a spirit, it's often very difficult to decide what that is.

Take an example from real life, out of a central tax planning conundrum. If you are running a limited company, the tax on your income, received by the company, is restricted to 19% unless and until you pay it out to yourself as income, for example as a dividend. If you do so pay it out, you will have a personal tax bill, once the dividends have exceeded £2,000, at rates between 7.5% and 38.1%. For this reason, many company owners simply leave the money in the company and don't pay it out as a dividend, with the result that a large cash balance builds up in the company.

This is clearly tax avoidance, in the sense of action deliberately taken to reduce tax, but is it within the "spirit" of the legislation or not? The legislation clearly has the result that profits retained within the company bear a lower rate of tax, at least initially, than profits paid out. So, is it therefore in accordance with the spirit of the law to retain profits?

Until the 1980's, there was a set of rules called "Close Company Apportionment" to stop precisely this. So, the letter of the law was contrary to building up reserves in a company then. It's not easy to discern precisely why the close company apportionment rules were abolished. (While they existed, they had the effect of taxing you as if you had paid dividends.) My own conclusion is that the rules were abolished because Mrs Thatcher's government, which abolished it, was more in favour of business, and less in favour of red tape, than the previous government which had introduced it. So, when governments keep changing their minds about tax, and our tax system consists of the various effusions of different governments at different times, where is the sense in talking about the spirit of tax legislation? It's like talking as though there were a discernible "spirit of the House of Commons" in all of its different actions over the last several hundred years. That is, it's complete nonsense.

My second objection to the principle that you should follow the spirit of the tax legislation is that this appears to be a completely one way street. Where, for example, the law gives an unfair result against the taxpayer, the attitude you will almost always get from HMRC, in my experience, is a sort of shrugging of the shoulders and a statement that they didn't make the law and have to administer it as written. So, it's one rule when HMRC might benefit from the "spirit of the legislation", and another rule when the taxpayer might have done.

For example, let's say that a mother gives a portfolio of quoted shares to a trust for her children. She fails to understand the difference between a "bare" trust and a "fully clothed" trust, and the fact that Capital Gains tax arises on a gift to a bare trust, but not to the other sort. Will HMRC let her off the tax because it is in the spirit of the law for gifts to trust to avoid CGT? Personally, I don't think so. An individual inspector might express sympathy, but say that he has no choice but to administer the law as it stands – that is, the letter of the law.

Right & Wrong In Taxation

So, where do I personally stand? You'll probably have gathered, from the above discussion, that I think Lord Clyde is right, and that there is no "morality" in taxation other than the duty to act honestly. The government has a legal right to tax us, rather than a moral right. We have no duty to pay more tax than is legally due, and we can rearrange things to reduce the amount that's legally due if we want to.

But where does this leave the subtitle to my book, which promises to show the reader how to save tax legally and ethically? On this view, anything which is legal and honest is also ethical by definition.

My answer to this apparent contradiction is that, whilst number four is my own view, number three, or something like it, is a view which is also very commonly held, and perhaps more commonly held, indeed, than mine. In order to make this book as useful as possible to those who have scruples of the kind expressed by the phrase "the spirit of the law", I have generally sought to put forward ideas, or justify the ideas I have put forward, by reference to what could be seen as the spirit of the law, thus hopefully satisfying those who hold to this view. I would have looked to justify everything that has been put forward by way of tax saving suggestions in this book by reference to view number two as well, (the "fair share of tax") if I could have done. Unfortunately this view seems to me impossible to make any sense out of once you look an inch below the surface, and even though no doubt a lot of people do hold this opinion, it seems impossible to apply it sensibly to any real life tax situations.

Part I: Rates & Allowances

	2020/21	2019/20
INCOME TAX		
Personal Allowance	£12,500	£12,500
(Reduced by £1 for every £2 of income over £100,000)		
10% starting rate for interest – band	£5,000	£5,000
20% band up to	£37,500	£34,500
40% band up to	£150,000	£150,000
45% band above	£150,000	£150,000
(Note marginally different rates apply in Scotland)		
Dividend Allowance	£2,000	£2,000
Dividend rates		
- Equivalent to 20%	7.5%	7.5%
- Equivalent to 40%	32.5%	32.5%
- Equivalent to 45%	38.1%	38.1%

	2020/21	2019/20
NATIONAL INSURANCE CONTRIBUTIONS		
Employee		
- Threshold	£9,500	£8,632
- 12% band up to	£50,000	£50,000
- 2% rate above that figure		
Employer		
- Threshold	£8,784	£8,632
- 13.8% rate above that figure		
Self Employed		
- Threshold	£8,632	£8,632
- 9% rate up to	£50,000	£50,000
- 2% rate above that figure		
- Plus £3 (2018/19 £2.95) a week if profits exceed	£6,475	£6,365

CAPITAL GAINS TAX

Annual Exemption		
- Individuals	£12,300	£12,000
- Trusts	£6,150	£6,000
Rates for residential property		
- Within income tax 20% band	18%	18%
- Higher rate	28%	28%
Rates for other assets		
- 20% band	10%	10%
- Higher rate	20%	20%
CORPORATION TAX	19%	19%

STAMP DUTY LAND TAX

	Rates 8 July 2020 to 31 March 2021		
	First Residential Property & Main Residence	Additional Residential Property	Non-Residential Property
Up to £40,000	0%	0%	0%
£40,000 - £125,000	0%	3%	0%
£125,001 - £150,000	0%	3%	0%
£150,001 - £250,000	0%	3%	2%
£250,001 - £500,000	0%	3%	5%
£500,001 - £925,000	5%	8%	5%
£925,001 - £1,500,000	10%	13%	5%
Above £1,500,000	12%	15%	5%

INHERITANCE TAX

Nil rate band	£325,000
Death rate	40%
Lifetime rate (to trusts)	20%

ANNUAL TAX ON ENVELOPED DWELLINGS

(2020/21 RATES)

Property value

£500,001-£1 million	£3,700
£1,000,001-£2 million	£7,500
£2,000,001-£5 million	£25,200
£5,000,001-£10 million	£58,850
£10,000,001-£20 million	£118,050
More than £20 million	£236,250

APPENDIX
PART II: VAT CATEGORIES

Outside the Scope

- Non business supplies.
- Supplies made outside the UK (but there may be a liability in the country of supply).
- Transfers of businesses as a going concern.

Exempt

- Sale or rent of land and buildings, except for new residential buildings, or commercial where there is an option to tax.
- Insurance and insurance booking.
- Postal services by a "universal service provider".
- Betting, gaming, and lotteries.
- Finance (investments, loans, and the services of intermediaries).
- Education in schools etc.
- Medical services and supplies by certain qualified practitioners.
- Undertakers.
- Subscriptions to trade unions and professional bodies.
- Sporting facilities.
- IHT exempt works of art.
- Fundraising events by charities.
- Cultural services by government and non-profit making bodies.
- Supplies where the supplier could not recover input tax.
- Investment gold
- Services by a group of exempt businesses to its members.

Zero-Rated

- Food (but not catering).
- Sewerage and water.
- Books, newspapers and magazines, including e-books from 1 May 2020
- Talking books etc for the blind.
- Sale and construction of new dwellings.
- Sale of dwellings created by conversion of non-residential buildings.
- Sale of "substantially reconstructed" listed buildings.
- Export of goods outside the EU and associated services.
- Passenger transport.
- Houseboats and (BS3632 complaint) large caravans.
- Gold.
- Bank notes.
- Drugs, medicines and aids for the disabled.
- Charity shops, advertisements etc.
- Children's clothes.
- Supplies to ERIC (European Research Infrastructure Consortium).
- Women's Sanitary products.

Reduced Rates (5%)

- Domestic fuel or power.
- Installation of energy saving materials.
- Grant – funded installation of heating equipment or security goods, or connection of gas supply.
- Children's car seats.
- Conversions that change the number of dwellings in a building.
- Conversions to multiple occupancy dwellings.
- Conversions to residential homes, children's homes, and other residential institutions.
- Conversions of "empty homes".

- Contraceptives.
- Welfare advice by charities or public sector equivalents.
- Other large caravans.
- Cable cars.

Standard Rated (20%)

- All other supplies!

PART III:
THE DEFINITION OF "PLANT", ELIGIBLE FOR CAPITAL ALLOWANCES

As well as machinery used in trade or property businesses, (which are called "qualifying activities") "plant" also qualifies for Capital Allowances, that is phased write off of the capital expenditure against profits. What is plant? As well as obvious things like JCB's, and the various types of equipment and vehicles, it includes (not necessarily exhaustively) the following:

- Thermal insultations of buildings.
- Capital expenditure on security for those facing a "special threat".
- Integral features in building, including electrical systems (including lighting), cold water systems, space or water heating systems, ventilation and air conditioning and purifying systems, lifts, escalators and moving walkways, and external solar shading.
- Software.
- Some film expenditure.
- Gas and sewerage systems providing mainly to meet the particular requirements of the qualifying activity, or to serve particular plant or machinery used for the purposes of the qualifying activity.
- Manufacturing or processing equipment; storage equipment (including cold rooms); display equipment; and counters, checkouts and similar equipment.
- Cookers, washing machines, dishwashers, refrigerators and similar equipment, washbasins, sinks, baths, showers, sanitary ware and similar equipment; and furniture and furnishings.
- Sound insulation provided mainly to meet the particular requirements of the qualifying activity.

- Computer, telecommunication and surveillance systems (including their wiring or other links).
- Refrigeration or cooling equipment.
- Fire alarm systems; sprinkler and other equipment for extinguishing or containing fires.
- Burglar alarm systems.
- Strong rooms in bank or building society premises; safes.
- Partition walls, where moveable and intended to be moved in the course of the qualifying activity.
- Decorative assets provided for the enjoyment of the public in hotel, restaurant or similar trades.
- Advertising hoardings; signs, displays and similar assets.
- Swimming pools (including diving boards, slides and structures on which such boards or slides are mounted).
- Any glasshouse constructed so that the required environment (namely, air, heat, light, irrigation and temperature) for the growing of plants is provided automatically by means of devices forming an integral part of its structure.
- Cold stores.
- Caravans provided mainly for holiday lettings.
- Buildings provided for testing aircraft engines run with the buildings.
- Moveable buildings intended to be moved in the course of the qualifying activity.
- The alteration of land for the purpose only of installing plant or machinery.
- Dry docks.
- Any jetty or similar structure provided mainly to carry plant or machinery.
- Pipelines or underground ducts or tunnels with a primary purpose of carrying utility conduits.
- Towers to support floodlights.
- Any reservoir incorporated into a water treatment works, or any service reservoir of treated water for supply within any housing estate or other

particular locality.

- Silos provided for temporary storage, or storage tanks.
- Slurry pits or silage clamps.
- Fish tanks or fish ponds.
- Rails, sleepers and ballast for a railway or tramway.
- Structures and other assets for providing the setting for any ride at an amusement park or exhibition.
- Fixed zoo cages.
- Alteration to buildings to accommodate "plant"

Printed in Great Britain
by Amazon